Property

D0882659

Gift From Glad Day Books
1992

The Homosexualization of America,
The Americanization of the Homosexual

The Homosexualization of America,

The Americanization of the Homosexual

DENNIS ALTMAN

ST. MARTIN'S PRESS, NEW YORK

for Assia Altman
and
Allan Hildon

Copyright © 1982 by Dennis Altman.
For information, write: St. Martin's Press,
175 Fifth Avenue, New York, N.Y. 10010
Manufactured in the United States of America

Library of Congress Cataloging in Publication Data

Altman, Dennis.
  The homosexualization of America.

  Bibliography: p.
  Includes index.
    1. Homosexuality—United States.   I. Title.
HQ76.3.U5A4   306.7'6'0973   81-23193
ISBN 0-312-38888-8   AACR2

Design by Manuela Paul

10 9 8 7 6 5 4 3 2 1

First Edition

Contents

INTRODUCTION   vi

ONE   The Invention of the New Homosexual   1

TWO   Homosexuals and Homosexuality
The Problems of Definition   39

THREE   Sex and the Triumph of Consumer
Capitalism   79

FOUR   The Movement and Its Enemies   108

FIVE   The Birth of a Gay Culture   146

SIX   Sexual Freedom and the End of Romance   172

SEVEN   A Personal Conclusion   208

BIBLIOGRAPHY   227

INDEX   237

Introduction

In the summer of 1980 I was in Washington, D. C., for the celebration of Gay Pride Day. It was a hot day, and perhaps 10,000 people had jammed into P Street Park, just down the road from the gay bars near Dupont Circle, to listen to music and speeches; buy badges, T-shirts, and books; eat hot dogs, homemade cookies, lemonade, even Jewish delicacies (at the Bet Mispuchah stand); or have their hair cut, all in the interests of raising money for the Whitman-Walker clinic. In all, the organizers listed thirty-eight booths, plus an open-air art fair and a softball match between the Lesbian/Gay team and the City Council Homerulers.

The day began with a marching band, an echo of all those school and college bands in which the boys had longed to twirl the batons (but that was too sissy) and the girls to beat the drums (too butch). Here they were, the D. C. Different Drummers, players in dark-blue uniforms, women and men, marching boys in red satin matched with white mock construction helmets, and the crowd parted, applauding, to let them through. (Gay marching bands and choirs are a particularly American phenomenon that have come into existence in a number of cities, often with patriotic names like the Great American Freedom Marching Band.)

It was more like a traditional country fair than the commercial street fairs in New York and San Francisco, and the crowd was appropriately mixed: almost as many women as men, large numbers of blacks, even a few children wandering through with their parents. The speakers included some city councillors and the mayor of Washington, who knew very well the political importance of the gay community. (The gay vote was an important factor in the election of Marion Barry as mayor in 1978, and he has sought to pay his debts.)

"I can't stand all these clones together," hissed my friend David, who was working one of the booths. *"Look* at that one"—

pointing at a man who wore a miniature rollerskate suspended from a ring pierced through his nipple—"would you go home with *him?*"

But that man was the exception; such extravagance seemed out of place in a gathering whose motto proclaimed, "We Are Family." The crowd was good-humored and ready to applaud anyone who made them feel good, as befitted a family outing; the speakers, whose speeches were duly translated into sign language, stressed a sense of community among lesbians and gay men. We need to encourage and develop our own culture, our own businesses, exhorted emcee Robin Tyler, and the crowd cheered.

The next day there was not one mention of the event in either the *Washington Post* or the *Star.*

What does this mean, gay pride and the explosion of events celebrating it? In a sense Gay Pride Day was a testimony to both the growth and the fragility of the culture and business to which Tyler referred, and evidence of the two-pronged impact of the gay movement, on gays themselves and on the broader society.

"Okay," said David. "There are 10,000 gays here. So where are the other 190,000 in the Washington area?"

It's hard to tell who are the more significant, those who come out and by so doing proclaim their homosexuality, or the large majority who stay away. The fact remains that a decade earlier such a gathering would have been inconceivable, for there existed neither the desire for self-affirmation that produces gay religious groups, marching bands, and softball teams, nor the recognition of a gay minority that leads politicians to court their support just as they seek to win that of Polish-Americans and trade unions.

A year later I was in San Francisco for the same event. The week began with a tumultuous welcome home for the San Francisco Gay Men's Chorus, whose tour across the country had been hailed as an enormous affirmation of gayness and a symbol of the role of San Francisco as the gay center of the United States. It ended on the following Sunday with a parade and demonstration in the center of the city at which something like a quarter of San Francisco's population was present; the march, which included thirty-six floats and several hundred groups, took over two hours to pass along Market Street and was led by "dykes on bikes," complete with American flags. Once again the annual lesbian/gay freedom day parade was the largest mass celebration or demonstration in the United States since the heady days of the antiwar movement.

The marches, the bands, the softball teams, the floats (ranging from gay rodeo groups with horses to the Anarcho-Magical Faggots and Dykes), the events in Washington and San Francisco that are duplicated in numbers of cities throughout the United States and indeed other parts of the world, sum up the two themes of this book: the emergence of homosexuals as a new minority with our own culture, life style, political movement, and claim to legitimacy, and the impact of this minority on the broader society. In a country where people identify themselves by reference to ethnicity and religion, it is not surprising that homosexuals have increasingly come to see themselves as another ethnic group and to claim recognition on the basis of this analogy.

The development is rooted in widespread socioeconomic changes over the past several decades and corresponding changes in the dominant values and structures of sexuality in modern liberal capitalist societies. That such changes would produce a developing sense of minority identity among those people who are homosexual was not, of course, inevitable; the breakdown of rigid rules about sexual behavior could just as well have made sexuality seem an irrelevant social criterion, and sexual preferences relevant. That this has not happened, despite the forecasts of a number of sexual liberationists in the sixties, underscores the reality that in Western societies homosexuality is far more than a matter of whom one goes to bed with; it is rather something that affects the whole fabric of everyday life. Yet comparatively few homosexuals have fully come to terms with the radically different ways of conceiving and living their lives that recent changes have made possible.

Over the past decade homosexuals, both women and men, have become much more visible and their status far more problematic; as homosexuals assert the legitimacy of our life style—"We show the straight community that we're just as normal as they are," proclaimed the leader of the New York Gay Men's Chorus[1]—this creates the basis for conflict with the makers and guardians of cultural, moral, and social norms. A whole new range of images has been added to the traditional stereotypes of the lisping hairdresser and the cigar-chomping diesel dyke; nowadays gay business, professional, and religious groups meet with mayors, members of Congress, and even (under Jimmy Carter) presidential aides; gay spokespersons appear regularly on television, speak at colleges and schools, and demand equal time in the press; and gay marches have become major events in a number of cities each summer. The very diversity of gays revealed in this new openness—the fact that the gay community cuts across divisions of sex, race, class, and geography—has helped make homosexuality an increasingly important political issue in contemporary American life. At the same time the various groups who make up the misnamed Moral Majority see in the new affirmation of a homosexual culture and identity a threat to their most cherished values, to their children, and to the prevailing sexual order. Over the past decade there has been a simultaneous development of both a gay minority and community *and,* as a response, a growing battle for its legitimacy as part of the American way of life.

Whether homosexuals will win this battle for legitimacy goes to the heart of what America is all about. On the one hand the development of a sense of gay identity is a phenomenon peculiar to America, where the tendency to perceive oneself as part of a group rather than a class underlies the whole liberal notion of politics and society. (In this, America differs from a number of European and Latin American societies, in which class and ideology are considered much more significant and where accordingly it is less easy to develop the idea of one's sexuality as a basis for social and political identity.) On the other hand, the acceptance of group diversity in America has always existed within very severe limits. Indeed, groups are allowed to maintain their identity within American society only to the extent that they are prepared to subscribe to the dominant values of the society; to go outside these values is to be denounced as un-American.

It was not by accident that in the fifties McCarthyism linked homosexuality with communism as a threat to "the American way"; this rhetoric is revived in the attacks of the Moral Majority today. Genuine acceptance of the gay minority implies acceptance of a group that asserts values and behavior that differ in many ways from the most deeply held views about the organization of private life and sexuality, and it therefore goes beyond a purely liberal notion that the state should refrain from interfering in private behavior (a notion by no means universally subscribed to). The way in which American society comes to terms with the challenge of the emergent gay minority is as much a test of its ability to live up to its ideology of freedom and the right to happiness as is its response to the demands of nonwhite minorities.

My focusing on homosexuality does not mean that I am concerned only with that minority of women and men who identify themselves as part of the gay community. Homosexuality cannot be understood without understanding sexuality in general, and while the past decade has seen the emergence of a self-identified gay minority and life style, this should not lead us to ignore the extent to which homosexual behavior, emotions, and desires are a part of all sexuality. We need to speak of both homosexuals and homosexuality, and the two are not necessarily the same.

In current discussions about homosexuality there are two major theoretical traditions, the one largely psychoanalytic and European in character, the other more sociological and most developed in America. The former stresses, as did Freud, the inherent polymorphous nature of sexual desire; we all have the potential to be both homosexual and heterosexual, and only a complex pattern of social pressures ensures that so few of us act out this potential. The other tradition, clearly the dominant if often unarticulated view of most gay Americans, stresses the existence of a separate homosexual identity, culture, and life style, and blurs the links to sexuality in general.

Certain issues raised by the part played by homosexuality in social life are better understood within one tradition than the other. Thus the *repression* of homosexuality has considerable importance, especially if one is prepared to accept the Freudian dynamics of repression and sublimation. Equally, the stress on homosexual desire, as in the radical liberationist theories of Guy Hocquenghem and Mario Mieli, ignores the day-to-day experiences of millions of homosexual people. What may be a psychological truth (that there is no clear distinction between homosexual and heterosexual desire) is no longer a commonly experienced social fact in this society. It seems equally probable that homosexuality is different for women than it is for men. Women often define their homosexuality in terms of an identification with other women in which sexuality is far less important than it is for men. As Holly Near put it, lesbianism has less to do with questions of sex and more to do with "commitment, loving women, caring for one another. And that can happen with or without sex."[2]

It must seem at times that no more can be said about homosexuality. (There are at least a dozen bookstores in North America devoted exclusively to gay publications.) Yet both as part of human sexuality and as the developing culture of a new minority, homosexuality poses certain crucial questions about society and culture as a whole. The tendency to ghettoize homosexuality, to assume that it is only relevant to the gay minority, means that these more general questions are rarely posed. Unlike the constant preoccupation of American intellectuals, at least since World War II, with the meaning of being Jewish, the universal applicability of the homosexual experience has only reluctantly and grudgingly been accepted in America; books like Gay Talese's *Thy Neighbor's Wife* (the wife, it is assumed, must be heterosexual) and Christopher Lasch's *The Culture of Narcissism* ignore homosexuality even when it would strengthen their case.[3]

This has been far less true in Europe. Thomas Mann used homosexuality as a universal theme in *Death in Venice*, and it was Jean-Paul Sartre who saw in Genet the genius that most American critics were too squeamish to recognize. As Vito Russo has demonstrated (in *The Celluloid Closet*), the difference has been reflected in films since the pretalkie era.

But homosexuality is both more central and more problematic a matter than Jewishness, for everyone can be homosexual, not metaphorically (as in the cry of the Paris students in 1968 that "we are all German Jews") but actually. And it is the repressed recognition of this fact that does so much to fuel homophobia, but equally acts so as to promote male bonding and certain crucial authority structures. Indeed Freud saw sublimated homosexuality as the basis of most social organization, though he ignored female homosexuality in his sociological writings.

The new self-assertion of homosexuals, particularly of male homosexuals, has made sexuality itself a political issue; the new gay culture represents an affirmation of sexual play and experimentation that goes far beyond the repressive norms most people in this society, including many homosexuals, have internalized. The constant linkage in New Right rhetoric of homosexuality and abortion, the ERA, drugs, pornography, and "secular humanism" reveals a deep-seated fear that the social fabric is being threatened by an assertion of sexual diversity, or even by the search for sexual pleasure.

If we want to ask what is happening to sex in our time, we need to consider the gay world a key barometer, for it is here that the changes are most evident. This is not necessarily a chauvinistic statement; I am personally uncomfortable with some forms of the new male gay sexuality and do not necessarily consider backroom bars or orgy rooms a mark of unalloyed progress. But an examination of American popular culture, above all of its films—who can fail to see the homosexual influence on *Looking for Mr. Goodbar* or *American Gigolo?*—demonstrates how sexual mores are being homosexualized. Both sadomasochism and child/adult sex, for example, are largely conceived of in a gay context, though they are fundamentally neither homosexual nor heterosexual issues. Among gay women and men there is considerable experimentation aimed at discovering forms of relationships that could reconcile our needs for both security and independence better than the existing models. Such experiments are of considerable relevance to nonhomosexuals.

The idea that America is being homosexualized, and not only in its sexual mores, is a complex one. I do not mean by this what Leslie Fiedler had in mind when he spoke of the strong homoerotic bonding in American literature, nor what may be implied by a blurring of gender roles and expectations, though such matters are clearly related themes. Rather I would suggest by homosexualization the adoption of styles and fashions associated with an increasingly visible and assertive gay minority. In the introduction to the anthology *A True Likeness,* Felice Picano writes: "Anyone, gay or straight, who has ever entered for even a few hours into a predominantly lesbian or gay male milieu has been immediately struck by a fully blown, variable and multi-levelled culture: *from which much cultural and social patterns seen elsewhere first emanated and were developed*" (my emphasis).[4]

On one level style and fashion are not very important; what we wear next season has limited effect on our lives. But at the same time there is a sense in which style and fashion mold behavior, and to this extent the impact of gays is changing American society in important ways. This is most obvious in the gay impact on the "gentrification" of decaying urban areas, a source of not inconsiderable tension between gays and other minorities.

Much of what I have to say applies to other Western countries; the new homosexual affirmation can be found in Sydney, Strasbourg, and even São Paulo, as well as in San Francisco. In part this is because America has become a cultural model for the rest of the world. At the same time there is in America both a more pronounced sense of gay identity and a greater degree of social hostility toward homosexuals than in any comparable country. No other country seems as divided around issues of sexuality: the conflict between a repressive puritan heritage and the ethos of contemporary hedonism creates a tension that is reflected in the passion and all too often the violence that surrounds debate over sexuality in America. Perhaps this is just an exaggerated feature of all frontier societies; the myths and fears that surround homosexuality in Australia, in South Africa, in Canada, and in Argentina are different from those of the United States, yet there are common elements in the bonding established between men in the settlement of a new land and the wars against the indigenous inhabitants.

It is difficult to make sense of a phenomenon as large and as elusive as the interrelationship between homosexuality and the broader society. As George Steiner wrote: "Neither sociology nor cultural history, neither political theory nor psychology has even begun to handle authoritatively the vast theme of the part played by homosexuality in Western culture since the late nineteenth century. The subject is so diffuse and of such methodological and emotional complexity that it would require a combination of Machiavelli, de Tocqueville and Freud to produce the great missing book."[5]

Maybe there is no one book, but the story is gradually being charted as novelists, historians, sociologists, and psychologists wrestle with the problems involved. Many of the writers that I discuss and quote in the following pages are friends of mine; all are, in a real sense, colleagues in a mutual exploration.

Much of my discussion rests ultimately on concepts derived from Marx and Freud. Since neither of these traditions is dominant in American discourse, it might be worth noting that I do not regard either as a sacred text, but rather as the work of theorists whose perception of the world has helped shape social debate in this century. No discussion of social change can ignore Marx; no discussion of sexuality can ignore Freud. This does not mean, of course, that we need accept their theories, nor their implications, in Marx's case for political action, in Freud's case for therapy. Equally, we cannot write honestly about sexuality without drawing on our personal experience, and my experience is reflected in much of this book. At the same time, to make sense of that experience requires theory, for it is out of the marriage of lived experience, empathy with the experience of others, and theoretical speculation that we can develop an understanding of the world and a politics and ethics for dealing with it.

It is difficult to single out individuals to acknowledge, for it is in conversations with literally hundreds of people over the last few years that the ideas in this book have been molded. However I wish to thank Mark Blasius, Larry Bush, Tim Curnow, Michael Denneny, Paul Dinas, Peter Ginsberg, Doug Ireland, Craig Johnston, Larry Maas, Lenore Manderson, Barbara Mobbs, Rosemary Pringle, Vito Russo, Mark Thompson, Scott Tucker, Simon Watney, and Edmund White; the collectives of *Body Politic* (Toronto), *Christopher Street* (New York), *GCN* (Melbourne), and *Le Gai Pied* (Paris); and the people in various parts of the world with whom I've stayed over the past few years, particularly Wes Downey, Adrian Driggs III, David Harman, Antoine Pingaud, Sam Schoenbaum, and Ivan Walker.

NOTES

1 Quoted by Guy Trebay, "Talking Heads: Choral Numbers," *The Village Voice*, May 27, 1981, p. 61.

2 Interview with Holly Near by Simone George, *New York Native*, June 1, 1981, p. 26.

3 See Dennis Altman, "Thy Neighbor's Wife Revisited," *Christopher Street*, March/April 1981, and Lawrence Mass, "The New Narcissism and Homosexuality," *Christopher Street*, January 1980.

4 Felice Picano, "Introduction," *A True Likeness* (New York: Seahorse Press, 1980), p. xi.

5 George Steiner, "The Cleric of Treason," *The New Yorker*, December 8, 1980, p. 180.

CHAPTER ONE

The Invention of the New Homosexual

By the beginning of the eighties a new type of homosexual man had become visible in most large American cities and could also be found, to a somewhat lesser extent, in most other Western urban centers. No longer characterized by an effeminate style, the new homosexual displayed his sexuality by a theatrically masculine appearance: denim, leather, and the ubiquitous key rings dangling from the belt. The long-haired androgynous look of the early seventies was now found among straights, and the super-macho image of the Village People disco group seemed to typify the new style perfectly, even if the group strenuously denied this identification[1] and later abandoned the style to make it in Las Vegas.

For homosexual women the changes were more complex. As with homosexual men, there was a considerable shift in self-image, even if this was less reflected in external appearances. For gay women, however, this shift was closely bound up with very major changes in self-perception brought about by the feminist movement, which itself had allowed large numbers of women to discover a capacity for sexual and emotional involvement with other women. In a quite new way one's sense of gender identity was important for homosexuals, both women and men, who no longer felt it necessary to adopt the characteristics of the opposite sex as a sort of apology for failing to act out conventional sexual norms. If some women now adopted a butch style, or men wore earrings, it was no longer due to a sense of inadequacy in meeting conventional expectations.

The new visibility of homosexuals was not exactly what gay liberationists had envisaged in the early days of the radical gay movement at the beginning of the seventies. Their views of the change were summed up in an editorial comment of the English journal *Gay Left* that "the ghetto has come out,"[2] seeing in this new visibility a lack of any real challenge to the dominant social order. Yet it was partly the demands and activities of the early activists that produced one of the key social changes of the decade, a change not fully understood, perhaps, by those who had helped bring it about, namely the establishment of a new definition of homosexuals, both female and male, as a new minority, comparable to other minorities and deserving of the same rights, legal and civil.

The seventies saw the beginning of a large-scale transition in the status of homosexuality from a deviance or perversion to an alternative life style or minority, as remarkable a change in the characterization of "the homosexual" as was the original invention of that category in the nineteenth century. Along with this change, homosexuals were being cast increasingly in the role of the vanguard of social and sexual change, worthy of considerable media attention. Some homosexual writers and artists have speculated that the eighties would see overt homosexuals dominating much of cultural life, while conservatives grumble that this is already the case. And "gay chic" emerged as a phrase in newspaper columns.

It is difficult for the generation approaching adulthood amid the disco-drugged recession of the early eighties to realize just how much has changed over the past fifteen years or so. During my first stay in the United States (1964–1966), when I was beginning to come to terms with my sexuality, homosexuality was both hidden and stigmatized; ironically the Village People's ode to YMCAs would have been much more appropriate at a time when they were often de facto gay meeting places because of the lack of any others. Until the end of the sixties, to be a homosexual in most Western countries, and especially in the United States, was to experience a life that was largely furtive, shameful, and guilt-ridden; most homosexuals shared only too strongly the social condemnations against them. Even the various social and cultural upheavals of that decade seemed to offer very little to the homosexual; "This is the dawning of the Age of Aquarius," promised *Hair*, but much of the sixties counterculture was as sexist and homophobic as the mainstream culture.

And yet it was under the pressures of change in that decade that both the image and the self-image of the homosexual began to change (note the more open treatment of homosexuality in *Hair* when it was filmed at the end of the seventies.) "Pity," commented Tom Burke, "just when middle America finally discovered the homosexual, he died."[3] In a real way the end of the sixties *was* the dawning of something new for those of us who lived, or wanted to live, as homosexuals. Ironically, despite the widespread political conservatism of the seventies, it was during this period that the changes really gathered momentum.

What exactly has changed for homosexuals over a decade that seems marked by repression and conservatism? Most noticeably we became much more visible. When I was at Cornell University in the mid-sixties it was very difficult to find other homosexuals, who were as hidden and scared of being found out as I; now there are gay groups on large numbers of campuses—though a number have had to fight legal battles for recognition—and gay dances are common. (In 1979 this began to percolate down to the high schools as several high school students claimed the right to take dates of the same sex to their school proms.) Paul Robinson has claimed that it is the search for visibility that underlies the gay push for antidiscrimination laws: "Visibility is important, psychologically, because of the profound role played by its opposite in the life of every homosexual—that is, secretiveness."[4]

But it is not just visibility per se that is important; a certain type of queen or butch dyke had long been visible but in a way quite unlike that of the new homosexual. (Quentin Crisp in his biography recounts both his undoubted bravery in flaunting his homosexuality and his simultaneous self-loathing, which seems largely responsible for his popularity with straight audiences who are reassured to see someone who matches so perfectly their expectations of homosexuals. The success of the film *La Cage aux Folles* suggests that this recipe still applies.) The new sort of visibility was the reflection of a new sense of self-worth; when we hid our homosexuality in the past, it was not only because of fear of social pressure but even more because of deeply internalized self-hatred. This self-hatred was very pervasive and still persists among many today; it was epitomized in Somerset Maugham who, while deeply in love with a man, could not bear to think of himself as homosexual.[5] Or Michael Davidson, himself homosexual, who in his autobiography could refer to the limited amount of homosexuality in Italy as proof of sexual health.[6]

Thus the visibility of the new homosexual woman or man was an affirmation that we no longer considered our sexuality a matter of which to be ashamed. The taunt that heterosexuals don't find it necessary to parade *their* sexuality in the street misses the point; in our society the depiction of sexuality is *always* in heterosexual terms, and any affirmation of homosexuality is an attack on the prevalent values. Hence, to declare the validity of homosexuality, to reject the judgment that it is sick, evil, a maladjustment, a deviance, or a

perversion, is a political statement, and the assertion of a homosexual
identity is as much a political act as was the assertion of a Czech or
Romanian identity in the nineteenth century.

Ever since the term "homosexual" came into use toward the
end of the nineteenth century and was taken up enthusiastically by
doctors and psychiatrists, two things could be said about it: experts
rather than homosexuals themselves decided how we would be
viewed, and with a few exceptions these experts were in agreement,
however they framed this view, that homosexuality was a less acceptable form of sexual behavior than heterosexuality.

Several traditions came together to fix the status of "the homosexual" as the term existed between its coining by the Hungarian
doctor Karoly Benkert (also known by his pseudonym Kartbeny) in
1869[7] and the major reappraisals that began in the 1960s. Oldest of
these was the Judaeo-Christian condemnation of "crimes against
nature," which is derived from the assumption that the only acceptable form of sexuality is that which can lead to procreation. This sort
of condemnation places great stress on the (supposed) absence of
homosexuality among animals, which is rather odd given that the
people using such arguments are prone to brand free expression of
sexuality as "animalistic," and comes from a view of sex that should
have been firmly ended by Freud's revelations of infant polymorphous perversity. As a gut reaction, however, it persists surprisingly
widely.

Among those of religious inclination this could very easily lead
to a condemnation of homosexuality as sinful, especially when bol-
stered by selected quotations from the Bible. Paul's epistles, which
are often cited to support this view, also condemn women with
braided hair and gold, pearls, or costly array (1 Tim. 2:9) which
would seem to describe a number of our more prominent homophobes. As John Boswell has shown in *Christianity, Social Tolerance,
and Homosexuality,* it took a long time for the Catholic church to
adopt a rigid condemnation of homosexuality, and there is need for
considerable research to explain just why the Christian churches did
indeed come to adopt such a strong antihomosexual position. Since
the Middle Ages, however, homosexuality has been firmly established as a sin, a powerful factor in a society as marked by religiosity
as the United States.

The concept of homosexuality as an "illness," a "perversion,"
or a "maladjustment" belongs to the gradual development of medicine as both a science and an ideology, with the power to define
and categorize certain key areas of human behavior. Such terms

reflect the growth of expert control over our lives achieved through the apparatuses and discourses of power during the past several centuries, which is the chief theme of Michel Foucault's writings. The adoption of these negative terms underlies both the strengthening of the role of medicine and psychiatry as institutions of power, and simultaneously the developing idea of a homosexual identity, found in the late nineteenth-century writings of men such as Karl Ulrichs and Edward Carpenter. (It was not until well into the twentieth century that women began to define themselves as homosexual, although there is, of course, a much longer history of passionate friendships between women.)[8] Even today many homosexuals accept uncritically the expert definitions of their identity; one of the most significant actions of the early gay liberation movement was to call into question the power of science to define normality.

Partly because of such challenges, an increasing number of medical, psychological, and psychiatric authorities no longer define homosexuality as an illness or maladjustment. A crucial step was taken in 1973 when the American Psychiatric Association and the American Psychological Association both declared that homosexual orientation was not, in itself, an illness, although the psychiatrists retained the category of "dystonic homosexuality" for people who are disturbed by or who wish to change their homosexual orientation. As a popular belief, however, the concept that homosexuality is a sickness that should be "cured" remains very widely held. (A French survey in 1978 found that 38 percent of the respondents saw homosexuality as an illness, considerably more than believed it to be either a vice or an alternate form of behavior.[9] There seems no reason to believe an American survey would produce very different results.)

The idea of sexual deviance is, in a sense, the sociological equivalent of the medical concept of illness and is particularly associated with liberal American sociology. Despite the protestations of social scientists like Howard Becker and Erving Goffman that this is not their intention, the idea of deviance ties in very well with many prevailing antihomosexual myths: homosexuals as morally irresponsible, as bizarre, as different. But there is no such thing as a value-free concept of deviance; to say homosexuals are deviant because they are statistically a minority is, in practice, to stigmatize them. Nuns are rarely classed as deviants for the same reason, although if they obey their vows they clearly differ very significantly from the great majority of people.

During the late sixties and seventies all these ways of seeing homosexuality—which, whatever their framework, agreed that it was a condition that if sometimes unavoidable was certainly less preferable than heterosexuality—came to be challenged. (The old prejudices were remarkably widespread. One doctor, referred to as "a sort of guru" to the New Left journal *Ramparts*, expressed the hope that "as society and psychiatric techniques advance, the number of homosexuals will dwindle to the irreducible minimum of emotional derelicts.")[10] Of course many people still cling to such views. However, the condemnation of homosexuality is today under sufficient challenge, above all from homosexuals themselves, to have become problematic.

Two quite new and connected ways of looking at homosexuality came into being in the seventies: the concept of the alternative life style and that of a gay people or minority. Seeing homosexuals as a minority, with a specific life style, meant taking a major step away from the categorization of them as evil, criminal, sick, or deviant. After all, murderers are not usually seen as a minority, nor tuberculosis as a life style. I suspect there is a much more significant change here than merely the growing use of the word "gay," though this parallels the broader changes in some ways. In 1969 *The Village Voice*, which refused to use the word, was "zapped" by the newly formed Gay Liberation Front. Today the term has become a common newspaper heading—though as late as 1981 *The New York Times* report of the Gay Pride March avoided the word—leading to expressions of regret from those who feel the "innocent" meaning of the word has been usurped.

The growing use of the concepts of minority and life style reveals a fundamental reappraisal of what being homosexual means, and a tendency to see it in social rather than individual terms. Once the homosexual is perceived as part of a people with his or her particular life style, s/he will likely be treated as are other members of recognized minorities and accorded a particular identity that is a far cry from the stigmatized one implied in earlier definitions. Moreover the impact on homosexuals themselves is enormous; the sense of being isolated, exceptional, doomed to a lonely and miserable life, which was the experience of so many gay women and men in the past, is far less likely in a society that acknowledges the existence of a homosexual minority and culture.

Ironically, homosexuals themselves long resisted the idea of being somehow distinct from other people; as a character mused in Mary Renault's *The Charioteer*, a novel of the forties:

He kept telling me I was queer and I'd never heard it called that way before and didn't like it. The word I mean. Shutting you away, somehow: roping you off with a lot of people you don't feel anything in common with, half of whom hate the other half anyway, and just keep together so that they can lean up against each other for support.[11]

The expression of self-hatred in the rejection of being in any way part of a separate group still exists today, but it is far less common. Indeed both the visibility and the politicization of homosexuals is most apparent in the growth of a sense of community, which has meant a vast increase in the size and impact of the homosexual world. This growth has not occurred only in the urban liberal enclaves of the two coasts, but in almost all the cities of North America and, to a lesser extent, Western Europe and Australasia. A 1979 report about Phoenix, Arizona, for example, found not only the usual complement of bars and baths (predominately male) but also a wide range of political, religious, and social welfare groups, plus two gay publications; in that year the Citizens for Constitutional Rights, a gay political group, organized a fund-raising party, the Metropolitan Community Church raised $22,000 for a new building, and there were positive programs dealing with homosexuality on local television.[12] None of these activities would have been conceivable ten years earlier.

Not that hostility toward homosexuals and homosexuality has disappeared: the new church was needed because the old one was burned down, and homophobia remains rife among state politicians, especially those with fundamentalist backgrounds. What is important is that these hostilities are now being countered by homosexuals themselves; whereas the gut reactions against homosexuality were based on a general consensus, shared even by the great bulk of homosexuals themselves, such attitudes are now under attack.

Phoenix illustrates a development found in most larger cities of the Western world, namely the development of a sense of gay community with its own institutions, values, and means of communication. In embryonic form such communities existed in eighteenth-century Paris and London, in particular cafes or salons where homosexuals gathered. (While these were generally reserved for men, reflecting the different status and freedoms of the two sexes, there was some sign of a recognizable lesbian world; in 1889 a Parisian *Guide des Plaisirs* referred to a lesbian restaurant in Montmartre.) There are records of self-consciously homosexual groups at the end of the nineteenth century, and quite famous ones early in the twentieth. Compton Mackenzie, for example, satirized the lesbian circles of pre-World War I Capri in his now-forgotten novel *Extraordinary Women* (which should be read in conjunction with Roger Peyrefitte's *The Exile of Capri*).

Such groups were generally furtive, and membership was confined to small numbers of wealthy eccentrics. It is extraordinary to consider that, with the possible exception of pre-Hitler Berlin, no city in the world had a gay communal life before the late sixties equivalent to that now found in Phoenix or any one of perhaps a hundred Western cities. By the beginning of the eighties, Albany, New York, had a sufficiently developed gay commercial and movement scene for Richard Stevenson to use it as the basis of a detective novel, *Death Trick,* and the gay community in Lincoln, Nebraska, organized a large-scale public welcome for the San Francisco Gay Men's Chorus.

As these examples suggest, a real gay community is more than bars, clubs, baths, and restaurants, important as these are. Nor is it merely an elaborate network of friendships, though these too are important. Rather it is a set of institutions, including political and social clubs, publications and bookstores, church groups, community centers, radio collectives, theater groups, and so on, that represent both a sense of shared values and a willingness to assert one's homosexuality as an important part of one's whole life rather than something private and hidden as was traditionally the case.

The roots of such a communal sense and organization predate the sixties (in Germany they go back to the 1920s and in Holland to the 1940s). But over the last decade the gay community has become much bigger, more varied, and more visible. In 1968 Martin Hoffman compared the homosexual community (in whose development his book *The Gay World* played some part) to "the early Christian communities during the time that Christianity was persecuted by the Romans."[13] This comparison seems less accurate as visibility and self-assertion increase.

The idea of a specific gay community—though with some ambivalence as to whether there are in fact separate male and female communities—is the logical extension of seeing gays as possessing a particular culture, a minority status, and a life style. As an advertisement in *The New York Review of Books* proclaimed:

> Modern gay life would make no sense to the homosexual of the past. To be sure there have always been men who have had sex

with other men. And there have always been stories of great and touching, even passionate, friendships between members of the same sex. And there have even been, in many societies and in different epochs, men who have been willing to face public scorn in proclaiming their love for other males. Even so, none of these earlier homosexuals would have felt comfortable in our company, nor we in theirs.

The Joy of Gay Sex is by gays, for gays, about the gay subculture that comes equipped with its own rituals, its own agonies and ecstasies, its own argot. Therefore in this book the authors in the main speak to gays in their own language, using words and terms not accepted everywhere but natural to gays.[14]

Oddly enough, few of those hostile to the growing acceptance of homosexuals have fully appreciated the meaning of the new stress on a homosexual identity, community, and life style. One of the paradoxes of the present situation is that even where the old laws defining homosexual behavior as a major crime remain, there is a growing de facto recognition of a gay minority, deserving of full civil and political rights as a minority. Thus for years the mayor of New York could proclaim an official Gay Pride Week while the very people being honored remained criminals under state law, or the government-owned airline in Australia could become the official carrier for several national homosexual conferences at a time when all but one of Australia's state governments refused to remove the criminal sanctions against (male) homosexual behavior.

The greatest single victory of the gay movement over the past decade has been to shift the debate from behavior to identity, thus forcing opponents into a position where they can be seen as attacking the civil rights of homosexual citizens rather than attacking specific and (as they see it) antisocial behavior. President Reagan apparently recognizes the distinction: before his election he was quoted as saying, "My criticism of the gay rights movement is that it isn't asking for civil rights, it is asking for a recognition and acceptance of an alternative life style which I do not believe society can condone, nor can I."[15]

Such changes emerged out of the general radicalization that took place in nearly all Western societies during the mid- to late sixties, with the flowering of the hippy movement, the counterculture, student and antiwar protest, and a general assault on traditional values. At first, as Roger Baker wrote of his experiences in the "swinging London" of the sixties, "They were all heterosexual issues.

Whether just talked through or acted out, they were interpreted in entirely heterosexual terms. Through these years of social and sexual upheaval, the gay dimension was completely missing. We lacked a model for action, we lacked insight, and we most likely lacked confidence even if we did have them."[16] It was after the dramatic events of 1968 in a number of Western countries and the emergence of a reborn feminism, at least in the Anglo-Saxon societies, that the "gay dimension" emerged.

But it is not only a homosexual political movement that has developed, important as that is. Thousands of women and men who see themselves as totally apolitical, who may even express hostility to the gay movement, have discovered a new sense of self-identity and a new feeling that they belonged to a larger gay community. Does this mean that gays have become a new minority, equivalent, say, to Mexican-Americans or Bretons; that there is indeed a distinctive gay life style and gay culture? And if so, does it encompass both women and men?

*   *   *   *   *   *   *

It is clear that in popular usage "gay" means male, as indeed does "homosexual." (Which is why many women prefer to speak of "lesbians and gay men.") It is also clear that gay male identity is very different from female, and this seems due to both social and psychosexual reasons. While I shall postpone discussion of the latter, the former reflects the very different meanings of being homosexual for women and men in an essentially male-dominated society. For a man to be homosexual has always been seen as a relinquishing of his privileges as a member of the dominant sex. (Very macho societies such as those of the Mediterranean or Latin America have widespread male homosexuality, but few men who identify themselves as homosexual.) For women, on the contrary, homosexuality is often a way of affirming their position as women and rejecting the need to be defined solely in relationship to men.

But while such a view of lesbian identity has long existed among a small minority of women—it seems most obvious among the legendary group of lesbians who lived in interwar Paris, including Romaine Brooks and Natalie Barney as well as Radclyffe Hall, Gertrude Stein, and Alice B. Toklas[17]—it is also true that homosexuality, especially exclusive homosexuality, is less widespread among women than among men even today. Given the greater economic and social freedoms available to men, and the greater repressions surrounding female sexuality, this difference is hardly surprising. It certainly does not support the rather strange argument of John Leo in *Time* magazine that "the apparently greater number of male homosexuals points away from the theory that homosexuality is a random variation (which ought to be randomly distributed by sex) and towards the theory that it is heavily related to special problems of male development, which appears to be more complicated and disaster-prone than that of the female."[18] Leo ignores the fact that we do not know whether the apparent difference in the number of male and female homosexuals would change were social roles and expectations affecting the sexes to change.

The changes in the control, perception, and definition of homosexuality over the past decade have, of course, affected women as much as men, but in somewhat different ways. Women have been affected simultaneously by the impact of feminism and have created a lesbian-feminist culture quite distinct from the gay male world. As Karla Jay wrote:

> The flowering of culture in the past decade has been especially true for lesbians. I think in part this has happened because, while gay men had more of a subculture because of "camp's" acceptance in the mainstream culture . . . lesbians, since we are women, have been more subsumed and at the same time isolated in the straight culture. Therefore, theoretically, we started with a blank slate which, though it would appear to be a disadvantage, actually made it easier to build a new and different culture.[19]

However, as Jay herself goes on to argue, "I think that women's culture and lesbian culture are basically the same."[20] If this is true, it suggests that gay men do not have very much in common with gay women (for whom being women is more important than being gay), that gay men are either part of the dominant male culture or separated, at least to some extent, from both it and the lesbian-feminist culture, which is probably true. Jay, I think, tends to place too much emphasis on economic factors: "As women, lesbians don't have access to the kind of money men have always taken for granted."[21] It is not poverty that explains why there are no lesbian saunas or backroom bars, but rather a whole set of assumptions and values that women hold about sexuality.

It is in the creation of a whole network of women's centers, coffee houses, rap groups, dances, bookstores, newspapers, rape crisis centers, etc. that one sees most clearly both the development of a lesbian identity and its links with straight feminists. (When the women in Jane DeLynn's novel *Some Do* come together, first in a rap group and then to form a coffee shop, it seems irrelevant that only a couple of the women are in any sense gay.) Indeed one might argue that for feminists the line between straight and gay is so much more blurred than such a division would be among a group of men that one cannot talk of gay female and gay male identities in the same way. One of the reasons lesbians often seem invisible beside gay men is that they tend to assert a feminist rather than a gay identity; in the program for the 1981 San Francisco Parade there appeared a guide to Valencia Street that identified twenty women's businesses and organizations. None of them include the words "gay" or "lesbian" in their names, though clearly a number are.

The growth of lesbian-feminism should not blind us to the continued existence of a traditional lesbian world, which remains apart from and often very suspicious of feminism. There may, indeed, be a greater gap between traditional and radical lesbians than is the case for male homosexuals, where the commercial scene is so much larger and tends to provide at least some common meeting places. For many lesbians there is little identity with straight women, and the difference in sexuality is crucial, as is shown in Jane Chambers's play *Last Summer at Bluefish Cove.* Even some lesbian-feminists acknowledge this. As Joan Nestle wrote:

> We lesbians from the 1950s made a mistake in the early 1970s: we allowed our lives to be trivialized and reinterpreted by feminists who did not share our culture. The slogan "Lesbianism is the practice and feminism is the theory" was a good rallying cry, but it cheated our herstory. The early writings need to be reexamined to see why so many of us dedicated ourselves to understanding the homophobia of straight feminists rather than to understanding the life realities of lesbian women "who were not feminists" (an empty phrase which comes too easily to the lips.)[22]

What does unite gay women and men is a new sense of self-assertion and a willingness to be publicly identified as homosexual. Over the past decade there has been an explosion in explicitly gay writing, art, and film; a demand for a new view of homosexuality in education and the media; and a vast increase in the number of homosexuals publicly demanding their rights. A substantial number of well-known figures have "come out" publicly, and there has been considerable controversy over the role of homosexuals in education and government. (The campaigns against homosexuals in such positions, associated with people such as Anita Bryant and Senator Briggs, linked lesbians and gay men together and helped produce a sense of common identity.)[23] The increase in "positive" gay writing over the past decade has been the work of women as much as of men; in addition to writers like Rita Mae Brown, Doris Grumbach, Bertha Harris, and Jane Rule, one is struck by the number of women (Mary Renault, Patricia Nell Warren, Marian Zimmer Bradley, and Marie-Claire Blais) who have written about gay men.

However, when lesbians assert themselves they are asserting themselves as women; when gay men assert themselves, it is, at least in part, in opposition to the expected superiority of men. Thus gay men are visible as gay in a way that is less true for lesbians, and their impact on the broader society is far easier to perceive. The contrast is epitomized in the macho cult, which became the vogue among American gay men in the seventies and was copied enthusiastically in a number of overseas countries. (The actor/model Jack Wrangler claims to have invented the "flannel shirt/Levi thing."[24] I suspect it had more to do with convenience, comfort, and cheapness.)

On the surface the macho look, with its Levis and leather, short hair and moustaches, seems like a reaffirmation of the most traditional male stereotypes; it even found an echo in sexual practices as the cult of leather and sadomasochism moved from a hidden minority to a central preoccupation of much of the overt gay male world. (It is probable that the term "sadomasochism" is somewhat misleading, and that there are important differences between homosexuals and heterosexuals in their acting out of these fantasies.)

Yet the macho cult is in a sense a new form of drag, a parody of the social expectations of homosexuals, just as was the more traditional queen. If the man dressed as a woman was in effect mocking the assumptions society makes about men and women, then the man dressed as a stereotypical man is also mocking the assumption that to be gay is to want to be a woman—and if this seems to contain a fair degree of misogyny, it also includes a fair amount of self-parody. When the Village People performed "In the Navy" on the deck of an American naval vessel as part of a Bob Hope television special, they came across as macho drag queens.

Even with the present cult of muscle building and tattoos, gay men retain a much different attitude toward displays of masculinity than do those who are ostensibly straight. A cult of the male body has always been a major part of gay male sensibility, often reflected in painting and sculpture. But whereas among straight men the sexual element in such interest must be repressed and denied, among gays it is much more open and hence much less likely to turn to aggression. Whatever else it may mean, the upsurge of interest in body building among gays at the turn of the decade can hardly be attributed to repressed homosexuality, as is often said of body building and indeed of sport in general. (Paul Hoch quotes Norman Mailer as saying that "the main reason for the tremendous popularity of football in America may be our subconscious fascination over the fact that each play starts with the quarterback squatting between the center's legs in 'the classical pose of sodomy.' "[25] The symbolism is perhaps less graphic in other versions of football.) Rather body building is part of the whole assertion of sexuality that makes up much of the new gay male style, and it underlies the fact that to be gay is not, as is often thought, to be a man who would be a woman.

If the new macho style is in some ways a parody of socially accepted roles, there is always the danger that it may turn on itself and become a way of reinforcing these roles. Just as the traditional queen or transvestite could be viewed as simultaneously mocking women *and* the expectations society makes of them, so the new macho style is both sending up traditional masculinity and asserting it in a way that seems to totally contradict the feminist critique common in the early days of gay liberation. The need to proclaim one's masculinity seems the central message of much of the new male gay culture, as revealed in strict dress codes and bars that will only admit men wearing at least some of the required fashions. The message that it's okay to be a fag provided you're also a man suggests some of the ambivalence felt about the changes of the past decade.

The expectation that the growth of gay self-assertion would lead to a much greater degree of androgyny and blurring of sex roles seems, at least for the moment, to have been an illusion. It is now in straight discos that one finds the soft-looking and long-haired males; gays are too busy striking masculine poses and flexing their pectorals. At the same time there is a change from the gays of the past who also admired the super-masculine (before there was overtly gay pornography, body-building magazines served as poorly disguised substitutes), for the new macho style is flaunted as a way of affirming one's (homo)sexuality rather than denying it.

There is no real counterpart to this development for gay women. If anything the impact of feminism has been to make the gulf in style between gay and nongay women less visible and less important. However, just as the queen style is dwindling among men —as early as 1971 Laud Humphreys pointed out that "few gay bars are now distinguished by the presence of limp wrists and falsetto voices"[26]—so too the traditional dyke, with her mimicry of traditional male costume, is disappearing. There is a common style among younger lesbians, but it is not really equivalent to the male parody/affirmation of traditional stereotypes. Deborah Wolf argues that there are certain subtle forms of dressing that distinguish lesbians from straight feminists,[27] but again the key division seems between feminists and nonfeminists. There is, however, something of a dyke macho style, captured perfectly in the opening lines of a story by Lynn Bahlmann:

> It's a pleasant Saturday night in Greenwich Village. I put on some
> tight jeans and a flannel shirt open all the way to the waist . . .
> satisfied that it's late enough to catch a peak crowd, I pull on some
> very sexy black leather cowboy-style boots. As I do I recall my past
> six years of experience at women's gay bars.[28]

Gay women can now borrow gay men's clothes rather than vice versa; I have seen women dressed in total macho drag, complete with key rings and colored handkerchiefs, and, just like men, they are asserting their (homo) sexuality. But if a macho style for men affirms a traditional concept of masculinity, the new lesbian is hardly likely to affirm traditional femininity, now confined to reactionary, and usually religious, spokespersons and transvestites.

Not all homosexuals, of course, welcome the appearance of the macho look. The French writer Guy Hocquenghem, for example, mourns the passing of "the traditional queen, likeable or wicked, the lover of young things, the specialist of street urinals," and his replacement by "the reassuring modern young homosexual (about 25 to 40 years old) with moustache and briefcase, without complexes or affectations, cold and polite, in an advertising job or sales position at a large department store, opposed to outlandishness, respectful of power and a lover of enlightened liberalism and culture."[29]

As Hocquenghem hints, the new homosexual belongs to the generation that became aware of sexual feelings before experiencing the impact of the sexual liberation movements of the seventies. Among those who are essentially products of the last decade, things are somewhat different. "They don't know," a friend of mine said in wonderment, "there was ever a time we couldn't turn up in discos and dance together." I suspect that quite a new style is emerging among younger gays, one in which a greater degree of bisexual behavior coexists with a greater willingness to identify as homosexual. If older gays often claimed to be bisexual for reasons of both social and self-respect, today's bisexuals are likely to proclaim themselves homosexual for political reasons. This has been particularly true among women, where there is strong pressure on those who are bisexual to identify as lesbians. Kate Millett, for example, was strongly attacked in the early seventies for her position—both by lesbians because she acknowledged her heterosexual desires and by straights because she refused to be limited to them.

The crucial problem in discussing the new homosexual and the stress on her/his identity as part of a specific community is that it ignores the large number of people who move in and out of that community and that identity. If there has been a marked increase in the number of people who affirm a homosexual identity, there are also increasing numbers of people who resist such categories. For the moment it seems worth suggesting that the image of the new homosexual—who populates the plays of writers like Robert Patrick or Doric Wilson and novels like *Faggots*, and who has seemingly replaced the sad, scared, guilt-ridden queens of *Boys in the Band* (even while persisting, in a somewhat modified form, in a book like *Dancer from the Dance*)—will in turn be replaced by a new generation who will act out its homosexuality in ways not yet clear.

The stress on gay community and identity is sometimes linked with the idea of some sort of inherent gay sensibility, a notion often associated with the theory that one is "born" homosexual (an idea that seems to be resurfacing in some gay rhetoric). What is involved is rather the gradual transformation of old stereotypes into a set of positive self-images, rather as was done by the black cultural movement of the sixties. This is particularly true of the new response to the attacks on gay men as sexually promiscuous, a theme that is used frequently by homophobes to brand us as morally irresponsible, immature, and doomed to loneliness in old age. Whereas most homosexuals tended to answer this by claiming both that it wasn't true ("Look at Jack and Dan—together for thirty years") or, if true, was only so because of social pressures, now there is a move toward claiming that this is part of a different, perhaps even superior, way of managing sexual relationships. Gay women, too, influenced by feminist attacks on the family and monogamy, are increasingly inclined to defend other approaches to relationships than one based on the model of heterosexual marriage.

It is not merely that so many commercial institutions are organized around the assumption of promiscuity (baths, backroom bars), and often more honestly so than, say, the singles' bars available to straights. Beyond this, the assumption that it is desirable to have frequent and varied sex partners is increasingly seen as a positive part of the gay life style. Any commercial gay paper will make this clear: it is not merely the existence of sex as a commercial enterprise that is striking (the straight press is also full of adds for prostitutes, massage parlors, and pornography), but the range of sexual venues available to gay men (not women) in any large Western city.

The popularity and importance of gay baths seems to me particularly revealing, for with few exceptions they have no real counterpart for either gay women or heterosexuals. (An occasion for regret on the part of some of my women friends.) Large-scale luxurious pleasure palaces where everyone is potentially an immediate sexual partner are a common sexual fantasy; only for gay men are they a commonplace reality. (In the very large survey reported in Jay and Young's *The Gay Report*, a majority of gay men answering had used baths, 20 percent of them frequently.)[30] The growth of luxury in baths—they are now likely to include restaurants, pools, entertainment, and even, in Paris, a hairdresser—can be seen as both a triumph of commercialism and a mark of the declining furtiveness about homosexual sex. (Which does not mean that more furtive and sordid places have disappeared; one of the ironies about the commercialization of gay sex in the seventies was the way in which some of the new ventures re-created the atmosphere of illicit cruising grounds, as in the fake trucks in a New York bathhouse or the "cornhole bars" popular in San Francisco.) That such places do not exist for gay women is almost certainly one of the reasons that lesbians are seemingly much less visible in this sex-obsessed society.

The new self-assertion of homosexuals is by no means ubiquitous. There are still many who remain guilty, ashamed, or unable to act out their desires; the old attitudes persist, often in peculiar synergy with the new. There remain, too, those who have persuaded themselves that there is no reason to "come out" or who, perhaps, enjoy a sense of being in some way underground. (This self-image is catered to by a magazine like *After Dark*, which at the beginning of the eighties had a large readership, mainly among gay men. But the magazine carefully characterizes its readers as "affluent, successful and single. With no strings to tie them down and money to live it up, any chance they get.")[31]

While my main concern is those homosexuals who share, at least to some extent, the new gay definitions and identity, we must remember that a majority of homosexuals, especially those outside a few large urban areas, remain largely invisible and generally afraid of being discovered. The success of Patricia Nell Warren's books, in which this fear is a central theme, illustrates the importance of that group. (It was only with her third novel, *The Beauty Queen*, that Warren began to include lesbians in her writing.) The proliferation of a gay commercial scene is one of the key ways in which such people are brought into the gay community and often serves as a transition path toward the acceptance of a gay identity. Indeed, talk of "gay community" often seems more a product of commercialism and conspicuous consumption than of the sort of political identity associated with the gay movement of the early seventies. As one Toronto paper summed up the new gay market: "A buck is a buck. Who the hell cares if the wrist holding it is limp?"[32] Yet the invention of the gay minority as a definable consumer market is itself a step toward acceptance, even if it is acceptance defined by narrow economic criteria. From perceiving a gay market in areas such as travel, clothes, and entertainment, it is a short step toward recognizing a gay minority with political rights. Indeed, some gay activists see economic power as the basis for political clout, and inflated claims are being made for gay "consumer power"; one article in 1981 claimed that homosexuals controlled 34 percent of California's buying power.[33]

The link between the commercial world and the new homosexual, as well as the impact of both on society at large, is symbolized in the growth of discos. Almost every discussion of the disco phenomenon, which swept most of the Western world in the late seventies, stresses its connections with gays (in fact with gay men), thus reinforcing the idea of a self-evident gay culture and minority:

> "There is a big cultural difference between rock and disco," says Casablanca's promotional wizard, Kenn Friedmann. "And it's gayness. Disco began in gay clubs. These were the first entertainment institutions of gay life." Adds John Luongo, one of Boston's top disco entrepreneurs: "In the beginning there was the gay audience. The primo disc jockeys were gay. Disco was high energy, emotional, physical; liberation made gays much more loose that way. Now there's gay chic, so it's hard to tell what part of disco is essentially gay and what part has been stolen by the straights."[34]

It is easy to be snide about disco and to predict its imminent decline; in fact, the phenomenon of discos as technologically sophisticated and loud places for dancing can quite well survive the decline of disco-style music. The connection between discos and a whole ethos of deliberate hedonism, as in the widespread use of drugs (some of which, such as MDA and angel dust, seem clearly linked to the gay world), is often used to attack gay male culture; I have friends who see places like The Saint in New York as an expression of gay fascism. But discos also represent for many gay men an important way of expressing both a sense of solidarity and a celebration of their sexuality; at their best, discos generate a communal eroticism that is very powerful. For gay women, often excluded from places like The Saint, the equivalent seems to be women's dances and music festivals, less dependent on high technology and more self-consciously political. (There are many more openly gay women singers than men.) The disco phenomenon sums up very clearly the role of commercial ventures in the development of gay male culture, and their lesser importance for lesbians.

The development of "gay chic" is a sign of both the new openness about homosexuality and the ambivalence that still clings to it. (Thus the word "decadence" is frequently used to describe it.) Gay chic is found particularly in such places as the New York disco Studio 54 and its numerous imitations, places that are in some ways openly gay while catering to a status-conscious straight public. Such chic is often a parody of the reality of homosexual life; it stresses conspicuous consumption (of clothes, drugs, entertainment) and a sense of self-presentation and artifice, reflected in the exaggerated leather, punk, and glitter fashions associated with such places. Without the stress on either political or cultural revolution that marked the rhetoric of earlier "radical chic," the new gay male chic combines elements of traditional homosexual stereotypes, such as the cult of glamour and style, with the commercial products of the past decade, for example drugs, electronic music, and strobe lighting. The disco culture demonstrates that gay men are not only part of modern technetronic society but are often its vanguard; it is here that are developed such products as amyl-nitrite substitutes—now packaged (surely with irony) as "room odorizers."

The development of the gay commercial scene over the past decade is to a large extent a reflection of the new openness and self-affirmation by homosexuals, and thus markedly different from the more traditional forms of gay businesses, which were often controlled by people closely linked to criminal syndicates. What is striking is the profusion of services and institutions, many of which straddle both movement and commercial activities. A gay bookstore, for example, might be run as a business venture, but it could not exist without the new sense of identity—and literature—that is the product of social and political change. Starting a business is often a way

of integrating one's working and one's social life, and to start a gay
hotel or a women's restaurant can be a way of expressing a commitment to the gay community. Large cities now have gay travel agen-
cies, gay medical and legal services, gay theater groups, gay alcoholic
and counseling services, gay bookstores, gay publishing houses, and
so on.

Among professional and academic organizations there are a
number of gay caucuses, sometimes, as in the case of the American
Library Association, with a considerable effect on their parent body.
Gay sports are being increasingly organized: in 1980 the Canada
Cup (for softball) brought together teams from New York, Mil-
waukee, Boston, Los Angeles, Vancouver, and Toronto; in 1981
there was a gay rodeo in Reno; and a gay olympics is scheduled in
San Francisco in 1982.

To look through any gay magazine or paper (*Blueboy* and *The
Advocate* have themselves become large-scale ventures with quite
impressive circulation and advertising revenues) is to see something
of the scale of overtly gay businesses. Increasingly, businesses and
professionals in areas far removed from the traditional entertain-
ment-related ones are seeking out gay clientele and emphasizing
their gay ownership and/or employees. In a number of cities gay
businesses have formed organizations, such as the Gotham Business
Council in New York, and there is now a National Association of
(gay) Business Councils.

One of the best examples of these developments was the Gay
and Lesbian Lifestyles Expo at the Los Angeles Convention Center
in December 1980. With several hundred exhibitors (including such
nongay businesses as the Pacific Telephone and Telegraph Company
and Aspen Airways) and with an official proclamation from Mayor
Tom Bradley, the exhibition showed both the extent to which gays
are seen as an attractive market and the way in which some people
see this factor as a basis for political influence. As Scott Anderson
wrote of the National Association of Business Councils shortly after
the swing to the right in the 1980 elections: "(This) could well
become the most potent force for gay liberation in the 1980s. More
than any other group the 1500 members of the NABC may be in
the best position to influence conservative policy-makers through the
medium they best understand: dollars."[35] To date, the best example
of this sort of strategy has been gay participation in a boycott of
Coors beer, which helped from alliances between gay activists and
some trade unions.[36]

No other minority has depended so heavily on commercial

enterprises to define itself: while the role of movement papers, dances, and organizations has been significant, it has been overshadowed, especially for gay men, by the commercial world. One of the ironies of American capitalism is that it has been a major force in creating and maintaining a sense of identity among homosexuals, and so far such identity seems attainable only within existing capitalist societies. In a sense the shifting stress from the language of oppression, liberation, and the movement to one of discrimination, rights, and community indicates the new integration of gays through the commercial world into mainstream society.

A major reason for this is the lack of the family as the basic unit of social life, in the way it is for ethnic minorities. For homosexuals, bars and discos play the role performed for other groups by family and church. As one gay woman wrote:

> The bars have been and remain, even now, the focal point of the gay and lesbian community. They are the most stable institutions in a frequently unstable world. As such they shape the culture of gay life, even as they are shaped and changed themselves. They contain within them all the contradictions and weaknesses of gay life. They, nonetheless, are our territory, even with all the control that the outside world exerts.[37]

Thus gay bars are not really comparable to straight bars, or at least they perform a much larger role than is true for most others. (There may be a parallel in the role of taverns for immigrant groups in which there were large numbers of single men.) It is here that most homosexuals first meet others like themselves and are able to express themselves in ways denied them in other areas of their lives. If there are some unhappy consequences, most particularly a high rate of alcoholism, it is also true that the commercial scene provides a sense of identity and even community that only a relatively small number of homosexuals find in alternative institutions. Attacks by movement people on the commercial scene, or on novels such as *Dancer from the Dance* in which the commercial scene of discos and baths is such an important element, miss this point.

Is the stress on a "gay minority," a "gay life style," merely a reconceptualization of how people see what they (and others) are doing, or does it also involve, as many of our opponents claim, an absolute increase in the number of homosexuals? In fact there is no data to answer this question (though a duplication of the Kinsey studies in the eighties would be very suggestive). What is clear is that very many more people are now able to accept their homosexuality and to integrate it into their lives. The need to repress one's homosexuality is declining, and there is less necessity for the enormously painful barriers erected by so many people against recognizing this potential within themselves. There may still be those who, like Lionel March in E. M. Forster's powerful story "The Other Boat," feel a gentleman should shoot himself if he gives way to "unnatural" feelings, but they are surely declining. And the women's movement has enabled more women to come to terms with homosexual desires than has probably ever been the case. It is not surprising that there appears to be an increase in marriages breaking up because one partner is gay, or that this is becoming a theme of contemporary books and film.

As homosexuals become more visible and more assertive, a new hostility is created among people who find themselves confronted by homosexuality. It has always been the claim of homosexual militants that if all homosexuals "came out" it would create a dramatic change in attitudes and reactions. Just as homosexuals can only be blackmailed as long as they fear disclosure of their homosexuality (a real fear for many, most obviously when there is the possibility of police prosecutions), so in a more general sense the stigma against homosexuals depends upon our remaining largely invisible.

This argument now seems to me fairly dubious. It is true that the traditional stereotypes cannot easily survive a widespread recognition that for millions of women and men homosexuality is a perfectly ordinary and unexceptional way of living their lives. To come out publicly is, according to the liberationist argument, the one potentially radical act for every homosexual, which is why homosexual militancy cannot be simply measured by organized movement activity. But as more homosexuals come out, new stereotypes are created; the assertion of homosexuality has in turn created new forms of homophobia. This is not an argument for remaining closeted; the psychic damages of social invisibility are too great. It is, however, an argument against the liberal belief that greater knowledge necessarily leads to greater acceptance.

Coming out can occur at all sorts of levels and among all sorts of groups: family, friends, fellow students, colleagues, even casual acquaintances. The growing openness of homosexuals means that more and more people are coming into contact with us, and this leads to a major confrontation of prejudices and hang-ups. Whether it be the lesbian who wears a badge to work, the two men with their arms around each other in the street, the woman who tells a man

who's bugging her that she prefers women, or the men who start
dancing together at an office party, in all sorts of small and everyday
ways homosexuals are becoming visible and hence demanding recognition at this everyday level.

*   *   *   *   *   *   *

Today the dominant view of homosexuality has become problematic, suspended as it were between the traditional condemnation
(whether in religious, legal, medical, or psychological terms) and the
new concepts of minority and alternative life style. These changes
are by and large the product of the past two decades and are particularly marked in the Anglo-Saxon world where condemnation of
homosexuality had been remarkably savage. (A book produced in
England in 1955, including contributions by Establishment figures
in law, medicine, religion, and politics, could pronounce in its introduction that, "There can be no question about the potential evil, in
varying degrees, resulting from the practices associated with homosexuality."[38] This sort of extravagant language seems much less
common in continental Europe, except under totalitarian regimes,
and indeed in most other parts of the world.)

Thus it is in the Anglo-Saxon world that the changes have been
most dramatic; if in the fifties Britain and the United States were
seen as extremely repressive societies from which homosexuals were
forced to flee, often to Paris, in the seventies it was the United States
that became the new gay mecca, with Parisians looking to it as the
epitome of liberated sexuality.[39] (To a lesser extent London shares
some of this reputation, although it seems to me oddly undeserved.)

Yet we must reiterate that old attitudes coexist with the new
self-affirmation, and it is often difficult to disentangle the two. The
lesbian who strides in a Gay Pride March may not have come out
to her parents or work mates; the gay man who wears a gay button
at his school or neighborhood may also harbor self-doubts that scar
his personal relationships. In the same way social attitudes have only
changed in part and have, if anything, become more unpredictable.
This was illustrated in the media coverage after the tennis player
Billy Jean King was sued by a former female lover; the press seemed
very confused about whether to condemn her for lesbianism (or, in
some cases, for adultery) or to congratulate her for bravery.

There has clearly been a marked increase in self-acceptance by
homosexuals over the past decade; there has probably also been an
increase in social acceptance, often as a result of pressure by homosexuals themselves, all the more remarkable because this has not

seemed a period generally hospitable to ideas of social change. To draw up a scorecard of progress is very difficult; the score would depend on sex, class, and locale. Clearly for a middle-class male homosexual in San Francisco the progress made during the seventies is much more apparent than for a poor lesbian in rural Arkansas (and the differences are duplicated elsewhere; a study for the French group Arcadie highlighted the gap between, say, the Midi and the much more conservative west).[40] But reality is more complex: the San Francisco man still risks real physical violence and the Arkansas woman may have experienced very basic changes in her life as a direct result of new opportunities to meet other women.

On some criteria there can be no doubt about the changes of the past decade. The most obvious is law reform. It is not merely that during the sixties and seventies many of those countries that retained punitive sanctions against homosexual behavior (in most cases exclusively between males) abolished these laws; this was true of England and Wales (but not of Scotland until 1980 and not of Northern Ireland even now), both West and East Germany, Austria, Canada, and a minority of American and Australian states. After all, in practice the state usually retained enough legal weapons to continue persecution of homosexuals for "soliciting," "offensive behavior," or whatever; Britain, Canada, and states like Illinois can all furnish graphic examples of how changes in the law by themselves do not necessarily end police harassment. In the same way, even in countries that, often because of the influence of the Napoleonic Code, had not classified homosexual behavior as a crime, all sorts of restrictions on homosexual meeting places and organizations remain (for example in Spain, Finland, and much of Latin America). The whole area of legal and police persecution of homosexuals is very complicated and underresearched.

More significant may be something that only occurred in the seventies, namely the creation of positive protection of homosexuals by the legal system. This takes two forms: recourse to the police to protect homosexuals against private vigilantes and punks (at the end of 1980 one of the major complaints of the New York gay movement was the inadequacy of police protection in gay areas), and the move to include homosexuals within the ambit of various antidiscrimination and human rights ordinances. The latter marks the most significant recognition on the legal front of the concept of a gay minority.

In a number of American cities, in several states, in Quebec, and within a different legal framework in Norway, Holland, and most recently France, governments have with varying degrees of efficacy declared their commitment to gay rights. Most often this is done by means of antidiscrimination laws, although it may also involve executive orders, such as that issued by Governor Brown in California which banned discrimination against homosexual personnel in state government employ. Equally, and again largely in the United States, the courts have extended at least certain legal protection to cover homosexuals. Thus, while the Supreme Court has so far refused to rule on the constitutionality of antisodomy laws, which have been challenged under the Court's own doctrine of the right to privacy, various judgments, for example over dismissal from the armed services and immigration restrictions, have begun the gradual process of extending legal protection for homosexuals.[41] These, in turn, contribute to the creation of a recognized minority status for gays.

That this is largely an American phenomenon is not surprising; both recourse to legal protection of civil rights and state action to protect minorities have a special place in American politics and jurisprudence. Similar moves have been pushed for in Canada, and to a lesser extent Australia and New Zealand; in Holland the government has stated it will not discriminate against homosexuals, and in some areas of housing and welfare it recognizes the existence of homosexual couples. Norway, which has a national antidiscrimination law, and Sweden are moving in this direction. (It is worth reflection that the most enlightened governments are in those countries where social democracy is most entrenched.) At the moment legal acceptance of homosexual partnerships, of the rights of homosexual parents to child custody, and of the possibility for homosexuals to adopt children are before the courts in a number of countries.

Yet even after law reform and antidiscrimination ordinances, a whole fabric of discrimination remains. This is clearest in the case of employment: in most American states homosexuals are legally barred from such varied occupations as cosmetologist, electrician, and plumber. Of course, most of the time such requirements are discreetly ignored. Similarly, while United States immigration laws bar known homosexuals from the country, I have been admitted on several occasions for the purpose of promoting books on gay liberation. (Since a court ruling in San Francisco in June 1981 the status of the immigration laws has been uncertain.) Particularly in the fields of education, medicine, and certain public services, however, being known as a homosexual is a real barrier. Even though federal employment rules theoretically preclude discrimination based on sexual orientation, the attitude of many administrators is similar to that of President Carter's Special Trade Representative, Reuben Askew, who at his confirmation hearings in mid-1979 declared, "I will not have a known homosexual on my staff."[42] To the best of my knowledge the CIA and State Department still seek to exclude homosexuals, while the position of homosexuals in the military is an extremely murky one following a number of court cases, the best known of which concerned Sergeant Matlovich, who after six years of litigation following his dismissal accepted a cash settlement from the Air Force.

The impact of social attitudes toward homosexuality can affect the whole pattern of our working lives. Howard Brown, chief health officer of New York City in the 1960s, wrote:

> It was my homosexuality that determined my choice of profession —I hoped to solve the riddle of my sexual identity in medical school. It was my homosexuality that determined which city I would live and work in—New York would allow me to lead the sort of life, social and private, that my staunchly gay nature impelled me to. And it was my homosexuality that impelled me to resign some eighteen months after I had attained the pinnacle of my profession. At the same time my professional life repeatedly impinged upon my life as a homosexual, ultimately damaging the relationship that meant more to me than any other—indeed more to me than anything else in the world; my long-term love affair with Thomas.[43]

At this point being gay clearly becomes a dominant part of one's identity.

Among the ideological institutions of society, the most important changes in attitude toward homosexuality have occurred among psychiatrists and psychologists. The abolition of the definition of homosexuality as a mental illness by the American Psychiatric Association has had considerable impact; not the least result was to throw the whole policy of excluding homosexual aliens into disrepute. Many psychiatrists, however, remain unconvinced by the change, and Ronald Bayer concludes his study of the shift with a warning that the decision is bound to become increasingly vulnerable.[44] (The World Health Organization has retained the classification of homosexuality as a disease.) Psychiatrists are found among both the allies and the opponents of those who argue that homosexuality should be understood as an alternative life style.

Churches, in many ways the bulwark of homophobic ideology,

are by no means monolithic in their condemnation. Quakers, Unitarians, and Disciples of Christ have all moved toward an acceptance of homosexuality, and the United Church of Christ was the first in America to ordain an openly homosexual clergyman (William Johnson in 1972.)[45] In Britain a report of the Anglican Synod in 1979 called for the Church of England to do likewise (perhaps it would be unkind to suggest that this church is already renowned for the number of closeted clergy in its midst). Fundamentalist and Catholic hostility has been less affected. The present pope has reaffirmed the Catholic church's resistance to any recognition of homosexuality as valid, and most rabbis have adopted similar positions.

In response to these prejudices many gay religious groups have grown up over the past decade, ministering to homosexuals of all denominations who are unwilling to accept the teachings of their churches. The most significant of these is the Metropolitan Community Church (M.C.C.), which claims about 30,000 adherents in some 170 churches throughout the world. While the church's leader, the Reverend Troy Perry, perhaps the most charismatic leader yet produced by the American gay movement, protests that the church is open to all, it is clearly directed at those who identify themselves as homosexual and has succeeded in attracting many people who are searching for a sense of gay community. Often the M.C.C. will be the only gay meeting place apart from a bar in a particular town.

Crucial to any change in social perceptions of and by homosexuals is the role of the media. It would be a massive job to analyze how the media depiction of homosexuality and homosexuals has changed over the past decade, yet it is an important one. That the media reinforces oppression and self-hatred is now almost a liberal cliché, yet the stock homosexual figures of ridicule, fun, and pathos conveyed by the great bulk of television programs and the popular press are probably the most direct image of homosexuality available to those growing up in contemporary Western societies. They are nicely summed up in the title of one of the few relevant studies, "How to Be Immoral, Ill, Pathetic and Dangerous All at the Same Time."[46]

Very little systematic study has been made of the way in which these popular images may be changing; the only safe generalization is that there has been a marked increase in visibility over the past ten years. Several articles have discussed this in terms of television,[47] where there have been some attempts to portray homosexuality positively in plays like "That Certain Summer" and serials like "Alice," "Soap," "All in the Family," and "Rock Follies" (in Britain). So far there have been no such serials with homosexuals as central characters, except for the Australian "Number 96," for a long time considered unsuitable for American viewers. (The NBC sitcom "Love, Sidney" manages to ignore the sexuality of its central character.) At the same time there have been a number of special documentaries, often sensational and of dubious value in challenging prejudices about homosexuals. One such documentary, CBS's "Gay Power, Gay Politics," was even criticized by the National News Council for its distortion.

Among major newspapers the trend over the past ten years has been quite clearly toward increasing the coverage of gay news (even allowing for the fact that there is much more to report than there was ten years ago). It has been a long, and by no means always victorious struggle, to convince editors and journalists that there *is* gay news other than murders and scandal. Today a few newspapers —the *San Francisco Chronicle,* the *Minneapolis Star,* and the *Los Angeles Times,* for example—are reasonably aware of the need for coverage of gay movement and cultural events. Unfortunately this is not true of *The New York Times,* whose neglect of gay-related stories is quite remarkable in a paper claiming the most extensive news coverage in America.[48] The newsweeklies have been more aware; *Time* magazine devoted three cover stories over a decade (in 1969, 1975, and 1979) to changing views of homosexuality and clearly modified its moralizing during the period.

Nonetheless homophobia still surfaces in a way unlikely for more socially disapproved prejudices like anti-Semitism. The same newspaper that gives fair and adequate coverage to, say, debate on an antidiscrimination ordinance is likely to carry an advice column full of undisguised prejudice, book reviews that can only see homosexual relations as "immature" or "unsatisfying," or social pages with coy references to "housemates" and "companions." But even where the media sensationalizes, trivializes, and exaggerates, the general thrust of media attention has been to help consolidate a sense of homosexual identity and community. It may also, as some activists feared of the CBS documentary or the film *Cruising,* help create greater hostility. As David Rothenberg has stressed, the omission of stories is often as crucial as the way stories are reported (antigay violence, for example, is very rarely analyzed by the media).[49] Often the press is only interested in the most extreme forms of sexual hedonism, homosexuals being portrayed entirely in sexual terms. A good example of this comes from the Australian edition of *Playboy*:

> Simplified, straights have their golf, their tennis, their bridge and stamps. Gays have their leather bars, hotel lavatories known as the beat . . . gay libbers . . . the drag queen society and the very, very quiet gays.[50]

The medium that has had the most difficulty coming to terms with homosexuality is the film industry, which, in America at least, only rarely depicts homosexuals as other than villains or victims. This is less true of Western Europe, where there are many more films that show homosexuals as complex and human characters. But even a decade of major social change has had little impact on the way in which homosexuals appear in Hollywood; if they are not portrayed as evil, as in *Windows* or *Cruising*, they will be lonely and self-hating, as in the film *Fame*. The beginning of 1982 saw a number of films with homosexual themes, but of these *Personal Best* was largely a heterosexual male fantasy and *Partners* an American version of *Cage aux Folles*. Only *Making Love*, the story of a man whose marriage collapses because of his homosexuality, suggested a willingness to portray homosexual relations as equally valid as heterosexual ones, and the wariness with which the film was promoted suggests real change will be slow. Indeed, the American film industry provides a fascinating case study of self-hate (no one questions that there are large numbers of gays at all levels of the film industry) and of commercial and artistic judgment being subordinated to traditional moralizing. Since a great many of our concepts about sexuality and relationships come from the movies, a real change in these attitudes would be extremely important.

As gays are increasingly being perceived as a minority in the best American tradition, it is hardly surprising that they have come to claim a political role based on this fact. In New York, San Francisco, Los Angeles, Washington, Houston, Seattle, and a number of smaller cities, gay political clubs, often linked to the Democratic Party, have provided the basis for direct intervention by homosexuals in electoral politics; in San Francisco it seems accepted that one of the city supervisors should be recognizably gay. (There was a tragic irony in the fact that the first person to hold that position, Harvey Milk, was shot, along with the mayor, George Moscone; the light sentence awarded their killer, ex-supervisor Dan White, led to major riots the following year.) In 1979 the *Washington Post* could comment that "they (homosexuals) are now ranked by city politicans with such traditional power blocks as organized labor, the black church and the business community. . . . Gays have money, votes and a sense of persecution. Gay issues to them are like Israel to Jews. The sense of persecution binds them together."[51]

So far this seems a largely American phenomenon; the pattern of American politics is particularly appropriate for locally based pressure-group politics. Gay intervention in mainstream politics in other Western countries has been much more sporadic, although openly gay candidates have contested elections in a number of countries, and in Britain, Holland, and Norway parliamentarians have "come out" publicly. (The British M. P. Maureen Colquhoun was challenged for preselection in her local Labor branch, a challenge in which antigay prejudice was clearly involved, but it was the general swing against Labor in 1979 that cost her her seat.)[52] In Italy the largest organized gay movement, FUORI, is closely associated with the Radical Party, and at least one openly homosexual deputy has been elected. In Spain there are close ties between the gay movement and sections of the non-Communist left, ties forged during the underground period of Franco's reign, and in some South American countries such as Mexico, Colombia, and Brazil there are signs of this sense of a new politicized minority.

The new sense of homosexual identity/community is most visible in large cities; in 1979 Arthur Bell wrote of Dayton, Ohio, which he argued represents the American heartland:

> To the average straight Daytonian, a gay subculture does not exist. To that same straight, gay is "drag." Since drag is out of the question in Dayton, homosexuality is invisible. What is visible is the male couple who have lived next door for the past 20 years. They're a little weird, but they're witty and harmless, so they're invited to straight cocktail parties. The word, I believe, is assimilation. Most individuals look to straights for models in terms of career, dress, attitude. Naturally Dayton is without a gay sensibility.[53]

Over the past ten years what would once have been true of the entire country is no longer the case in its big cities, where certain areas—the most famous being the West Village in New York, the Castro area of San Francisco, and West Hollywood—have become distinctively gay in the way that other areas of American cities are

Italian or black or Chinese. These new gay neighborhoods are characterized not only as centers of homosexual night life (such areas are common in most large Western cities), but also as places where increasing numbers of gay men, if far less frequently women, live and work. As a consequence, one of the most important impacts of the changing nature of homosexuality over the past ten years has been on the very appearance and nature of the inner city.

Such areas are marked by a certain sameness: they seem at first sight to be populated almost entirely by men under the age of forty-five, dressed in a uniform and carefully calculated style and dedicated to a hedonistic and high-consumption life style. The main streets of what are often termed the ghettos—Christopher Street and Columbus Avenue in New York, North Wells in Chicago, Castro and Polk in San Francisco, Santa Monica Boulevard in Los Angeles—are lined with shops selling high-camp postcards, coffee pots, pillowcases, T-shirts, and even food (in the ice cream parlors and "Erotic Bakeries"), with dim, noisy, and smoke-filled bars, and with the new-style gay restaurants, full of potted palms, with large front windows and health-food menus.

In a way that is rapidly declining elsewhere, these neighborhoods remain oases of sidewalk life, with constant movement in and out of shops and bars and a twenty-four-hour ritual of cruising, meeting friends, and in some cases buying and selling drugs. (Every afternoon a little stall is set up near the end of Christopher Street, where an emaciated man dressed in black sells various forms and replicas of amyl nitrite.) By midnight on Saturday the main streets of the gay ghetto in any American city will be packed with thousands of men seeking thrills, sex, conversation, escape, or perhaps lifetime love. Unlike all other neighborhoods these contain almost no children (though there are numbers of teenagers searching for both love and money), few old people, and not very many women, though there are more than may appear, for women are less likely to cruise the streets. Lesbians often live in these areas; the West Village, for example, has long been a center for gay women as well as men and features in a number of lesbian pulp novels, and in San Francisco Valencia Street is fast becoming a lesbian equivalent to Castro. Like other neighborhoods, these areas represent both the affirmation of a particular culture, in this case an embryonic one that is still in the process of being invented, and a subtle form of social control: as the gay ghettos become better known and are recognized by politicians looking for votes and tourist guides to the city, they also suggest a particular confinement of homosexuality to certain areas and certain styles, just as the original purpose of the ghetto was to restrict Jews to certain areas so that their presence could not weaken the faith of the Christian majority.

But the word "ghetto" is perhaps misleading, even though it has been adopted by gays themselves. (There are plans to open a gay bookstore in Sydney called Ghetto Books.) As Alain Sanzio put it, "the homosexual space is both the expression of the place assigned to homosexuals by society and the possibility of living openly, thus destroying this social reality—[the ghetto] is a territory of desire and in this sense it escapes the heterosexual model."[54] Such spaces are as much neighborhoods as they are ghettos, for people move to them voluntarily as places where they can live openly as gay. Their development is an essential part of the growth of a sense of homosexual identity.

The changes in the inner city that allow the creation of new neighborhoods have always led to friction, whether because blacks and Puerto Ricans displace Jews and Italians in Harlem or the Lower East Side, or because gays displace blacks and Puerto Ricans in West Side Manhattan or Chicanos in Silverlake (Los Angeles). As San Francisco Supervisor Harry Britt pointed out: "The displacement creates anomie, and people look for a scapegoat. The speculation business creates real bigotry—and the bigotry is encouraged in some quarters. If a land speculator is Italian or whatever, he is never identified as such in the newspapers. But if the real estate speculator is gay, the major papers are quick to point it out."[55] Enthusiasm for the "gentrification" of certain once run-down areas should not lead us to overlook the costs, both for those pushed out and for those who move in.

Of course it is an error to attribute "gentrification" to gays alone; the trend is a broader middle-class phenomenon in which gay influence varies considerably from area to area. In San Francisco, for example, where the gay presence is most obvious, there is a clear demarcation between areas around Castro and the Haight on the one hand, and the almost exclusively straight area around Union Street. Armistead Maupin's serial, *Tales of the City*, shows very well the complexity of changes in the social composition of various parts of the city. But the very visibility of gays, especially gay men, in the process has made such urban developments a symbol of homosexualization.

There is a further category of gentrification, namely the development of certain resort areas as openly gay. The first and still most famous of these is Cherry Grove on Fire Island, which has been known as a gay area for thirty years (and more recently was joined by the Pines). Since the 1960s, Provincetown, Key West, Russian River (in northern California), and Palm Springs have all developed a visible gay scene, often with tensions between local residents and gay vacationers as the homosexual tourists are less and less willing to remain closeted.

The new gay neighborhoods represent the most visible sign of a larger process I have already termed homosexualization. It might be objected that the word is inappropriate, that, indeed, what is happening is the more sophisticated control of a newly defined minority rather than the impact of that minority on society as a whole. Yet as homosexuals grow both more visible and more distinct, it becomes possible to talk about their overall effect on American life in a way that was not possible until a decade ago. While homosexuals have long exercized a considerable influence on style and fashion, this was a different phenomenon from the impact of a self-conscious minority whose presence is now openly asserted. "New York," claimed a friend of mine, "is now a gay city, just as it used to be a Jewish one." He did not mean by this that there were necessarily more homosexuals and fewer Jews (the two are not, of course, mutually exclusive, although one would never guess it from the rhetoric of the Jewish right), but rather that the dominant style of New York, or at least of Manhattan, is set by visible homosexuals.

Such homosexualization is apparent in a number of areas—the remaking of the inner city, the development of certain forms of urban life and entertainment (such as disco), and the use in decor of high technology. Overall there seem two major areas where one can most accurately speak of homosexualization; fashion, and attitudes toward sexuality and relationships.

One of the common clichés about homosexuals is our role in defining fashion, and it is in those professions that are concerned with setting style (for example, for clothes, hair, and interior decoration) that the traditional stereotypical male homosexual is still most visible. It is easy to dismiss such matters as being of little importance, and as falling within those areas of life often dismissed as feminine (one reason why they have been open to male homosexuals). Yet this would be a mistake. How one presents oneself to the outside world is not merely a matter of individual taste; it is also a product of certain social pressures, and when we choose to adopt certain fashions rather than others we are often less free than we imagine. That the gay world is the source of a number of styles and fashions that become dominant throughout society is not due to conscious decisions made by either homosexuals or nonhomosexuals but seems rather to be a result of the social roles played by homosexuals and their corresponding importance in the style-setting businesses (fashion, photography, advertising). The diffusion of the macho style through advertising (for jeans, for example) and entertainers like the Village People led to its being adopted by millions of straight men unaware of its origin. In the same way the sadomasochistic references that have been common in much female fashion over the past few years owe much of their inspiration to the gay world.[56] What is common to both of these styles is an assertion of sexuality, and one could speculate that since much of gay self-assertion involves such open expressions of sexuality, this is influencing larger social mores through fashion.

In his novel *The Lure* Felice Picano uses the redecorating of Noel's apartment as a symbol of his accepting his gayness:

> His stark white walls became different shades of grey and brown, with satiny hues of blues and pinks that only emerged at night or in different lighting. Old, much painted-over pipes and mouldings —formerly hidden behind white paint—stepped forward as design elements when he painted them in chocolate and charcoal grey. He ordered a dozen plants of various sizes from a plant store . . . and was building in planters for the larger ones, hanging the smaller ones. He tore down his loft bed and put the bedspring and mattress on the floor in the middle of the studio, heaping it with large pillows, surrounding it with small wooden cubes he'd bought, unfinished and painted to match the walls.[57]

What could seem trivial and no more than surface fripperies here becomes important as a means of expressing a basic psychological change.

Just as in earlier times homosexuals were identified by tennis shoes, scarves and jewelry for men, shoulder bags, and floral shirts, so a new set of styles came to be identified as gay during the seventies: restaurants with plants and plate-glass windows; an art deco revival; greeting card shops; wicker furniture; high tech style; leather fashions; earrings for men and army fatigues for women; Perrier water. No doubt as the decade progresses these will be replaced by others. The crucial point is that as gays become more open, so too does their impact on fashions as a whole.

Even language takes on terms derived from the gay culture. The word "gay" itself is the classic example, but so too is the use of "cruising," meaning the search for sexual partners, and the term "out of the closet." My favorite example (from an in-flight music program) is the country and western singer who had "come out of the closet to show his natural talent here on TWA."

But there is another sense in which American society is being homosexualized, and this is the sense in which more and more people, especially those who are young, educated, and urban, are behaving in ways long thought typical of homosexuals. The growth of singles' bars, "wife-swapping" parties (despite the sexist term), computer dating, and so on suggest the way in which casual and recreational sex, so long condemned as "promiscuous" and "irresponsible" and thus proving the undesirability of homosexuality, is becoming a heterosexual as much as a homosexual norm.

It might seem ironic to argue that there has been an increase in the homosexual impact on social mores at a time when gay self-assertion is creating a greater degree of separation, symbolized by the development of gay ghettos. In fact it is the new openness of homosexuals that makes such an impact possible and that means we can speak both of the invention of a homosexual minority and of the homosexualization of the society at large. No longer sinners, criminals, perverts, neurotics, or deviants, homosexuals are slowly being redefined in less value-laden terms as practitioners of an alternative life style, members of a new community. In a self-proclaimed pluralist society like the United States, this is probably the most effective way to win tolerance, if not full acceptance. In the process the gay impact on the rest of society, once something spoken about in whispers, becomes much more open and visible; but if gays are seen as the pioneers of new life styles, rather as was the counterculture in the sixties and feminists in the seventies, this brings in its wake attacks as well as imitation. Moreover, there are some surprising implications to the process of redefinition, as we shall see.

NOTES

1   See Ken Emerson, "The Village People: America's Male Ideal?" *Rolling Stone*, October 5, 1978; William Franklin, "Morali," *The Advocate*, December 27, 1979.

2   "Within These Walls" (editorial statement), *Gay Left* (London), No. 2, Spring 1976, p. 4.

3 Tom Burke, "The New Homosexuality," *Esquire*, December 1969, p. 74.

4 Paul Robinson, "Invisible Men," *New Republic*, June 3, 1978, p. 10.

5 See Robin Maugham, *Conversations with Willie* (New York: Simon and Schuster, 1978).

6 Michael Davidson, *The World, The Flesh and Myself* (London: Quartet, 1977), p. 191.

7 See Jeffrey Weeks, "Discourse, Desire and Sexual Deviance," in Ken Plummer (ed.), *The Making of the Modern Homosexual* (London: Hutchinson, 1980).

8 See the discussion in Lillian Faderman, *Surpassing the Love of Men* (New York: William Morrow, 1980).

9 See Alain Sanzio, "Homosexualité et Société," *Masques* (Paris) No. 9/10, Summer 1981, p. 82.

10 Quoted by Arno Karlen in *Sexuality and Homosexuality* (New York: W. W. Norton, 1971), p. 198. The doctor in question was Gerald Feigen, a proctologist.

11 Mary Renault, *The Charioteer* (London: Longmans, 1953), p. 176.

12 Lenny Gitteck, "The Face of Gay Phoenix," *The Advocate*, May 17, 1979.

13 Martin Hoffman, *The Gay World* (New York: Basic Books, 1968), p. 153.

14 *New York Review of Books*, May 31, 1979, p. 37.

15 Quoted in *Campaign* (Sydney), November 1980, p. 17.

16 Roger Baker, "Times They Were A-Changin," *Gay News* (London), December 14, 1978, p. 22.

17 See Bertha Harris, "The More Profound Nationality of Their Lesbianism," in P. Birkby et al. (eds.), *Amazon Expedition: A Lesbian Feminist Anthology* (New York: Times Change Press, 1973).

18 *Time*, January 8, 1979.

19 "No Man's Land," in Karla Jay and Allen Young, *Lavender Culture* (New York: Jove/HBJ, 1979), p. 51.

20 Ibid., p. 52.

21 Ibid., p. 55.

22 Joan Nestle, "Butch-Fem Relationships," *Heresies*, No. 12 ("sex issue"), p. 23.

23 See for example the interview with Amber Hollibaugh, *Socialist Review*, No. 45, May–June 1979.

24 Quoted by Charles Hix, *Male Model* (New York: St. Martin's Press, 1979), p. 185.

25 Paul Hoch, *White Hero, Black Beast* (London: Pluto, 1979), p. 81.

26 Laud Humphries, "New Styles in Homosexual Manliness," *Transaction*, March–April 1971, p. 41.
27 Deborah Wolf, *The Lesbian Community* (Berkeley: University of California Press, 1979), p. 86.
28 Lynn Bahlman, "Game Ladies," *Christopher Street*, September 1977, p. 41.
29 Guy Hocquenghem, "We Can't All Die in Bed," *Semiotext(e)*, Vol. III, No. 2, 1978, pp. 30–31.
30 Karla Jay and Allen Young, *The Gay Report* (New York: Summit Books, 1979), p. 239.
31 *After Dark*, April 1978, p. 31.
32 Ken Waxman, quoted by Michael Lynch, "The Rise of Gay Capitalism," *Body Politic*, October 1976.
33 Shannon Steele, "Business Affairs," *The Voice* (San Francisco), March 27, 1981, p. 30.
34 Andrew Kopkind, "Disco Tech," *New Times*, August 1, 1979, p. 52.
35 Scott Anderson, "Money Muscle," *The Advocate*, December 25, 1980, p. 24.
36 On this see Randy Shilts, *The Mayor of Castro Street* (New York: St. Martin's Press, 1982).
37 Christine Riddiough, "Culture and Politics," in Blazing Star (ed.), *Working Papers on Gay/Lesbian Liberation* (Chicago: New American Movement, 1979), p. 14.
38 J. Tudor Rees and H. V. Usil, *They Stand Apart* (London: Heinemann, 1958), p. xi.
39 See my "The Americanization of the French Homosexual," *The Advocate*, October 2, 1980.
40 Jerome Bernay, *Grand'peur et Misère des Homosexuels Français* (Paris: Arcadie, 1977).
41 See E. Carrington Boggan et al. (eds.), *The Rights of Gay People* (New York: Avon, 1975), and "Homosexuality and the Law," *Journal of Homosexuality*, Vol. 5, Nos. 1/2, Fall/Winter 1979–1980.
42 *Time*, October 15, 1979.
43 Howard Brown, *Familiar Faces, Hidden Lives* (New York: Harcourt Brace Jovanovich, 1976), p. 142.
44 Ronald Bayer, *Homosexuality and American Psychiatry* (New York: Basic Books, 1981), p. 194.
45 *Time*, June 5, 1978.
46 Frank Pearce, in Stan Cohen and Jock Young (eds.), *The Manufacture of News* (London: Constable, 1973).
47 See, for example, David Mole, "Watching Them Watching Us,"

Body Politic, December 1980–January 1981; Larry Gross, "The Ethics of (Mis)representation" (paper delivered to the Edward R. Murrow Symposium, Washington State University, April 1981); Richard Levine, "How the Gay Lobby Has Changed Television," *TV Guide,* May 30 and June 6, 1981; Vito Russo, *The Celluloid Closet* (New York: Harper & Row, 1981), pp. 220–226.

48 See David Rothenberg, "Homophobia at the New York Times," *New York Native,* No. 13, June 1, 1981.

49 David Rothenberg, "Media Watch," *New York Native,* No. 4, January 1981, p. 7.

50 Daphne Guiness, "Sydney: Gay Capital of Australia," *Australian Playboy,* May 1981, p. 94.

51 Milton Coleman, "Washington's Gay Vote," *Washington Post,* April 21, 1979.

52 See Susan Hemmings, "Horrific Practices: How Lesbians Were Presented in the Newspapers of 1978," in Gay Left Collective, *Homosexuality: Power and Politics* (London: Allison & Busby, 1980), pp. 158–162.

53 Arthur Bell, "Gay American Gothic," *The Village Voice,* May 21, 1979, p. 38.

54 Alain Sanzio, "Les Espaces du Désir," *Masques,* No. 6, Autumn 1980, p. 108.

55 Quoted by Robin Hardy, "San Francisco: Hitting Back," *Body Politic,* July 1979, p. 24.

56 Kennedy Fraser, "On and Off the Avenue," *The New Yorker,* June 19, 1978.

57 Felice Picano, *The Lure* (New York: Delacorte Press, 1979), p. 353.

CHAPTER TWO

Homosexuals and Homosexuality: The Problems of Definition

If the thrust of most of the changes that took place over the past decade has been toward the construction and recognition of a homosexual minority, it is important to realize that this thrust is double-edged. On the one hand the recent changes have undoubtedly been important in developing a sense of self-confidence and acceptance among those who conceive of themselves as homosexuals; "gay pride" and "glad to be gay" were slogans that expressed this feeling very well. On the other hand, the more stress that is placed on the idea of a homosexual minority, the more difficult it is to recognize that homosexuality, whether acted out or repressed, is part of everyone's sexuality and has implications for many people other than those who conceptualize themselves as part of the gay minority.

This view of homosexuality is derived from Freud, who differed from most of his contemporaries in insisting that homosexuality was neither innate nor a discrete category. For Freud, homosexual desire was part of the infant's "polymorphous perversity"; that is, we are all born with an undifferentiated sexuality, in terms of both sexual object (the sought-after partner) and sexual aim (the sought-after act). Certain variations from the "normal" pattern of sexual development, somewhat different depending on one's gender, were advanced by Freud to explain why some people become largely or exclusively homosexual in terms of the sexual object, but Freud never regarded homosexuals as a discrete category and stressed the existence of repressed and/or sublimated homosexuality in everyone: "By studying sexual excitations other than those that are manifestly displayed, it [psychoanalysis] has found that all human beings are capable of making a homosexual object choice and have in fact made one in their unconscious."[1] Consequently Freud denied that there was such a thing as "innate inversion"[2] and rejected the ideas of those earlier writers, such as Ulrichs and Krafft-Ebbing, who had argued for it. Ulrichs had seen homosexuals as men with "a feminine brain in a masculine body," constituting a "third sex," a term already used by Gautier in 1835 of women, and by Balzac in 1844 of men.[3] (Ulrichs paid virtually no attention to lesbians.)[4] The idea of "urnings" (Ulrichs's term) who are innately quite different from heterosexuals in some unspecified way was strongly rejected by Freud.

Freud's view of homosexuality was both complex and changing, for he discussed it in a number of both clinical and theoretical works written over a long period of time. But the essential point is that Freud consistently rejected the notion of a defined group of people who were in some innate and unchangeable way homosexual, and it was probably the influence of Freud that ended the tendency of late nineteenth-century apologists to so define homosexuals. It was also a major reason for Havelock Ellis's disagreements with Freud, with Ellis clinging to the congenital theory of homosexuality.[5]

Freud remains a figure of considerable controversy, and even many people who employ his concepts remain unwilling to acknowledge his influence. Yet in certain key areas—the fluidity of sexual desire, the existence of the unconscious, the importance of sexuality, and the concepts of repression and sublimation—Freud's insights seem to me to have withstood attempts over the past half-century to discredit him. We may doubt (as I do) much of what he had to say about female sexuality, about the mechanisms of sexual development, about the workings of dreams, and especially about the therapeutic value of psychoanalysis, while recognizing that his remains overall the most satisfactory framework for understanding human sexuality.

Much gay hostility to Freud stems from a perception that he saw homosexuality as immature and a perversion. Yet it is important to stress that Freud was far less homophobic than the bulk of psychoanalysts who have followed him, particularly in the United States where psychoanalysis has become associated with considerable antipathy to homosexuality. American psychoanalysts like Irving Bieber, whose insistence on the pathology of homosexuality influenced a whole generation of analysts and psychiatrists, quite consciously rejected Freud's belief in innate bisexuality.[6] Freud, however, saw homosexuals as neither sick nor criminal, was careful to spell out that "inverts cannot be regarded as degenerate," and, indeed, claimed that some "are distinguished by specially high intellectual development and ethical culture,"[7] and he supported the early German and Austrian campaigns to decriminalize homosexuality.[8] In some ways he wrote about homosexuality with a degree of acceptance not found again among psychiatrists until the early seventies. For Freud, of course, sublimation of homosexual desire was a crucial part of both social and cultural life, as he argued in his study of Leonardo da Vinci. Wasn't this, indeed, reflected in his own life, in which there is evidence of very strong repressed homosexuality—his idealized relationship with his wife, his strong attachments to men friends (Freud actually fainted after his break with Jung), his paternalistic yet passionless relationships with women? Samuel Rosenberg has seen evidence for this claim in Freud's passionate friendship with Wilhelm Fliess, who suggested to him the idea of inherent bisexuality and whose wife became increasingly jealous of the friendship.[9]

Any discussion of sexuality must balance the contribution to our behavior and emotions of inborn desire and of social constructs. This balance is often posed as a simple conflict between two discrete alternatives: that of ethology and sociobiology, which seems to claim that our sexual behavior is genetically programmed, and that of cultural anthropology, which sees societies as regulating sexuality in very diverse ways. Thus the sociologists Gagnon and Simon have argued that "the sexual area may be precisely that realm wherein the superordinate position of the sociocultural over the biological level is most complete."[10]

But this is something of a false polarization: biology and culture are not alternatives, but rather dual factors that interact with each other to produce particular expressions of sexuality. Such sexual expressions can take many and varied forms (including abstinence), but ultimately they involve a universal need for body contact, erotic stimulation, and orgasmic release. While it is true that our sexuality is shaped and influenced to a large extent by social pressures, this can only occur within the real limits imposed by biology. Thus, however far one tries to get away from Freud's concept of natural drives that need be distorted in the interests of civilization, in almost any discussion of sexuality one is forced to fall back ultimately on some idea of a basic instinctual desire, even if such desire is not necessarily translated into what would commonly be regarded as sexual acts.

The most controversial part of Freud's analysis of homosexuality involves the concept of repression and the idea that everyone has experienced homosexual desire that, in most cases, is more or less successfully repressed. To argue that homosexuals are genetically determined would seem to reject this view, but Edward O. Wilson, the best-known exponent of sociobiology, has written that "there is a potential for bisexuality in the brain, and it is sometimes expressed

fully by persons who switch back and forth in their sexual preference."[11] What happens to such potential in those people who do
not so switch is not clear.

There is considerable evidence that people are capable of very
fluid sexual response; in the Kinsey surveys 37 percent of the men
and 19 percent of the women acknowledged at least one orgasm with
a partner of the same sex, though this says nothing about emotional
responses. Masters and Johnson's study *Homosexuality in Perspective* provides considerable support for the thesis that we all possess
the potential for bisexual desire; among the group studied, sexual
fantasies almost invariably included persons of both sexes.[12] As poets
have always known, our sexual desires are foreshadowed in fantasies,
dreams, and poetry, however unamenable these may be to empirical
research.

It is equally evident that the way such desires are expressed will
depend to a large extent on social organizations. There is a great gap
between the meaning and experience of being homosexual lovers in
ancient Sparta or of being a *bedarche* in an Amerindian tribe, and
between the nineteenth-century view of female sexuality and friendship and that promulgated by magazines like *Cosmopolitan* today.
This is demonstrated by the fact that while homosexual behavior
among men is very widespread among different cultures, it is only
in comparatively modern Western societies that exclusive homosexuals exist in any significant number.[13] And if lesbianism seems far
less common across different cultures, this seems due less to any
innate difference between the sexes than to the much more severe
repression of female sexuality in almost all societies.

Whether the variety of homosexual expression demonstrates
the accuracy of the repression hypothesis is less clear. There is more
persuasive evidence in the extraordinary preoccupation with homosexuality among so many allegedly heterosexual men. Norman
Mailer was speaking for many when he wrote (in the early homosexual magazine *One*): "There is probably no sensitive heterosexual
alive who is not preoccupied at one time or another with his latent
homosexuality, and while I had no conscious homosexual desires, I
had wondered more than once if really there were not something
suspicious in my intense dislike of homosexuals."[14]

The very term "homosexual" is a product of the nineteenth
century and is one that many people in the Freudian tradition have
seen as essentially a limitation and restriction of a universal bisexuality. Gore Vidal, for example, claims that the word should always be
used as an adjective and never a noun, because it describes particular

acts rather than particular people,[15] and Kinsey, too, stressed that one should never speak of homosexuals as if such an identity were inherent rather than the product of social labeling. Yet at times Kinsey spoke of homosexuals in a nominal rather than an adjectival sense, and his stress on behavior as opposed to emotion could be used, ironically, to strengthen the concept of the homosexual; as Paul Robinson points out, Kinsey's behavioral categories extending over a scale between exclusive heterosexuality and homosexuality are easily collapsed into the commonsense view of people as heterosexual, homosexual, or bisexual.[16] Certainly there are enormous problems of definition; does one include as homosexual the married woman whose heterosexual experience is far less satisfying than her unconsumated lesbian fantasies, or the married man, by no means uncommon, who occasionally seeks homosexual gratification in public toilets?

Yet it is equally true that, whatever the theoretical and definitional problems, a homosexual identity is a reality for many millions of people and can easily coexist with some bisexual behavior (just as men who engage in homosexual prison sex don't thereby necessarily give up their heterosexual identity). Indeed, some lesbians have told me that when they want quick sex they look for men, precisely because there is no emotional contact. The paradox of categorization is summed up by Ken Plummer, who wrote in the introduction to *The Making of the Modern Homosexual* that while such categorizations "control, restrict and inhibit [they] simultaneously provide comfort, security and assuredness. . . . This book . . . persistently strains to debunk the category of 'homosexual,' to show its relativity, its historical sources, its changing meanings and—overwhelmingly —its damaging impact on human experience. Yet *at the current moment* it also tacitly finds it hard to believe that 'liberated, joyful homosexuals' could ever have obtained their 'liberation' without that label."[17]

The fact that we are all potentially bisexual, both behaviorally and emotionally, and that large numbers of people have at least experimented with that potential, in no way invalidates the reality of a homosexual identity. Sexual behavior is, indeed, only one aspect of our sexual identity; to see oneself as homosexual is at least as much a matter of emotional as of physical response. There are people who engage in frequent homosexual behavior without considering themselves homosexuals, just as there are those without homosexual experience—perhaps with considerable heterosexual experience—who consider themselves homosexual.

A view that sees homosexuality as part of human sexual response that is acted out by certain individuals according to particular biographical and cultural factors—and repressed or sublimated by others with varying degrees of difficulty—does not tell us *why* certain people act out their homosexuality. My feeling is that there is no one answer, that the explanation will vary widely from individual to individual and is a compound of life experience and social and cultural factors. Nor am I necessarily convinced that, as psychoanalysis would have it, the direction of one's sexuality is fixed in the first few years of life. It is even possible, as Paul Robinson suggests, that "there is room for some theory of 'congenital predisposition,' "[18] though the evidence for this is not really very good so far. After studying what evidence is available, Masters and Johnson concluded that "we must acknowledge that in at least some instances—though clearly not in most cases—hormonal predispositions may interact with social and environmental factors to lead towards a homosexual orientation."[19]

Despite press reports suggesting firm evidence of a biological basis for homosexuality, the latest Kinsey Institute study, *Sexual Preference*, claims no more than "at the moment a large body of convincing research appears to suggest a biological foundation for homosexuality, at least among some people."[20] They are impressed by the considerable efforts of biologists, endocrinologists, and physiologists to prove this foundation; I am more impressed by the inability of many years of research to amount to more than "suggestions."

There is a political problem here: the great advantage of the idea that homosexuals are "born, not made" is that it suggests the condition is unalterable, and the identity innate. There is a certain comfort in being able to assert, as does Alec in Mary Renault's *The Charioteer*, "I didn't choose to be what I am, it was determined when I wasn't in a position to exercise any choice and without my knowing what was happening."[21] In fact such an assertion is consistent with orthodox psychoanalysis, as well as with attempts to prove genetic or hormonal causes. But psychoanalysts, like behavioral psychologists, can argue, given their assumptions, for the possibility of altering sexual orientation, which in practice is expressed as "curing" homosexuality, even by those who would not classify homosexuality as a disease. Yet this is hardly an objection to the theories as such, and in any case those who are seeking an endocrinological or hormonal explanation for homosexuality are usually equally spurred on by a zeal to alter it.

The greater problem with the idea of a discrete homosexual

identity is that it ignores the large numbers of people who are both behaviorally and emotionally bisexual and are therefore ambivalent about how far to adopt a homosexual identity. This ambivalence leads to their being attacked both by gays concerned to strengthen the idea of this identity, and by "experts" who seem affronted by ambivalence. Thus the psychoanalyst Hendrik Ruitenbeek sees bisexuality as the refuge of "those people who are unwilling to face up to their sexuality as part of their whole being,"[22] and Masters and Johnson have lumped together the phenomenon of bisexual desire with a rejection of "meaningful relations" to produce what they call "ambisexuals." This is the weakest and most moralistic part of their study, and one that requires considerable stretching of the data. One of their "ambisexuals" was a woman who had a four-month "marriage of convenience" and "maintained an open lesbian relationship during the brief marriage." At least the latter would seem incompatible with the claim that "ambisexuals have never evidenced interest in a continuing relationship."[23] Even in the film *Sunday Bloody Sunday* the bisexual character played by Murray Head was less sympathetically shown than either his male or his female lover.

Few arguments have caused as much controversy among gay audiences as the assertion of a universal bisexual potential. I was once interrupted during the taping of a gay radio program in Los Angeles by a producer very concerned by this position, which he said justified Anita Bryant's claim that all homosexuals could be "cured." He was only partially mollified by my pointing out that the reverse was equally true. Yet to assert this is not tantamount to arguing that the actualization of bisexuality is necessary for liberation, only that its potential must be recognized, at least in any theoretical discussion of sexuality. Gay women seem more likely to accept this than men, partly because much lesbian-feminist rhetoric assumes that all women can choose to be homosexual and should do so as a way of escaping dependence on men, partly, I suspect, because women's sexuality is more fluid.

Many people *do* act out their bisexuality, and this seems to create particular unease among those whose identity is exclusively either heterosexual or homosexual, perhaps because they see it as somehow calling into question the legitimacy of their sexuality. The exclusive homosexual (or heterosexual) can be defined as "the other": someone who is bisexual is too close to be so distanced. (It is also true that many homosexuals claim to be bisexual because they feel this is a safer persona to present socially.) I have had several involvements over the past few years with men who were very conscious of a bisexual desire—including one who moved from marriage to largely homosexual relationships, and another who moved in the opposite direction—and who felt an alienation from both mainstream straight and mainstream gay circles as a result.

One of the crucial questions to be asked about bisexuality is whether my suspicion that women are more fluid in their desires, better able to move between women and men, is true. This has been suggested by a number of feminists; a good example is in Kate Millett's *Sita*, where the two central women characters are involved with both women and men. Charlotte Wolff, in one of the very few works about bisexuality, has hinted that it is more common among women than men but unfortunately offers no explanation.[24] C. A. Tripp in *The Homosexual Matrix* quotes various studies of "swingers" to underline the point.[25] And in Jay and Young's survey there are more women than men who are bisexual, at least in behavior, though their samples of the two sexes are unfortunately not really comparable.

One may ask whether women's seemingly greater fluidity is due to an innate difference between male and female sexuality, or is due to social conditioning. One could argue that men find homosexuality more difficult to accept because their sexuality is more directly organized around the genitals, in particular around the erect penis (which for straight men looms as an enormous threat in a putative partner), whereas female sexuality involves a less direct concentration on the genitals and is therefore more easily fluid; but even if this is the case it could be as much the result of social expectations as of any inherent differences. In Western, particularly Anglo-Saxon, societies, women have tended to have closer emotional relations with each other than have men, which may facilitate a move into direct physical expression. The *Hite Reports* suggest that more women have thought about having sex with other women than is the case with men;[26] unfortunately Hite's samples also are not representative.

Some very interesting explanations for fundamental differences between the way the two sexes organize sexuality are raised by Nancy Chodorow, who has expanded on the psychoanalytic framework to argue that real differences in the raising of girls and boys explain later patterns. Boys, she argues, are taught to be masculine more consciously than girls are taught to be feminine,[27] and the nature of the girl's oedipal experience means that we would expect bisexuality to be more common among women than men:

Most women emerge from their oedipus complex oriented to their father and men as primary *erotic* objects, but it is clear that men tend to remain *emotionally* secondary, or at most emotionally equal, compared to the primacy and exclusivity of an oedipal boy's emotional tie to his mother and women. Second, because the father is an additional important love object, who becomes important in the context of a relational triangle, the feminine inner object world is more complex than the masculine. This internal situation continues into adulthood and affects adult women's participation in relationships. Women, according to [Helene] Deutsch, experience heterosexual relationships in a triangular context, in which men are not exclusive objects for them.[28]

Unfortunately Chodorow nowhere explains how these claims explain the apparently greater degree of exclusive homosexuality among men than among women, nor does she examine anthropological data which could measure these claims against the experiences of different cultures.

*   *   *   *   *   *   *

While homosexual behavior is widespread across both time and place, according to all available historical and anthropological evidence, the concept of a homosexual identity is a recent and comparatively restricted one. In many non-Western societies particularly, intermittent homosexual behavior is legitimate and given social recognition. Writing of a visit to Morocco in 1952, Marc Oraison observed, "The students of the Islamic university—which I was able to visit—practiced homosexual relations openly and publicly. This did not prevent them, having finished their studies, from marrying and settling down."[29] Such students quite clearly did not define themselves as homosexual. To so define oneself implies not just that one sleeps with another man or woman, but also that one derives a certain sense of identity from that fact. In many societies it is the act rather than the gender of one's partner that is seen as significant —in Freudian terms the sexual aim rather than the sexual object— so that a man who fucks other men but is not himself fucked is not viewed as a homosexual. There are strong echoes of this in the norms of many Western jails.

To identify as homosexual is to accept the desire for members of one's sex as valid in itself, rather than merely a poor substitute for heterosexuality, and involves the recognition of emotional as much as physical attraction. (For many men kissing another man takes on huge symbolic importance as a step toward accepting their homosexuality.) It is hardly surprising that societies that condone homosexual behavior in certain circumstances can simultaneously condemn those who are identified as homosexuals. As far as I can tell this is particularly true of the Islamic societies of North Africa and the Middle East, where there is considerable acceptance of certain forms of homosexuality—at least among men; the position for women is less clear—but strong hostility toward anyone who is perceived as a homosexual.

The existence of large numbers of women and men whose self-definition is homosexual, and who regard homosexual relationships as the primary ones in their lives, is largely confined to modern Western societies, and it seems to be possible only under the particular social formations of urbanization and industrialization. Traditional societies (which furnish almost all of Ford and Beach's examples) are organized in such a way as to disallow the possibility of a child's choosing a way of life other than that prescribed by tradition and her elders; thus exclusive homosexuals, where they exist, take on particular roles, often religious ones (as in the case of Amerindian *bedarches*), or become outcasts (which appears to be literally the case among some Hindus). It is only with the breakdown of the ascriptive family and the very narrowly defined social roles of traditional cultures that it becomes possible to live as a homosexual in other than this very rigid way. And only in urban societies, where social institutions can develop independently of the family and the clan, can a homosexual subculture develop. If Gagnon and Simon are correct about the "superordinate position of the sociocultural over the biological level," then for homosexuals to appear in a given society there must exist conditions under which one can both imagine homosexual acts and emotions and act them out by adopting an appropriate identity.

Moreover, as Lillian Faderman has stressed, there must also be a particular view of sexuality before this identity can be formulated. In recent years there has been considerable argument about just when homosexuals, as we understand the term, emerged as a social category. Those who use the concept fairly rigorously have argued for the birth of this category in eighteenth- and nineteenth-century Western Europe. Foucault's position in *The History of Sexuality* is representative:

> The nineteenth century homosexual became a personnage, a past,
> a case history, and a childhood, in addition to being a type of life,

a life form, and a morphology, with an indiscreet anatomy and possibly a mysterious physiology. Nothing that went into his total composition was unaffected by his sexuality. It was everywhere present in him: at the root of all his actions because it was their insidious and indefinitely active principle; written immodestly on his face and body because it was a secret that always gave itself away. It was consubstantial with him, less as a habitual sin than as a singular nature. We must not forget that the psychological, psychiatric, medical category of homosexuality was constituted from the moment it was characterized—Westphal's famous article of 1870 on "contrary sexual sensations" can stand as its date of birth—less by a type of sexual relations than by a certain quality of sexual sensibility, a certain way of inverting the masculine and feminine in oneself. Homosexuality appeared as one of the forms of sexuality when it was transposed from the practice of sodomy onto a kind of interior androgyny, a hermaphrodism of the soul. The sodomite had been a temporary aberration; the homosexual was now a species.[30]

Foucault is thinking here of male homosexuals, but the nineteenth century also saw the development of the lesbian as a personnage, a central one in much French literature of the period. Against this view is the desire to claim a history of "gay people" going back for thousands of years, the most respectable of these claims being in John Boswell's *Christianity, Social Tolerance, and Homosexuality* (subtitled *Gay People in Western Europe from the Beginnings of the Christian Era to the Fourteenth Century*). I think Boswell has grossly stretched his evidence to make this point; as he himself says, "Roman society, at least in its urban centers, did not for the most part distinguish gay people from others and regarded homosexual interest and practice as an ordinary part of the range of human eroticism."[31] If this were the case, even in much of early Christian Europe, does it then make sense to speak of "gay people" as if they were set apart from others? Boswell acknowledges in passing that the existence of "gay people" requires a gay subculture. "Individual writers recording their personal feelings in isolation, no matter how numerous, probably do not constitute a 'sub-culture' in its most common sense; but a network of such persons, conscious of their common difference from the majority and mutually influencing their own and others' perceptions of the nature of their distinctiveness, does indicate the sort of change at issue here."[32] While he can point to some striking examples of homoerotic writing in twelfth-century

Europe, it is not clear that this is sufficient to demonstrate the existence of such a subculture in either ancient or medieval Europe, and there is an unnecessary confusion in much of Boswell's writing between homosexual behavior and a sense of gay identity.

It is conceivable that, at least among small groups of upper-class men, a sense of homosexual identity and culture did exist, perhaps in ancient Greece, medieval France, and Renaissance Italy. It is very probable that a gay subculture can only emerge where sufficient social space exists for individuals to break away from customary expectations of marriage and procreation—or, more accurately, for their sexuality not to be limited by such expectations. In its early years such a culture will probably be very closed and furtive and tend to reflect the assumptions of the larger society that homosexuality is "unnatural." In particular this assumption will be expressed in the rigid role playing that produces effeminate "queens" and butch "dykes"; reflected in such role-playing is the belief, stressed by Foucault, that to "be" a homosexual is to take on the characteristics of the opposite sex. Among theorists Ulrichs's theory of a "third sex" may have died long ago, but it is an assumption that persists among some homosexuals, as witness this exchange, in Manuel Puig's *Kiss of the Spider Woman*, between the homosexual Molina and his cellmate Valentin:

> "Because a man . . . what he wants is a woman . . ."
> "And all homosexuals are that way?"
> "No, there's the other kind who fall in love with one another. But as for my friends and myself, we're a hundred percent female. We don't go in for these little games—that's strictly for homosexuals. We're normal women—we sleep with men."[33]

We will come back to the confusion revealed in such arguments. It is not accidental that Puig's novel is set in Argentina where, as in most of Latin America, a particular combination of Catholic teachings, political repression, and especially the Iberian macho tradition has restricted the development of the gay subculture and the growth of a sense of homosexual identity, though this is now changing, especially in Brazil where homophobia seems less pervasive than in Spanish America.[34] In fact when we speak of homosexuals we are using a concept that ceases to have much meaning outside the affluent developed countries of the First World (North America, Western Europe, Australasia, and perhaps Japan) and that seems dependent on a certain level of both economic development and political liberalism to flourish. It must be galling for those fundamentalist defenders of "the American way" to reflect that it is only their "way" that allows for the creation of a homosexual minority, and that the so-called socialist states of Eastern Europe are much more successfully repressive of public homosexuality than are those of the "free world." Cities like Warsaw and Budapest today have homosexual worlds rather akin to those of North America in the fifties.

In an odd way, the best evidence for the assertion that a homosexual subculture is the product of modern urban liberal capitalism is found in certain non-Western societies that have been exposed to the influence of Western imperialism. In the large cities of the Third World one finds male homosexual subcultures that have developed as a result of the infusion of Western values and Western tourists; pre-Castro Havana, San Juan, Tangiers, Bangkok, and Manila all have gay milieux that provide a transition for local youth between the traditional restraints of the national culture and the attractions of the West. In many cases a strong homosexual tradition predates the Western impact, but westernization introduces new forms and definitions, in particular the idea of a homosexual identity, so that the fundamentalist Islamic regime in Iran, where there is a homosexual tradition dating back thousands of years (popularized very effectively in Mary Renault's *The Persian Boy*) can attack homosexuality as a product of Western imperialism.

Not that they are altogether wrong, for imperialism has dramatically increased the role of prostitution and often makes for very demeaning and racist exploitation in which homosexuals may become the scapegoats for a broader phenomenon. This has been the experience of many North Africans, who since the late nineteenth century have been an object of considerable European male homosexual fantasy, as revealed by writers from André Gide to William Burroughs. It is summed up in the comment of the 1975 *Spartacus Gay Guide*, the Michelin and Baedekar of promiscuous gay travelers, that the boys at Kudu Beach, Bali, are "available for a cigarette." (Ironically, the 1980 edition of the *Guide* attacked homosexual imperialism in Third World countries, though without much sense of its own responsibility.) Such attitudes help explain, though not excuse, the hostility of many non-Western revolutionaries, both of the left and of the right, toward homosexuals, just as the experience of prison homosexuality helped create the homophobia of such writers as Eldridge Cleaver or as widespread male prostitution in pre-Hitler Berlin may have contributed to that of Wilhelm Reich.[35]

But there is a certain irony in that the nineteenth- and twentieth-century myth that homosexuality was far freer in non-Western societies, a myth attested to by several generations of European travelers and writers, has been superseded by a situation in which there is unparalleled freedom for homosexuals in Western societies, so much so that they are attacked as "decadent" by leaders from erstwhile "liberated" societies. The seeming paradox, however, has much to do with the difference between homosexual behavior and identity; the creation of a specific person known as "the homosexual" is a product of modern Western societies and runs contrary to traditional mores and values in even strongly homoerotic societies.

The development of this view of "the homosexual" is the result of a strange collusion between so-called "experts," primarily in the fields of medicine, law, and psychiatry, and homosexuals themselves. Indeed the whole discourse on homosexuality since the nineteenth century has been a remarkable example of Foucault's theses about knowledge and power; the ability of experts to name, codify, classify, and define and thus help determine how people see themselves is very clear. Many of the experts who have written about homosexuality since the late nineteenth century have themselves been homosexual, often closeted, and homosexual writers have frequently internalized expert judgments of their inferiority, as in the self-pity of Radclyffe Hall in *The Well of Loneliness*.

While early gay liberationists attacked experts for their presumption in naming and judging from the outside, the bulk of respectable homosexuals today appear to welcome the legitimization of their life style provided by some psychologists, sociologists, and clinicians over the past few years. Increasingly research into homosexuality is being justified in their terms; fairly typical is the large-scale Kinsey Institute study of homosexuals in San Francisco, carried out by Alan Bell and Martin Weinberg, which concluded that "perhaps the least ambiguous finding of our investigation is that homosexuality is not necessarily related to pathology."[36] Such a finding does not, of course, call into question either the concept of pathology or the ability of psychologists to determine it, and many homosexuals seem to accept that in such matters experts are more reliable judges than homosexuals themselves. There is a considerable market among homosexuals for studies of this sort, which are presumably read by people who need to combat the way we have been stigmatized by one set of experts with the reassurances of another. Academics who are otherwise openly gay do not acknowledge this when writing about homosexuality, not necessarily because they wish to hide it but because they have been socialized into the academic ideology that personal experience is not valid data.

One finds a considerable amount of silly, banal, and even mischievous discussion of homosexuality in the writings of those experts who pose as sympathetic. A very good example of this is the collection *Homosexual Behavior*, edited by Judd Marmor in 1980 and promoted as representing the "most advanced knowledge and thinking that presently exists on the subject of homosexual reactions and behaviors in both men and women."[37] By and large the gay press seemed to accept this claim, despite the fact that the book reeks of ignorance and prejudice, and the contributors almost entirely ignore the enormous amount of "knowledge and thinking" that has gone on in the gay movement and in gay publications over the past decade. The real world that homosexuals have been constructing for ourselves barely appears in this study; an excellent example comes in the opening of Barbara Ponse's chapter on "Lesbians and Their Worlds," which tells us that:

> The analysis that follows is based on three years of observation and interaction in secretive and activist lesbian worlds, informal talks with many women who relate sexually and emotionally with other women, and 75 in-depth interviews. In the course of these observations it became clear that lesbians or women-related women live in many different worlds.[38]

How much more instructive it would have been to ask someone like Rita Mae Brown or Charlotte Bunch or Jane Rule to write about "lesbians and *our* worlds." Their writings do not, however, accept the ideological criterion that expertise need be objective and unrelated to the experience of the writer.

The book is full of examples of ignorance and prejudice. One contributor who teaches both law and psychiatry, and whose expertise is therefore doubly certified, writes of the Soviet Union that, while there are certainly homosexuals, "there is rarely, if ever, to be seen a male who walks with a swishy gait or talks like a woman."[39] The same comment could be made about Christopher or Castro streets. Writing in the section, "The View of the Clinician" (which includes several overtly homophobic contributors), two psychiatrists repeat the old adage that "sadomasochistic practices and other deviant sexual behaviors (sic) are practically nonexistent among lesbians."[40] They have apparently never read the articles of Pat Califia, presumably because they appear in *The Advocate* rather than the *Archives of Sexual Behavior.*

Very little of the considerable output of the social and behavioral sciences on homosexuality over the past decade adds to any real understanding of the homosexual experience. While it is clearly preferable to the moralism of earlier periods, the recent literature reinforces the idea that homosexuality is something experienced by a discrete minority and separate from the experience of most people. Freud and Kinsey, although working in very different intellectual traditions, both stressed that homosexuality had to be understood within a continuum of sexual behavior, and Freud, like Havelock Ellis, began his general study of sexuality by discussing homosexuality. The idea of the universal relevance of homosexuality seems to have largely vanished from contemporary psychological and sociological discourses on sexuality, which by concentrating on homosexuality as something apart perpetuate the idea that it is a matter of concern only to those who identify themselves as homosexual.

There are very good reasons—psychological, social, and political—why homosexuals should stress a sense of separate identity, even if this means insisting on rigid definitions that are only particular social constructs. When such definitions are imposed by outsiders, they seem more clearly designed to control and limit homosexuality by denying that it is an integral part of human sexuality. But homosexuality is a much broader concept than homosexual identity, and it is in the interplay between the two concepts that lie some of the crucial questions to be asked about sexuality. Rather than yet another study of a gay bar or the "treatment" (a word now used in preference to "cure") of homosexuals, we need studies of the connection between sexual repression and violence or between sexuality and gender roles. Questions about these are much more likely to be posed by feminist and gay writers than by the experts who contribute to works like Marmor's and who insist on the academic segregation of homosexuality from broader questions of sexual theory.

*   *   *   *   *   *   *

To the confused concepts of behavior and identity we can add two other areas that require clarification: the link between sex roles and sexuality, and that between innate and acquired patterns of sexual desire. Most discussion about homosexuality is marred by a confusion between gender and sexuality, as the extract from Puig's novel demonstrates. Even Freud, despite his rejection of the idea of a "feminine brain in a masculine body," was not immune to this confusion. In the *Three Essays* he speaks of mental "masculinity" and "femininity": "There can be no doubt that a large proportion of male inverts retain the mental quality of masculinity, that they possess relatively few of the secondary characteristics of the opposite sex and that what they look for in their sexual object are in fact feminine mental traits."[41] Freud made similar comments elsewhere about female homosexuals.[42] However, in *Civilization and Its Discontents* he seems to reject such a metaphysical view of gender: "Though anatomy, it is true, can point out the characteristics of maleness and femaleness, psychology cannot. For psychology the contrast between the sexes fades away into one between activity and passivity, in which we far too readily identify activity with maleness and passivity with femaleness, a view which is by no means universally confirmed in the animal kingdom."[43]

Here Freud points to two quite separate phenomena, the physical characteristics of gender and the mental traits associated with these, which, at least to some degree, are social constructs and hence mutable. Confusion about gender roles and sexuality dogs much of the popular use of the term "bisexual," which is used indiscriminately to mean having characteristics or traits of both sexes *and* being sexually attracted to both one's own and the opposite sex. The origin of this confusion lies, presumably, in the assumption that humans seek completion in the act of sex by restoring an original unity of male and female, and that is why heterosexuality is "natural." Freud commences his discussion of "the sexual deviations" in the *Three Essays* by reference to this myth, Platonic in origin, but there is no logical reason to assume that even if there is a different balance of traits between the sexes this in itself will necessarily create an attraction to the opposite sex.

Yet the belief that homosexuality is somehow a reflection of a blurred sense of masculinity/femininity remains central to the Western imagination, and to the extent that our concepts of gender have implied a heterosexual norm, this is important in understanding the development of homosexual identity. Vito Russo can begin his study of homosexuality in the movies by focusing on attitudes toward sissies and only gradually suggest that this is a distorted view of homosexuality, because the common depiction of homosexuals has been of men and women who reject commonly accepted gender roles. Historically the developing homosexual identity in Western societies was closely linked to a repudiation of sex roles, and feminism was often attacked as leading to mannish women and effeminate men, both of whom were likely to be homosexual. It is possible that the connection was less strong than historians have suggested, because it was those women and men who clearly rejected appropriate role behavior who were most visible—how effeminate, after all, were those cowboys who were homosexual? But it is only with the changes in self-image of homosexuals over the past decade that there has been any real challenge to the assumption that to be homosexual is to adopt some of the characteristics of the opposite sex. This view underlies a novel like Patrick White's *The Twyborn Affair* (1979), in which the central character shifts sex through the book and awakens desire in almost everyone s/he comes in contact with, as if to demonstrate the fluidity of both gender and desire. For White we are all androgynous: " 'True friendship,' Edith decided, after wiping off the cream and most of the hateful magenta lipstick, 'if there is anything wholly true—certainly in friendship—comes, I'd say, from the woman in a man and the man in a woman.' "[44] The problem is that White seems to extend this to an explanation of homosexuality, as if accepting that only desire between the sexes is fully explicable.

Even John Rechy, who would seem to epitomize the masculine homosexual, falls for this misapprehension:

> No, the artist doesn't have to be homosexual to produce good art; and certainly not all homosexual artists are "good." But the artist who represses either the male or female aspect of his or her being produces unfulfilled work. James Joyce, Shakespeare, Picasso, Flannery O'Connor, D. H. Lawrence and many, many other finally heterosexual artists have accepted, often joyously, the female and the male sides of themselves.[45]

But sexuality and gender are distinct concepts; you can be homosexual and reject all the traits associated with the opposite sex, or be heterosexual and express them. Homosexuality can just as easily be a way of asserting one's "femininity" (for a woman) or "masculinity" (for a man), even if in a society where masculinity brings with it certain privileges the latter is more common.

David Fernbach has argued strongly that while this distinction may be true, it is deviance from the gender system that separates gayness from homosexuality. "Gay men, in other words, really are effeminate. . . . Our gayness is a function of two things: a deviance from the gender system that is anchored in our personalities in the course of childhood experience, and the choice to build our lives around the homosexual preference that this induces."[46] In the same way Bell, Weinberg, and Hammersmith argue that "there is a powerful link between gender nonconformity and the development of homosexuality."[47] This assertion depends on the memories of their respondants, who are likely to have been influenced by social expectations of how far homosexuals should conform to gender roles (their data was collected in 1969–70, that is, prior to both the growth of the modern gay movement and the development of the macho style among gay men). Moreover, they are prone to confuse social roles with what is inborn. Thus they talk of "an inborn predisposition toward gender nonconformity"[48] which seems to imply that masculinity and femininity are far less social constructs than either I or Fernbach would argue.

To assert that gender nonconformity and homosexual identity are the same, rather than related through certain socially constructed norms and expectations, overlooks both those homosexuals who do conform, and those nonhomosexuals who deviate from the gender system; a play (and movie) like Robert Anderson's *Tea and Sympathy* treats the dilemma of such a boy who is perceived by others, quite wrongly, as homosexual. Clearly there is a connection between gender and sexuality. It is not, however, as simple or as complete a connection as Fernbach, in what seems something of a nostalgic longing for the early days of gay liberation androgyny, suggests.

It is transvestism that most powerfully illustrates the confusion, not least because in the popular mind it is always linked with homosexuality. In fact transvestism is both logically and often in practice distinct from homosexuality; it is rather related to finding erotic pleasure by dressing in the clothes of the opposite sex and is more frequently found among heterosexuals. When the person seeks to change sex physically, through chemical and surgical means, this is transsexualism.

It may well be that those transvestites and transsexuals who are behaviorally heterosexual are, in fact, repressing their homosexuality, and that in a society with rigid sex role distinctions and strong hostility toward homosexuality this becomes a particular way of acting out homosexual desire. (At the same time transvestism, in the form of "drag," is a classic way for some to assert their homosexuality, even if it does confuse sexuality and gender.) The view of these phenomena as expressions of repressed homosexuality has provoked considerable criticism of transsexualism among both psychologists and feminists,[49] and there is some support for this way of seeing it in the autobiography of one of the better-known, and certainly one of the more literate, transsexuals, Jan Morris: "I was walking along Jermyn St. one day when I saw, for the first time in twenty years, a member of the Everest team of 1953. My goodness, I said to myself, what an extraordinarily handsome man. I knew he had been handsome all along, but I had allowed myself to like him only for his gentle manners, and it was only now that I permitted myself the indulgence of thinking him desirable."[50]

It is hardly surprising that as sex roles become somewhat blurred and the stigma against homosexuals declines, there is a comparable decline in most Western societies of "drag queens." The world of exaggeratedly effeminate gay men that John Rechy portrayed in the early sixties in *City of Night* is fast disappearing, along with the buildings where they lived in downtown Los Angeles, and in so far as this world remains, it seems largely associated with poor and often nonwhite groups in which concepts of sex roles and sexuality are presumably more rigid.

Thus "drag queens" are most prevalent in those societies that combine rigid concepts of sex roles with sufficient freedom to allow at least this particular form of rebellion. (In some traditional societies, with very rigid role demarcations, transvestites were accorded a special role, often with semimagical status.) The best example may be Brazil, where transvestism is widespread—through publicly recognized only at carnival time—and seems the only socially accepted way of living as a homosexual for those who are not part of the westernized and educated middle class. Many homosexual prostitutes are transvestites, a fact Freud noted in pre-World War I Vienna and saw as a proof that homosexual men seek "feminine mental traits" in their partners.[51] However, since the Brazilian prostitutes are reported to often fuck their clients, things are less simple than this; like the case of Jan Morris, they suggest the distortions forced upon homosexual desire in a sexist society.

However, most homosexuals of both sexes are not transvestites (indeed, female transvestites are far rarer, perhaps because role expectations for women are ironically less rigid), and there are many transvestites and transsexuals who are determinedly heterosexual, whatever the reason. What is clear is that while the popular myths confuse gender, sex roles, and sexuality, they are quite distinct concepts that interact in a complex set of relationships.

Just as popular mythology ascribes certain characteristics to men and women that it then develops into social roles known as "masculinity" and "femininity," and that go much further than any physiological basis requires, so too it has become fashionable to suggest that there are "masculine" and "feminine" forms of sexual desire that are, if anything, found most clearly among homosexuals. In particular, it is argued that lesbians seek monogamous coupling while gay men are compulsively promiscuous. This stereotype is common in much contemporary writing; thus Martin Levine writes, "Lesbians are typically feminine in much of their behavior, for example they court each other for long periods of time, sex is approved of only when it occurs within an emotional relationship, the community is organized around couples. This is in complete contrast to gay men's often noted promiscuity and single status."[52] Similar views are put forward by C. A. Tripp, who has denied "any" lesbian interest in sadomasochism.[53] And reviewing a collection of recent gay plays, Don Shewey wrote:

> Another theme that emerges from *Gay Plays* as a whole is the difference between male and female sexuality (which probably underlies most conflicts between faggots and dykes). *Entertaining Mr. Sloane*, *The Madness of Lady Bright* and *T-Shirts* promulgate the typical gay man's promiscuity; *Confessions of a Female Disorder* and *A Late Snow* display the hyperromanticism/submerged sexuality that seem endemic to lesbians.[54]

The real question is to what extent these differences are somehow an innate part of male and female sexuality (as the term "endemic" suggests) and to what extent they are social constructs. The reference to conflict over sexuality is presumably a reference to the fact that many lesbians, especially feminists, see the male gay life style as unnecessarily promiscuous and full of sexist objectification, but this is a political critique of a particular form of male homosexuality, and a form that only exists, as already suggested, under certain social conditions. There is also no way of knowing how lesbians would behave in a society that imposed the same sort of restrictions on female sexuality that it does on male, but there is no real evidence that women are naturally or necessarily less promiscuous than men.

Indeed, what evidence does exist suggests that the differences are already less dramatic than is sometimes believed. In their survey, for example, Jay and Young found that lesbian relationships tended to be shorter-lived and male homosexual ones longer-lived than is often thought. The main difference they tapped was the ability of male homosexuals to have sex with far less emotional commitment than was true of women—but how does one know whether this is innate or cultural in origin?

It *is* true that by and large the new gay women and men do not have particularly good relationships with each other, and that this is largely because they tend to hold different values. Again this seems cultural rather than innate: gay women, especially those affected by feminism, are likely to be particularly conscious of anything that smacks of sexism, and gay men often assert their masculinity either through parody of or disdain of women. But there is another, deeper reason; if homosexuals are to be identified by their sexual interest in the same sex, the constant emphasis on this identity will increasingly separate gay women and gay men. What unites us is largely political (thus campaigns such as those against Anita Bryant's initiatives or the Briggs referendum in California brought together large numbers of women and men), and politics is less powerful than the strong social and cultural differences keeping us apart.

If gay women and gay men often have difficulty communicating, the reverse sometimes seems true for straight women and gay men, so much so that the term "fag hag" is used to describe straight women who often associate with gays. I am somewhat suspicious of the praise this particular relationship has sometimes been accorded;[55] it often rests upon uneasiness on both sides, gay men's with other men (except as sex partners), and straight women's with other women and straight men (again, except as sex partners). Gay men who proclaim, "All my friends are women" are often revealing a dislike and distrust of other gay men, and perhaps of themselves.

Today the more common claim is likely to be, *"None* of my friends are not gay": the new identity/community/culture is producing a separatism that tends to isolate gay men from straight men, from women, and from children (gay women are far more likely to have contact with children because of the relatively large number of lesbian mothers). Contacts between gay women and gay men, too, are declining. Even if gay women and men often mixed together in the past for their mutual camouflage, there were benefits to their interaction that we are now in danger of losing.

*   *   *   *   *   *   *

If one accepts the broad outlines of Freud's repression thesis, it helps explain both the role of homosexuality in everyday social life and the virulence of homophobia in societies such as ours, where homosexuality has been defined as a discrete form of identity. Freud saw the repression of homosexuality, where successful, as the basis of the sublimation upon which most of our social instincts are based: "In the light of psychoanalysis we are accustomed to regard social feeling as a sublimation of homosexual attitudes towards objects."[56] This idea reappears frequently in his writings. It is suggested in the famous myth of the brothers banding together to slay the primal father; the brothers' ability to coalesce "may have been based on homosexual feelings and acts, originating perhaps during the period of their expulsion from the horde."[57] (This may be bad anthropology, but it could be nonetheless true on a symbolic or mythic level.) More specifically it is found in Freud's comments written in 1911 on the Schreber case:

> After the stage of heterosexual object choice has been reached, the homosexual tendencies are not, as might be supposed, done away with or brought to a stop; they are merely deflected from their sexual aim and applied to fresh uses. They now combine with portions of the ego-instincts, and as "attached" components, help to contribute the social instincts, thus contributing an erotic factor to friendship and companionship, to "esprit de corps" and to the love of mankind in general. How large a contribution is in fact derived from erotic sources (with the sexual aim inhibited) could scarcely be guessed from the normal social relations of mankind.[58]

This argument views the repression of homosexuality as essential in the formation of male bonding, itself the psychological basis for authority and male dominance in virtually all existing societies. Both contemporary feminists and ethologists, despite some mutual suspicion, accept the thesis that male bonding is a dominant reality in social organization, even if they reject a Freudian explanation of its mechanics.[59] (Freud paid no attention to the repression of homosexuality among women, which still awaits psychoanalytic discussion. It seems likely that such an analysis would concentrate on the nature of female friendships and the much more frequent sublimation of female sexuality into mothering along the lines suggested by Nancy Chodorow.) It is my belief that sexual repression is a central part of male bonding, and one that is reflected in a number of male institutions. Competitive team sports, an essential part of male culture in Western societies, reveals very clearly the way in which straight male culture represses the homoerotic, as Philip Roth illustrated in *Our Gang*.

Both Bell and Weinberg and Charles Silverstein have commented on how little interest gay men show in competitive sport.[60] Neither seem able to explain it (a pity neither had read John Mitzel's pamphlet, "Sports and the Macho Male"). Yet if we accept the argument that competitive sports is one of the most common ways in which male homosexuality is sublimated, often through means that legitimize direct physical contact with other men, the paradox dissolves: in as far as this explains the motivation for competitive sport, it is less important for gay men, whose lack of interest is closely connected to their homosexuality. For gay women somewhat different psychological factors seem to operate, perhaps more closely related to a revolt against gender roles. If we also consider that in most authoritarian societies, above all Nazi Germany and the Communist countries of Eastern Europe, team sports are fostered with enormous enthusiasm by the government, the importance of an analysis of sport and its connections with repressed sexuality becomes evident.

If Freud's basic premises are correct, the hostility of armies, police forces, and fire brigades to admitting overt homosexuals is perhaps not as irrational as liberal civil libertarians like to argue. In an article on homosexuals and the military Andrew Kopkind hints at this: "Contemporary gay culture essentially denies the validity of much in the military order. Stripped of those attributes imposed by social discrimination and self-hate, gay consciousness disdains military machismo, downgrades regimentation, deplores insensitivity."[61] There is a certain homosexual chauvinism to this argument, but it is probably true that the recognition of homosexuality is a threat to that peculiar combination of male camaraderie and hierarchy on which most organizations depend; sexual desire is too anarchic, too disrespectful of established boundaries, to be trusted. At an everyday level male bonding is characterized by a strong degree of violence and aggression, which Paul Hoch has analyzed in terms of repressed homosexuality: "The more one retreats to an all-male environment, presumably the greater the homosexual temptation and hence the continued need to 'up the ante' in the way of violence to prove one's manhood."[62]

At the other end of the scale we can see the importance of sexual repression in religious institutions, above all in the Catholic church, which is based on both sexual denial and male domination. In *Group Psychology and the Analysis of the Ego* Freud suggested that institutions such as the church and the army—to which we might add the great bureaucracies of business and government that make up the "military-industrial complex"—are based upon the sublimation of libidinal energies into nonsexual energies, thus maintaining group ties that hold the organizations together, while displacing any overt sexual feelings outside the group.[63] If it is true, the homophobia of organized religion is not merely a matter of ideology, it is an essential basis for its continued existence. This leads me to argue that those people who seek change within the established churches are doomed to fail, for they could only really succeed were the institutions themselves to change radically.

Freud's concept of repression not only helps illuminate the mechanics of male bonding; it provides an explanation for homophobia as well. This term was invented and defined by George Weinberg as "the dread of being in close quarters with homosexuals";[64] I prefer Mark Freedman's formula of "extreme rage and fear reaction to homosexuals."[65] Weinberg attributes homophobia to five motives, of which only one is related to the Freudian concept of repression ("the secret fear of being homosexual"). His other reasons are the influence of religion, repressed envy, the image of homosexuality as a threat to established values, and an inability to accept those who live outside the norms of family and procreation.

The clearest analyses of homophobia in terms of repressed homosexual desire are found in the works of Martin Hoffman and Guy Hocquenghem. As Hoffman argued:

> The dread of homosexuality is a result of, and derives its tremendous force from, the wishes for homosexual expression which are present in our unconscious minds. In other words the fear is intimately connected with the wish, and the wish is only repressed because of the dread which is conjured up by the social taboo.[66]

Hocquenghem goes even further and argues that "anti-homosexual repression is itself an indirect manifestation of homosexual desire."[67] As he points out, one of the basic roots of paranoia in psychoanalytic terms is the need to repress homosexuality, and Hocquenghem traces the growth of this paranoia in tandem with the development of homosexuality as a separate category. It is not surprising that as the official definitions of homosexuality as something undesirable and inferior have become more problematic, so too a cruder form of homophobia has come to the surface, less able to rely on psychiatric or legal arguments, more likely to resort to the sort of extravagant denunciations associated with Anita Bryant or Jerry Falwell. The increase in visibility of and acceptance of the homosexual, and the general change in social values of which this increase is part, have made the homosexual more attractive as a target for various groups in need of an object onto which they can project their hates and anxieties.

The repression thesis seems to be most useful in explaining homophobia because of the irrational passion with which so much antihomosexual feeling is expressed. It is not uncommon to hear calls for castration and even the death penalty for homosexuals among some fundamentalists (the former was originally advanced as a progressive measure by Thomas Jefferson).[68] The language of homophobia is remarkable for its vehemence (why was homosexuality and not rape or murder long seen as "the unmentionable and abominable crime"?), and its frequency—Anglo-Celtic slang, in particular, is full of references to homosexuality: "cocksucker," "bugger," "pansy," "faggot," "poofter" are all common terms of abuse—is striking, as if the constant reiteration of homosexual words and references will somehow ward off the reality. Most clearly, homophobes constantly speak as if homosexuality were contagious and place great stress on "protecting" children from any contact with homosexuals; it is hard to explain logically how homosexuality can at the same time be "disgusting" and "unnatural," and yet so attractive that only the most severe sanctions will prevent its becoming rampant.

Nowadays the polite form of homophobia is expressed in terms of safeguarding the family, as if homosexuals somehow came into existence independent of families and were without family ties. It is true that much radical gay rhetoric has expressed hostility toward the nuclear family, pointing out the inadequacy of the nuclear family in coping with all the demands placed upon it and to this extent echoing feminist arguments. On the other hand, the estrangement between individual homosexuals and their families is a direct result of homophobia; it is ironic that the religious homophobes who talk so much of the importance of family ties are thus responsible for dividing family members from each other. The reality is that many homosexuals do maintain very close ties with parents, siblings, and children (their own and those of their sisters and brothers), and the homosexual totally cut off from all family is no more common than the one enmeshed in family ties, as depicted by James Baldwin in *Just Above My Head*.

One of the odder yet more revealing forms of homophobia is its expression as a distorted form of homosexual desire; thus, for example, there are men who seek out homosexuals for sex and then turn on them. Paul Monette has described such a case:

"He came in my mouth," he said. "And then he leaned over to the bedside table and picked up the lamp. I didn't believe it, so I didn't duck." . . . The damaged vision that mixed up sex and pain was what men risked when they lived in the closet.[69]

There are frequent examples of both men and women who crack up psychologically because of their inability to accept their homosexuality; this was the experience of the film actor Montgomery Clift, according to a number of observers.[70] Sometimes self-hatred and denial can lead homosexuals to seek out punishment in the form of danger. This seemed an element in the deaths of both the filmmaker Pier Paolo Pasolini and the Philadelphia publisher John Knight; writing of the former, Guy Hocquenghem invoked "the intimate, ancient and very strong bond between the homosexual and his murderer,"[71] a dubious argument to say the least, but a theme also found in works by Tennessee Williams and Jean Genet. This bond is clearly related to the need of those who attack homosexuals to "kill" the homosexuality in themselves.

The growing openness of male homosexuality has been accompanied by an apparent rise in homophobic violence, sometimes performed by those who are themselves behaviorally homosexual. There have been some quite extraordinary mass murders of homosexuals in recent years; indeed Patrick Franklin claims that "in this century the six most horrific, goriest mass murders in the U.S., now standing at a total of 166 victims, were committed in the course of homosexual rape and mayhem. Any one of these instances erased more lives than did Son of Sam, the Los Angeles Strangler or the San Francisco Zodiac Killer." (They include John Gacy's thirty-three victims, Dean Corll's twenty-seven, Juan Corona's twenty-five.) And, as Franklin points out, the media has been largely uninterested in the issues these murders raise.[72]

In one way the growth of antihomosexual violence that has been noticeable in the past few years, especially in New York, San Francisco, Los Angeles, and Houston, is the other side of partial acceptance. When the social strictures against homosexuality begin to decline, individuals most troubled by homosexuality will themselves become vigilantes, just as the Ku Klux Klan emerged—and reemerges—when there appeared to be a decline in segregation. John Money has referred to such violence as "the exorcist syndrome . . . when teenagers see something evil about themselves, one way to get rid of the evil is to destroy it."[73]

As Weinberg suggested, there are other factors involved in

homophobia, particularly in its institutionalized form, which is perhaps better termed heterosexism and which is maintained by people who do not share the extreme personal hostility of fag-bashers. Two factors seem to me most important, the general fear of sexuality so widespread in Western society and the apparent rejection by homosexuals, both men and women, of the institution of marriage and parenthood.

For Wainwright Churchill the roots of homophobia (he used the term "homoerotophobia") are essentially a "sex-negative environment," which he saw as particularly prevalent in the United States. Writing in 1967, Churchill saw such phobia as having reached "an apex that has no parallel in civilized society in modern times,"[74] and he believed this to be closely related to the poverty of interpersonal relations in American society. (Certainly no country makes such a cult of "meaningful relations" nor provides so many professional services to help foster them.) The argument that in societies where there is generalized fear and hostility to sexuality, there will be the strongest expressions of homophobia, is a persuasive one, and the apparent changes in sexual mores since Churchill wrote have tended to strengthen the tensions surrounding sexuality in Anglo-Celtic societies. One can see this factor at work in, for example, the constant reiteration of the idea that condoning homosexuality will increase the spread of venereal disease; even if this were true (and much of the argument is based on misleading statistics), one rarely finds the same objections to the use of automobiles and alcohol, both of which are responsible for considerably more deaths than syphilis and gonorrhea.

The peculiar fears, fantasies, and myths that surround sexuality are intimately connected in this society with the nature of Anglo-Saxon Protestantism, though this term is meant in more than a sectarian sense, since Irish Catholicism, the dominant form of Catholicism in the English-speaking world, has something of the same spirit about it. Condemnation of homosexuality, however, is something that seems ubiquitous in all monotheist religions—homosexuals were executed in Iran after the fundamentalist Islamic revolution, and in Israel pressure from orthodox rabbis has prevented repeal of the antihomosexual laws bequeathed by the British mandate.

Just why the Judaeo-Christian religious tradition has come to be associated with so strong a hostility to homosexuality is not altogether clear (John Boswell has demonstrated that such hostility was not an integral part of the early church's teachings). Quite apart from any general psychoanalytic speculation, one should note that in America the churches have played a particular role in teaching that morality is a matter of individual and private behavior; the excesses of capitalism, racism, and imperialism are by and large not defined as moral questions in the same way as are questions of sexual behavior. Many of the most ardent supporters of the Moral Majority disliked Jimmy Carter's attempt to apply moral criteria to American foreign policy. One might further ask whether religion, and particularly its fundamentalist and evangelical varieties, has a special appeal for those ill at ease with their own and other people's sexuality; in modern society the churches are likely to be refuges for people with particular fears and phobias, and with an inability to tolerate either rapid change or ambiguities.

Weinberg's second and third categories, fear and envy, overlap and seem to be expressions of the ambivalence about sexuality that is an integral part of Western culture (if Freud is correct, of all culture). Male homosexuals in particular seem to represent an expression of rampant and undisguised sexuality that is simultaneously threatening and attractive to those outside their world; as gays become more assertive and visible in their behavior there could well be an increase in homophobia born of fear and envy. Edmund White points out that gay men are seen as rich, selfish, and immoral:

> Some of the animosity must also be envy. Self-sacrifice doesn't come easily to anyone, nor does fidelity. If gays are seen as both rich and promiscuous, as capable of indulging their every whim as consumers and Don Juans, then they represent a temptation, an affront, which must be condemned. Moreover the very perversity of homosexuality must seem like a first step toward abandoning *all* moral strictures. . . . (The homosexual) has broken the social contract and is perceived as capable of anything.[75]

As a result homosexuals are thus very easily depicted as a threat to dominant social values and the homosexual comes to represent a scapegoat for the rapid changes in sexual mores that so many people find frightening. This has been suggested as one reason why voters in a number of American cities have repealed antidiscrimination ordinances; in a sense they were voting against all the changes of the past decade that have threatened traditional moral values. Kenneth Sherrill has found that homophobia accompanies opposition to a whole set of generally liberal issues, such as abortion, marijuana, open housing, and decreased military spending, and sees these issues as "sharing the common dimension of belonging to the new morality."[76]

This connection is particularly marked where acceptance of homosexuality seems to imply acceptance of blurring sex roles, which also touches very deep and repressed angers and fears. (Thus the quite extraordinary reaction to long hair for men in the sixties, as caught in *Hair* or the film *Easy Rider*.) A feminist analysis of homophobia tends to emphasize its link to the subordination of women and deemphasize its emphasis on sexuality. Thus in an article clearly influenced by feminist analysis Stephen Morin and Ellen Garfinkle argue: "The fear of being labelled homosexual serves to keep men within the confines of what the culture defines as sex-role appropriate behavior, and it interferes with the development of intimacy between men."[77]

Undoubtedly the threat of homosexuality to sex roles is a factor, but it is one that probably has been overstated, partly because of the political desire by many gay activists to link themselves to the women's movement. If the explanation for homophobia lay in the alleged blurring of sex roles, one might expect that the new macho style would be far more acceptable than that of the traditional queen. Yet this is not the case; what affronts others is the blatant *sexuality* of homosexuals, not merely their transgression of sex roles. Thus the macho homosexual creates more anxiety among straights than did the sissy type, who could more easily be dealt with as a figure of fun. Often one can find the most ardent upholders of traditional sex roles among homosexuals themselves, a paradox expressed in the dispute between drag queen and leather men in John Rechy's polemical novel *Rushes*.[78]

It is likely that the repression hypothesis is less important in explaining hostility to lesbians, and that here the threat to gender roles is more central. If this is so, it is because in a male-dominated society men play the major role in determining ideologies, and men are threatened in a different way by lesbians than by gay men. Lesbians, after all, do not represent that which men might be, but in their assertion that women can find satisfaction without men they threaten both the male heterosexual definition of sexuality and the various institutions, particularly the family, through which male dominance is expressed. Lesbian feminism, which sees in heterosexism "not only sex between men and women but patriarchal culture, male dominance and female subservience,"[79] suggests a connection that is more important in explaining hostility to gay women than to men, even if the current fashion among our opponents is to blur such distinctions.

This connection is related to the link Weinberg posits between homophobia and commitment to what has become the traditional family, a link that certainly exists at least on the rhetorical level; "reproduction and children and the promise of an after-life are utilized by some as magical devices to cope with the fear of death. To many, the homosexual, who does not appear to be wearing these amulets, evokes this fear."[80] Jan Morris, for example, argues that "the truth and pathos of (the homosexual condition) seemed to me exemplified by their childlessness."[81] Homosexuals can of course have children and often do—which ironically is physically impossible for transsexuals, who can play neither the male nor the female reproductive role. Nonetheless attacks on homosexuals for not being able to reproduce, and thus needing to seduce other people's children, are frequent, as in the campaigns of Anita Bryant.

It is worth noting that certain factors may help account for what seems particularly strong homophobia in the United States. Certainly one would look for a partial explanation in the extreme religiosity of American life, and the importance of fundamentalist Protestantism. (One might speculate that Protestant cultures are more likely than Catholic ones to produce both overt homosexuals and homophobia, but it is almost impossible to isolate religious from socioeconomic factors. A comparison of homosexuality in Catholic southern and Protestant northern Germany would perhaps throw light on this connection.) The existence of a frontier society, in which men were often thrown together in long-lasting and intimate relationships, is probably important. This is often argued in regard to Australian "mateship," though it is my impression that Australian homophobia is less intense than American. Moreover the extreme homophobia of American Jews—not necessarily found among other Jewish communities— would seem difficult to relate to the frontier thesis. But if Leslie Fiedler is correct in his psychoanalytic speculations about American literature, this is a society that is haunted by the specter of homosexuality and therefore has more need to repress it than most. It is possible, as Lillian Faderman suggests, that there was *less* fear of lesbianism in America than in Europe, which might be related to the more independent role of women in a frontier society.[82]

Fiedler saw unacknowledged homosexuality between white and black as the great American literary theme:

We can never shake off the nagging awareness that there is at the sentimental center of our novels, where we are accustomed to find in their European counterparts "platonic" love or adultery, seduction, rape, or long-drawn out flirtation, nothing but love of males! What awaits us are the fugitive slave and the no-account boy side by side on a raft borne by the endless river toward an impossible escape; or the pariah sailor waking in the tattooed arms of the brown harpooner on the verge of some impossible quest.[83]

Although there is a rather supercilious homophobia to much of Fiedler's analysis, it is an extremely suggestive one: we might hypothesize that just because same-sex comradeship was particularly important in American life (and often served as an escape from social demands to marry and raise a family), there was a particular revulsion for anything that exposed the sexual nature of such relationships. A good example of this revulsion would be the gallons of ink employed to try to establish the platonic nature of Walt Whitman's attachments to young men, despite the fact that Whitman has long been recognized by homosexuals as one of the founding fathers of contemporary gay culture.

During World War II, great effort was expended to exclude homosexuals from the military, and thousands of men and women were first classified as homosexuals by military medical examiners. For many people this was the determining factor that led them to conceive of themselves as homosexual, a fact of considerable importance in the post-war movement of homosexuals to certain large cities, especially San Francisco and New York.[84] It is ironical that to the best of my knowledge the United States was the only country other than Nazi Germany and its satellites to set out systematically to establish procedures for the classification of homosexuals.

* * * * * * *

David Fernbach is right that homosexuality and gayness are quite distinct, even if I disagree in part with his formulation of the difference. To be gay is to adopt a certain identity whose starting point is a physical and emotional attraction to one's own sex. Thus gayness is a particular social form of homosexuality, while homosexuality is best understood as a universal component of human sexuality, and one that manifests itself in a number of ways other than gayness. Despite the trend among some sections of the gay movement and some sociobiologists to restate the argument for a genetic predisposition to homosexuality, the evidence for a polymorphous and undifferentiated sexuality—repressed and sublimated along various lines due to both individual psychological experience and social pressures—seems to me more persuasive. I would attribute far greater emphasis than did Freud to the way in which sexuality is socially constructed, but this is not to refute Freud's basic view of sexuality. Even to see an increase in homosexuality as an evolutionary response to the need to limit the size of population, as Buckminster Fuller has asserted[85] fits quite easily into this framework; sexual repression will take different forms depending on the need of a given society to encourage or discourage reproduction.

Ironically, the Greeks and Romans were well aware of this view of sexuality; John Boswell has documented that the idea of universal bisexuality was held by writers such as Aristophanes, Xenophon, Plutarch, and Martial.[86] This view seems to me persuasive because of my own experience; I have known no one intimately, of either sex, who has not been aware at some point in his or her life of a potential attraction to both sexes.

If we are to posit the repression of homosexual desire among heterosexuals, we must also examine the effect of repressed *heterosexual* desire among people who are exclusively homosexual. Given their relative social position and power, this is unlikely to result in the equivalent of homophobia, though one might see glimmerings of "heterophobia" in the half-mocking attacks on the straight world, the mysogyny of some gay men, and the contempt for men of some gay women. But Freud allowed for sublimation as much as for repression—as he wrote of Leonardo, "the greater part of his sexual needs could be sublimated into a general thirst for knowledge and thus evade repression."[87]

As far as I know the only person to have speculated on the forms taken by repressed heterosexuality is Mario Mieli, who in *Homosexuality and Liberation* argues that repressed heterosexuality is the basis for the (male) homosexual aesthetic, so much of which is centered around "the sensual desire for the woman which is almost universally latent in us manifest homosexuals."[88] Mieli points to the role of "manifest homosexuals" in creating images of women through their role in fashion, photography, film, etc.; there is a very important insight here that helps explain at a psychoanalytic level the fascination that certain women hold for male homosexuals. (Note that this is a quite distinct phenomenon from the attraction to what society deems feminine, which is also a part of the male homosexual aesthetic.) Mieli speaks only of men, and there is much less evidence for the effect of repressed heterosexuality among gay women; again, whether this suggests social factors or a real difference in the way the two sexes organize their sexuality is by no means clear. Certainly it would not be difficult to argue for the existence of sublimated heterosexual desire in the writings of those lesbians who seem preoccupied with male homosexuals.

There may seem to be a basic contradiction in the development of a homosexual minority, particularly in the way in which it has evolved since the end of the sixties. On the one hand the minority represents an affirmation by millions of gay women and men of a common identity and community. On the other it represents a new form of social control, particularly effective because homosexuals ourselves participate in what can be seen as an excellent example of Marcuse's notion of "repressive tolerance."[89] Certainly this argument was true as long as homosexuals were prepared to accept their inferiority, as defined by experts and ideologues, and to request, rather than demand, that they not be persecuted. We have shifted away from this position over the past decade, in particular toward the growing emphasis that we, and not psychiatrists, criminologists, or other would-be experts, should define our status. The original purpose of the categorization of homosexuals as people apart was to project the homosexuality in everyone onto a defined minority as a way of externalizing forbidden desires and reassuring the majority that homosexuality is something that happens to other people. Once homosexuals begin to assert the equal validity of homosexuality, they will lead others, even those who do not necessarily feel a need to adopt a gay identity, to ask questions about their own sexuality, and if the growth of homosexual affirmation has meant a certain amount of social separatism, it has also and simultaneously meant an erosion in the rigidity of sexual definitions.

It is easy to see why, from the perspective of today's gay movement, the assertion of a gay identity is a positive advance. Richard Hall illustrated this advance very clearly in regard to theater when he wrote:

> What chiefly marks the pre-1960 plays . . . is the absence of this identity. The characters may engage in same-sex love, or come close to it—as in *Cat on a Hot Tin Roof, The Best Man, The Garden District, Ballad of the Sad Café, Children's Hour*—but there is little or no acceptance of gayness and its consequences. Homosexuality refers to an act imagined or performed in the dark and discussed only guardedly later, with little exploration of its non-sexual ramifications. Self-acceptance is almost always out of

the question. It is only towards the end of the 1960s, with *Fortune and Men's Eyes, Staircase* and *Boys in the Band* that the matter is confronted more broadly, with attention to the assumption of identity.[90]

Nonetheless there are certain problems with this stress on a separate identity, for it often means that people who are uncertain about their sexuality, particularly the young, feel excluded from both the gay and the straight worlds. This is why the conservatives are absolutely right to see the depiction of homosexuality in schools and on television as crucial (a central argument of the antigay movement since the campaigns of Anita Bryant and John Briggs), and why the gay movement must be as concerned with the discussion of homosexuality in the broader society as with the development of an inward-looking culture.

This development of the concept of a gay identity and an accompanying deemphasis on universal homosexuality is most pronounced in the United States; European homosexuals tend to be more aware of the Freudian tradition and the way in which homosexuality has been socially constructed. The difference is nicely symbolized in two attempts to illustrate a gay theme on postage stamps. In the American case an article in *Gay Community News* spoke of "gay and lesbian history in stamps." By this was meant no more than portraits of famous homosexuals, some of whom, such as Beethoven and Shakespeare, can be so categorized only with difficulty.[91] The French gay newspaper *Le Gai Pied* approached the subject quite differently, heading its correspondence column for a while with copies of stamps that are homoerotic in nature (in most cases this has meant surprisingly seductive pictures of young boys, which some readers of *Gay Community News* would find ideologically dubious).

Yet if there are theoretical reasons to be sceptical of the concept of "the homosexual," the reality is that a combination of social pressures and self-definition are creating a strong sense of identity based on homosexuality. This is a reasonably new development; there may have been forerunners of it among small groups since the end of the nineteenth century, but only in the last decades have people been able to say, as did Michael Denneny, that "I find my identity as a gay man as basic as any other identity I can lay claim to. Being gay is a more elemental aspect of who I am than my profession, my class, or my race."[92] It is ironic that the "tribalization" of modern society that McLuhan foresaw as a consequence of the diffusion of electronic media should lead to the construction of a homosexual "tribe" (a term first used, I suspect, by Christopher Isherwood).[93] As one artist wrote: "These [gay men] are his travel companions. If not for them he would live in a prison, not a closet. . . . The pattern of tribal formation begins as a product of advanced urbanization."[94]

NOTES

[1]   Sigmund Freud, *Three Essays on the Theory of Sexuality*, trans. and rev. by James Strachey (London: Hogarth Press, 1962), p. 11.

[2]   Ibid., p. 6.

[3]   Théophile Gautier, *Mademoiselle de Maupin*, quoted by Lillian Faderman, *Surpassing the Love of Men* (New York: William Morrow, 1981), p. 266, and Honoré de Balzac, *Splendeurs et Misères des Courtisanes*, quoted by J. P. Aron and R. Kempf, "Triumphs and Tribulations of the Homosexual Discourse," in G. Stambolian and E. Marks, eds., *Homosexualities and French Literature* (Ithaca, N.Y.: Cornell University Press, 1979), p. 144.

[4]   See Hubert Kennedy, "Karl Heinrich Ulrichs: Pioneer of Homosexual Emancipation," *Body Politic*, Nos. 41 and 42, March and April 1978.

[5]   See Phyllis Grosskurth, *Havelock Ellis* (New York: Alfred A. Knopf, 1980).

[6]   See R. Bayer, *Homosexuality and American Psychiatry*, pp. 30–34.

[7]   Freud, op. cit., pp. 4–5.

[8]   See Herb Spiers and Michael Lynch, "The Gay Rights Freud," *Body Politic*, May 1977.

[9]   See Samuel Rosenberg, *Why Freud Fainted* (Indianapolis: Bobbs Merrill, 1978), pp. 189–203.

[10]   J. H. Gagnon and William Simon, *Sexual Conduct* (Chicago: Aldine, 1973), p. 15.

[11]   Edward O. Wilson, *On Human Nature* (New York: Bantam Books, 1979), p. 149.

[12]   William Masters and Virginia Johnson, *Homosexuality in Perspective* (Boston: Little, Brown, 1979), pp. 186–188.

[13]   The comparative data is found in Clellan Ford and Frank Beach, *Patterns of Sexual Behavior* (New York: Harper and Row, 1951). See the analysis of this data in David Fernbach, *The Spiral Path* (Boston: Alyson Publications, 1981), pp. 71–75.

14 Norman Mailer, "The Homosexual Villain," *Advertisements for Myself* (New York: G. P. Putnam's Sons, 1959), p. 203.
15 See for example my interview with Vidal in *Christopher Street*, January 1978, p. 4.
16 Paul Robinson, *The Modernization of Sex* (New York: Harper & Row, 1976), p. 74.
17 Ken Plummer, "Building a Sociology of Homosexuality," in *The Making of the Modern Homosexual* (London: Hutchinson, 1981), p. 29.
18 Robinson, op. cit., p. 189.
19 Masters and Johnson, op. cit., p. 411.
20 Alan Bell, Martin Weinberg, and Sue Kiefer Hammersmith, *Sexual Preference* (Bloomington: Indiana University Press, 1981), p. 220.
21 Mary Renault, *The Charioteer* (London: Longmans, 1953), p. 232.
22 Hendrik Ruitenbeek, *Homosexuality: A Changing Picture* (London: Souvenir Press, 1973), p. 202.
23 Masters and Johnson, op. cit., pp. 146, 148.
24 Charlotte Wolff, *Bisexuality* (London: Quartet, 1977), esp. Ch. 6.
25 C. A. Tripp, *The Homosexual Matrix* (New York: Signet, 1976), p. 255.
26 See Shere Hite, *The Hite Report* (New York: Macmillan, 1976), p. 262.
27 Nancy Chodorow, *The Reproduction of Mothering* (Berkeley: University of California Press, 1978), p. 176.
28 Ibid., p. 193.
29 Marc Oraison, *La Question Homosexuelle* (Paris: Seuil, 1975), p. 96.
30 Michel Foucault, *The History of Sexuality* (New York: Vintage Books, 1979), p. 43.
31 John Boswell, *Christianity, Social Tolerance, and Homosexuality* (Chicago: University of Chicago Press, 1980), p. 333.
32 Ibid., p. 243. See my review of this book in *Gay Information* (Sydney), No. 5, Autumn 1981.
33 Manuel Puig, *Kiss of the Spider Woman* (New York: Alfred A. Knopf, 1979), p. 203.
34 On Latin American attitudes see E. A. Lacey, "Latin America: Myth and Realities," *Gay Sunshine*, No. 40/1, Summer/Fall 1979.
35 See Juliet Mitchell, *Psychoanalysis and Feminism* (New York: Vintage Books, 1975), p. 141.
36 Alan Bell and Martin Weinberg, *Homosexualities* (New York: Simon and Schuster, 1978), p. 231.
37 Judd Marmor (ed.), *Homosexual Behavior* (New York: Basic Books, 1980), p. xi.

38   Barbara Ponse, "Lesbians and Their Worlds" in Marmor, op. cit., p. 157.

39   Ralph Slovenko, "Homosexuality and the Law," in Marmor, op. cit., p. 198.

40   Marcel Saghir and Eli Robins, "Clinical Aspects of Female Homosexuality," in Marmor, op. cit., p. 286.

41   Freud, op. cit., p. 10.

42   See, for example, Sigmund Freud, "The Psychogenesis of a Case of Homosexuality in a Woman," *Standard Edition of the Complete Works of Sigmund Freud*, James Strachey (ed.), Vol. 18 (London: Hogarth Press, 1955).

43   Sigmund Freud, *Civilization and Its Discontents*, ibid., Vol. 21, p. 106.

44   Patrick White, *The Twyborn Affair* (London: Jonathan Cape, 1979), p. 360.

45   John Rechy, *The Sexual Outlaw* (New York: Grove Press, 1977), p. 195.

46   David Fernbach, *The Spiral Path* (Boston: Alyson Publications, 1981), pp. 83, 84.

47   Bell, Weinberg, and Hammersmith, op. cit., p. 188.

48   Ibid., p. 218.

49   See Michael Ross, Lesley Rogers, and Helen McCulloch, "Stigma, Sex and Society," *Journal of Homosexuality*, Vol. 3 (4), Summer 1978. The most extreme feminist position is that of Janice Raymond, *The Transsexual Empire* (Boston: Beacon Press, 1979).

50   Jan Morris, *Conundrum* (New York: Harcourt, Brace, 1974), p. 144.

51   Freud, *Three Essays*, p. 10.

52   Martin Levine (ed.), *Gay Men* (New York: Harper & Row, 1979), p. 12.

53   See C. A. Tripp, op. cit., pp. 116–117.

54   Don Shewey, review of William Hoffman (ed.), *Gay Plays*, in *Christopher Street*, May 1979, p. 78.

55   See Roberta Pliner, "Fag-hags, Friends or Fellow Travellers," *Christopher Street*, October 1979, and Seymour Kleinberg, *Alienated Affections* (New York: St. Martin's Press, 1980), Ch. 4. A very different view is found in Elizabeth Kaye, "Straight Women and Gay Men," *New West*, April 1981.

56   Sigmund Freud, "Some Neurotic Mechanisms in Jealousy, Paranoia and Homosexuality," *Complete Works*, Vol. 18, p. 232.

57   Sigmund Freud, *Totem and Taboo* (London: Routledge and Kegan Paul, 1950), p. 144.

58 Sigmund Freud, "Psycho-analytic Notes on an Autobiographical Account of a Case of Paranoia," *Complete Works*, Vol. 12, p. 61.

59 See my discussion in "The State and the New Homosexual," *Coming Out in the Seventies* (Boston: Alyson Publications, 1981), pp. 109–113.

60 Bell and Weinberg, op. cit., p. 182; Charles Silverstein, *Man to Man* (New York: William Morrow, 1981), p. 103.

61 Andrew Kopkind, "The Boys in the Barracks," in Jay and Young, *Lavender Culture* (New York: Jove/HBJ, 1979), p. 381.

62 Paul Hoch, *White Hero, Black Beast* (London: Pluto, 1979), p. 85.

63 Sigmund Freud, *Group Psychology and the Analysis of the Ego*, in *Complete Works*, Vol. 18, pp. 122–123.

64 George Weinberg, *Society and the Healthy Homosexual* (New York: St. Martin's Press, 1972), p. 4.

65 Mark Freedman, "Homophobia: The Psychology of a Social Disease," *Body Politic*, No. 24, June 1975, p. 19.

66 Martin Hoffman, *The Gay World* (New York: Basic Books, 1968), pp. 181–182.

67 Guy Hocquenghem, *Homosexual Desire*, trans. by Daniella Dangoor (London: Allison & Busby, 1978), p. 41.

68 Jonathan Katz, *Gay American History* (New York: Thomas Y. Crowell, 1976), p. 24.

69 Paul Monette, *Taking Care of Mrs. Carroll* (New York: Avon Books, 1978), p. 211.

70 See the comments of Arthur Miller, quoted by Robert La Guardia, *Monty* (New York: Avon Books, 1977), p. 198.

71 Guy Hocquenghem, "We All Can't Die in Bed," *Semiotext(e)*, Vol. III, No. 2, 1978, p. 29. On Knight see Arthur Bell, *Kings Don't Mean a Thing* (New York: William Morrow, 1978).

72 Patrick Franklin, "Essay," *The Advocate*, August 21, 1980. There is a very homophobic account of the Gacy case in Clifford Linedecker, *The Man Who Killed Boys* (New York: St. Martin's Press, 1980).

73 Quoted by Doug Ireland, "Who Kills Gay People?" *Soho News*, November 26, 1980.

74 Wainwright Churchill, *Homosexual Behavior Among Males* (New York: Hawthorn Books, 1967), p. 155.

75 Edmund White, *States of Desire* (New York: E. P. Dutton, 1980), p. 151.

76 Kenneth Sherrill, "Homophobia: Illness or Disease," paper delivered to the 1974 American Political Science Association Meeting, Chicago, p. 24.

77 Stephen Morin and Ellen Garfinkle, "Male Homophobia," *Journal of Social Issues*, Vol. 34, No. 1, 1978, p. 41.
78 See also P. Pehrson, "The Gay Male Feminist," *Fag Rag* (Boston), No. 25, 1979.
79 Faderman, op. cit., p. 411.
80 Weinberg, op. cit., p. 18.
81 Morris, op. cit., p. 61.
82 Faderman, op. cit., p. 298.
83 Leslie Fiedler, *Love and Death in the American Novel*, rev. ed. (New York: Stein and Day, 1966), p. 368.
84 See Alan Berube, "Marching to a Different Drummer," *The Advocate*, October 15, 1981.
85 "Out and Around," *Christopher Street*, December 1980, p. 11.
86 Boswell, op. cit., pp. 49, 50, 73.
87 Sigmund Freud, *Leonardo da Vinci* (New York: Vintage Books, 1955), p. 112.
88 Mario Mieli, *Homosexuality and Liberation*, trans. by David Fernbach (London: Gay Men's Press, 1980), p. 56.
89 I have discussed the relevance of Marcuse to gay liberation theory in *Homosexual: Oppression and Liberation* (New York: Avon Books, 1973).
90 Richard Hall, "The Elements of Gay Theatre," *Gay Sunshine*, No. 36/7, Spring/Summer 1978, p. 16.
91 Louis Paul Hennefeld, "Gay and Lesbian History on Stamps," *Gay Community News*, January 17, 1981.
92 Michael Denneny, "Gay Manifesto for the 80s," *Christopher Street*, January 1981, p. 13.
93 Christopher Isherwood, *Christopher and His Kind* (New York: Farrar Straus & Giroux, 1976).
94 Sam Schoenbaum, "Program Notes," mimeographed pamphlet distributed at the Leslie Loman Gallery, New York in February 1980.

CHAPTER THREE

Sex and the Triumph of Consumer Capitalism

I have already referred to the importance of the baths in the male gay world. Let me take one example, a bathhouse in the northern section of Chicago, beyond the Loop and the Gold Coast, in an area where Puerto Rican bars rub shoulders with Thai and Vietnamese restaurants. An inconspicuous two-story building, noticeable only for its lack of windows, it is set in a cul-de-sac off the main road where a policeman stands watch (to protect the gays or the straights?), the Midwest's largest, most luxurious sauna.

But it is not just a bathhouse, for you can eat snacks here, buy leather gear and inscribed T-shirts, even watch live cabaret performances on certain nights (this being a tradition first established by the New York Continental Baths, where Bette Midler launched her career).[1] Most striking is a large disco floor on the top story, surrounded by enormous soft pillows, where men dance clad only in towels, their movements jerky under the strobe lights. In the basement there is a small swimming pool, showers, and steamrooms; the main floor is largely occupied by a maze of small rooms that people hire for eight hours at a time; there is always a door or two open, with men, all-but-naked, lying inside in wait for a temporary partner. The place is strangely quiet, disturbed only by the background noise of disco music from upstairs and the constant, muted plodding of bare feet. Men in bathhouses rarely talk much, and it is quite common for sex to take place without words, let alone names, being exchanged. Yet even the most transitory encounters are part of a heightened eroticism that pervades the building; there is a certain sexual democracy, even camaraderie, that makes the sauna attractive. The willingness to have sex immediately, promiscuously, with people about whom one knows nothing and from whom one demands only physical contact, can be seen as a sort of Whitmanesque democracy, a desire to know and trust other men in a type of brotherhood far removed from the male bonding of rank, hierarchy, and competition that characterizes much of the outside world. It is equally true, however, that age and physical beauty set up their own hierarchies and barriers.

It is this aspect of male gay life, with its acceptance of immediate sex, that most infuriates homophobes. As Robert Boyers fulminated:

> One need not defend a repressive sexual morality or the conventions of bourgeois marriage to be appalled at the way in which (Robert) Martin blithely says of Whitman's encounters that they "could well be repeated in almost any steam bath of a modern large city."
>
> Is it, again, too obvious to suggest that the people who frequent those steam baths are not likely to enjoy the robust and equable nature actually celebrated by Whitman? That they are likely to be disturbed, yes, disturbed and crippled people enacting fantasies of release or liberation that can at best relieve momentarily the fear or impotence they experience when they confront real people capable of making complex emotional demands?[2]

It is worth noting that the author of this diatribe is a respected member of the American intelligentsia and editor of *Salmagundi*. His reaction is part of a much broader liberal backlash against the new visibility and assertion of homosexuality.

For baths such as the one in Chicago are the almost perfect symbols of the changes in the expression of homosexuality that have already been discussed. So far they exist almost exclusively for men —although there is at least one women's bath in San Francisco— which highlights the fact that these changes have meant very different things for women and men. The older bathhouses, such as the famous Everard Baths described in *Dancer from the Dance*, were usually dirty and tawdry—appropriate, given the sense of guilt and furtiveness associated with homosexuality. Their successors are clean, luxurious, and sensual, replete with the latest technology (electronically programmed music, strobe lighting, the ubiquitous smell of amyl), and part of a much broader trend in Western societies, that of a growing acceptance of recreational sex.

Two elements are involved in this development: increased sexual expectations and the commercialization of desire. The very idea of a gay bathhouse, where despite all the accoutrements of steamrooms, gymnasiums, and bars the essential object is to find partners for immediate sex, allows for the gratification of sexual desire without either emotional or financial consequences. (This does not mean that there may not be such consequences; a surprising number of long-term relationships have begun in steamrooms.) In this respect the baths resemble to some degree the massage parlors of which Gay Talese has written so approvingly,[3] except that a bathhouse is not a brothel, for everyone pays the same admission and this buys not sex itself but an environment in which there is the possibility of finding a partner or partners. It is this possibility that so enrages critics, who cannot imagine that the enjoyment of such sex can coexist with long-term and committed relationships. One rarely finds the same vituperation directed against prostitution, although there is surely more degradation involved in buying a sexual partner than in freely choosing to take part in transitory sexual encounters. But the baths undermine conventional morality in that they are predicated neither on the subordination of women to men, nor on the direct exchange of sex for money.

In fact, the bathhouse is the logical extension of a powerful trend in modern society and one of the most common of all sexual fantasies, namely the possibility of what Erica Jong called the "zip-less fuck." ("For the true, ultimate, zipless A-1 fuck, it was necessary that you never got to know the man very well. . . . So another condition for the zipless fuck was brevity. And anonymity made it even better.")[4] It is possible that even critics like Robert Boyers (and there are echoes of his attack in articles by other literati such as Joseph Epstein and Paul Cowan)[5] share these fantasies, and that there is a tinge of envy to their vituperation.

. Modern society has placed on sexuality demands far greater than have been made in most periods of human history; not only do we recognize the importance of sexuality, but we demand an end to sexual repressions (which Freud never did). As a number of commentators, most perceptively Michel Foucault and Richard Sennett, have pointed out, sexuality has become a central focus for the individual's sense of self:

A great sexual sermon—which has had its subtle theologians and its popular voices—has swept through our societies over the last decades; it has chastised the old order, denounced hypocrisy, and praised the rights of the immediate and the real; it has made people dream of a New City. The Franciscans are called to mind. And we might wonder how it is possible that the lyricism and religiosity that long accompanied the revolutionary project have, in western industrial societies, been largely carried over to sex.[6]

This development is strengthened by the sheer size and anonymity of modern society, and the corresponding stress on the private sphere of life as our real freedom to affect our work and politics seems to decline. Sex remains one of the few areas of life where we feel able to be more than passive spectators. It is a feature of modern society that we increasingly define achievement in terms of immediate gratification, and the move to burden sexuality with greater expectations is closely related to the stress on ideas of "self-fulfillment" and "personal actualization." A number of social commentators have stressed that ours is a time of increasing demands for private and immediate gratification, often without recognizing how these values are in large part the product of modern consumer capitalism. Henry Fairlie, for example, wrote that the seventies "deserve to be called a Decade of Reaction, because behind the conservatism lies an amorality in the individual's association with his society that reaches back to the primitive."[7] (How much truer of the Reaganite eighties.) Haynes Johnson points to the image of "self-improvement" in the best-seller lists in the late seventies—in addition to books on cosmetics, clothes, and jogging, "the book that had been on the best-seller list twice as long as any other spelled out a symbolic message for the times. It was entitled *Looking Out for Number One.*"[8] Tom Wolfe, who called the seventies the "me decade," did at least see the link to consumer-based affluence and referred to the "boom-boom seventies."[9]

Increased sexual freedom and the stress on individual gratification have also increased the ways in which sexuality is incorporated into the marketplace; going to the baths to have sex represents an integration of sexuality into consumerism in a way that encounters in parks or on the streets do not. Of course these latter continue, but in general there seems increasing reliance upon the marketplace for sex and sexual encounters. As gay bathhouses have both proliferated and become more luxurious, they are being recognized as central institutions of male gay life, a recognition that is double-edged, for it leads both to the legitimizing of gay life styles (when entertainers perform and politicians campaign in them) and to their becoming targets for attack (as in raids on the baths in Toronto and Albany in early 1981).

The realm of sexual consumption is one in which the differences between the sexes are very marked, for there are relatively few exceptions to the rule that in the commercialization of sex men both control and buy the services of women. (This helps explain the rage of many feminists against pornography.) Gay men may seem to occupy an intermediate position between straight men and both gay and straight women, for we probably rely less directly on buying sex. But the differences are less clear-cut than one might imagine. There is a highly developed male prostitution network, ranging from the escort services glamorized in William Snyder's soap opera *Tory's* to the kids selling themselves for bed and breakfast in Times Square. Equally one might object that there is nothing new in the selling of sex or of sexual venues; quite apart from their possible Roman antecedents, gay bathhouses existed in the United States from the beginning of the century.[10] But as in other areas where sexuality has become a commodity, the increase in scale has been so vast as to suggest qualitative, not just quantitative, change.

In contemporary consumer societies sex is both equated with "private" as distinct from "public" life and seen as a solvent of all problems. Note the ubiquitous theme of articles, usually in women's magazines, on "how to save your marriage" that assume the centrality of a "good sex life." The irony is that the growing stress on sexual fulfillment almost certainly promotes discontent with marriage, as more women come to share with Isabelle Wing "all those other longings which after a while marriage did nothing much to appease."[11] Edmund White summed up much of the tenor of our times when he wrote:

> If I were to venture my own generalizations, I would say that with the collapse of other social values (those of religion, patriotism, the family and so on), sex has been forced to take up the slack, to become our sole mode of transcendence and our only touchstone of authenticity. The cry for scorching, multiple orgasms, the drive towards impeccable and virtuoso performance, the belief that only in complete sexual compatability lies true intimacy, the insistence that sex is the only mode for experiencing thrills, for achieving love, for assessing and demonstrating personal worth—all these projects are absurd. I can picture wiser people in the next century regarding our sexual mania as akin to the religious madness of the Middle Ages—a cooperative delusion. I feel that homosexuals, now identified as the element in our society most obsessed with sex, will in fact be the agents to cure the mania. Sex will be restored to its appropriate place as a pleasure, a communication, an appetite, an art; it will no longer pose as a religion, a reason for being. In our present isolation we have few ways beside sex to feel connected with one another; in the future there might be surer modes for achieving a sense of community.[12]

That the stress on sexual fulfillment is seemingly most common in the male gay world is due to several factors. The fact that men are more likely to seek out sexual adventure than women, whether for biological or for social reasons (and possibly—but only possibly—for both), means that there can be much greater sexual freedom in an all-male world; there is much less fear of rape and exploitation. Just as important, I suspect, is the fact that having broken one of the great sexual taboos, homosexuals feel free to break others, to become, in John Rechy's term, "sexual outlaws." And their general independence and lack of children means that gays, including many gay women, are freer to act out this belief in the all-encompassing importance of sexuality.

But the increased sexual expectations of modern life are by no means confined to homosexuals. They are reflected in a vast proliferation of sexual signs in the media and advertising that constantly bombard us with ideas of constant sexual adventure. This in turn creates demands for greater sexual gratification: Tom Wolfe has suggested that, far from the hydraulic theory of libido that Freud seemed to imply (i.e., we have a fixed amount of sexual energy that must be acted out, repressed, or sublimated), a more accurate theory would be a neurophysiological one: "Behavior is determined, instead, by which lines are open, and which messages get through. According to this model, what is the effect of pornography—or group sex—or 'massages'—or orgasmic regularity? Far from being a safety valve releasing energy that has built up inside the system, any such pastime is more like an input that starts turning on the YES gates . . . to the point where its message (sex!) closes out all others and takes over the entire circuit."[13] But such an observation does not necessarily disprove Freud's major theses, for it merely indicates how precarious is sexual repression and suggests that under contemporary conditions we can dispense with much of the repression of earlier periods. Herbert Marcuse developed this explanation in his concept of "surplus repression."[14]

The United States, with its heritage of distrusting sex and its hedonistic present, in which sex is treated as both a commodity and a stimulus to consumption, has been particularly vulnerable to the overburdening of sex with expectations that cannot reasonably be met. A book like Gay Talese's Thy Neighbor's Wife, with its simplistic thesis that sexual liberation is a matter of having more and better orgasms, is the respectable side of the proliferation of sex shops, pornographic movie houses, and massage parlors over the past decade. It is trite to point out that the commercialization of sex does not necessarily equal liberation. Indeed one feature of much so-called "liberated" sex is that it bolsters the traditional prejudices that sex must be dirty and furtive: the appearance of the great majority of such places, and their location in the decaying areas of the inner city, reinforces the feeling that going to them is surrendering to one's baser instincts. In recent years there has been a marked improvement in amenities and appearance at some gay saunas and straight massage parlors; their new respectability suggests just how closely sexual expression is tied to the workings of consumer capitalism.

It is ironic that as we have become freer in our sexuality we seem to have become more reliant on business institutions to provide us with the means to express this freedom; one might have expected that growing sexual freedom would mean the withering away of bathhouses and massage parlors as people relied less on them as places to make contact and to have sex. Indeed, while there is no concrete evidence of this, it is my hunch that the reverse has occurred, and that there has been a decline in street cruising, for example, with the growth of sex palaces. (The irony is underlined by the fact that many of the pornographic movies shown in such establishments are set out of doors, in woods, beaches, etc.) Much so-called sexual liberation has not, by and large, made for a genuine eroticism of everyday life as much as it has meant the creation of a set of specialized institutions within which people can, for a certain time that is quite consciously divorced from their everyday lives, act out sexual fantasies. Deeper changes in our sexual behavior and feelings must be more complex.

* * * * * * *

The first question to be asked is whether the apparent sexualization of modern society indicates any real changes in behavior or whether this sexualization has taken place largely in terms of images and rhetoric. No longer are there any absolute standards covering sexual behavior, a frightening prospect for many Americans. The idea of a pluralist society has traditionally allowed for religious and ethnic divisions while assuming agreement on one particular moral code. Thus Utah was only admitted to the Union after the Mormon church renounced polygamy, and there has been frequent persecution of Jehovah's Witnesses when their concept of religion has conflicted with broader American values. As Tocqueville wrote:

"American society is not averse to regularity of morals, for good morals contribute to public tranquillity and are favorable to industry."[15]

In fact the changes have occurred both in behavior and in the area of morality and values. This is reflected for example in advertisements, such as one from *TV Guide,* the magazine with the largest circulation in the United States, which proclaimed:

OLD MAID—DO YOU DARE TO NEGLECT HER?
The number of women putting off marriage for education or a career has risen 70% in the last decade. Men aren't rushing up the aisle, either. Over 17 million people now live alone.[16]

Or in the launching of the Reader's Digest magazine *Families:*

Today's family is:
Mom, dad and 2.4 kids
A couple with 3 kids—his, hers, theirs
A 26-year-old secretary and her adopted son
A couple sharing everything but a marriage license
A divorced woman and her stepdaughter
A retired couple raising their grandson.[17]

One might note that the people at Reader's Digest are still unwilling to recognize homosexual families, but even the changes to which they refer went unacknowledged until recently.

Figures from the Census Bureau provide some indication of how much real change there has been in the past decade. Between 1970 and 1979 there were large increases in the numbers of divorced couples, single-parent families, and the never-married. (Among women aged twenty to twenty-four, nearly half had not married, as against just over a third ten years earlier.)[18] Another study suggested that percentage of non-married will steadily increase, even among older age groups, and that only *one-fifth* of the new households likely to be established over the next decade will be married couples, the rest being made up of the never-married, the divorced, or the widowed.[19] Such figures lead to cries of alarm, such as this one by Ronald Kotulak: "As the traditional family bursts at the seams, a new specter of childlessness, singleness and 'second-career' marriages is beginning to creep over the country."[20]

Such changes do not, in themselves, make for a sexual revolution. There is considerable evidence that many of the non-married are living together in situations that effectively replicate marriage, and divorced people are likely to remarry with amazing haste. But there is further evidence of deeper changes that supports the claim that "recreational sex" and sex outside ongoing relationships is becoming more common.

In a mid-decade study of changing sexual mores, Morton Hunt itemized a large number of areas in which he saw change occurring, including the growth of sex therapy and encounter groups, the increasing acceptance of premarital sex (as in the growth of coed domitories on campuses), singles bars and "swingers" groups, open discussion of sexual unorthodoxy, the gay movement, sexual exhibitionism at rock concerts, the growth of massage parlors, greater discussion of alternatives to marriage, the legalization of abortion, etc.[21] Many of these changes have been sufficiently accepted to become staples of movie and television comedies; a whole range of movies, ranging from Woody Allen's self-reflections to formula comedies like *The Last Married Couple in America,* has explored at least some of the shifts in sexual mores. The married woman in *Stardust Memories* who turns up in Allen's bed with the blessing of her husband is a long way from the occupant of twin beds of the fifties. Thus one "single swingers sex club" could boast in its advertising—"Revel in our famous fur-lined swing room, play in our heated fountain"—that it had been featured on both ABC and NBC.[22] "One-night stands" are emphatically no longer the preserve of homosexuals.

Indeed the "singles scene" that Hunt mentions has become in some ways very much like the stereotypical gay male scene (though there are subtle differences, as Richard Price explored in his novel *Ladies' Man*). So big is the scene that the *Los Angeles Times* runs a column telling its readers "where singles meet," and as an article in that paper made clear, there are large numbers of people, both women and men, who like Theresa in *Looking for Mr. Goodbar* want their sex without major emotional involvements.[23] For growing numbers of Americans, sex can be casual and guilt-free and does not require a "meaningful relationship" to justify itself. Again there is statistical evidence of these changes. In the 1950s, Kinsey's studies showed that only 20 percent of unmarried women under nineteen had had intercourse; in 1971 the figure in a comparable survey was nearly 50 percent.[24] Between 1969 and 1973 the number of Americans who believed sexual relations before marriage was wrong declined from 68 to 48 percent.[25]

Hunt, unlike the more impressionistic Talese, whose book be-

longs to the uncritical "Gee Whiz Isn't Sex Great" school, is sufficiently cautious to avoid overstating the impact of these changes:

> It is our contention, based on our survey data, that the frequent
> assertions that a sexual revolution has conquered America is some-
> thing less than accurate, for the changes that have taken place
> both in attitudes and in actual behavior have not, by and large,
> created any real break with the fundamental Western tradition
> linking sexual activity with love, nor have they brought about the
> existence of new social institutions competing with or preempting
> sexuality from marriage and family life.[26]

In the same way, some observers have argued that it is not marriage
itself that is declining; rather, there is a precipitate decline in both
the expectation of and the reality of permanent monogamous marriages and their replacement by a growing number of divorces and
remarriages. But this still suggests a major shift in the dominant
ethos. As Molly Haskell put it: "The idea of marital love that we
inherited from the novel—marriage as the ultimate destiny, the
salvation and consolidation of virtue, the redemption of the profane
—has been shattered. It is still a possibility, but only that. And love,
romantic love—well, quite possibly that is all a mistake. The Happy
Ending has ceased to have even mythic resonance."[27]

Moreover the market for sex in its various forms (pornography,
massage parlors, "sex aids," prostitutes, swingers clubs, baths, and
backroom bars) is immense. One estimate suggests that about $5
billion is involved every year (but the Rev. Bruce Ritter, director of
a New York mission for runaways, estimates that $1 billion is spent
in the Times Square area alone). The very high spending on pornography—it is estimated that there are 20,000 "adult bookstores" and
800 full-time sex cinemas in the United States[28]—suggests that
much of the "sexual revolution" exists on the level of masturbatory
fantasy; it may even be that a large part of the pornography and "sex
aids" is dedicated to improving marital sex. As the emphasis in
capitalism moves more and more toward consumption, sex inevitably
becomes big business. There are no figures available on what share
of this market is gay. I suspect it is relatively small and, of course,
highly concentrated in large urban areas.

It is not difficult to see how all these changes affect the ways
in which homosexuality is expressed. Social change involves shifts in
both values and mores, and perhaps the most important change of
all is the decline in an absolute standard to be imposed on everyone;

in the seventies it became increasingly possible, even legitimate, to talk of a fulfilling life outside marriage and children. Single women were no longer stigmatized as spinsters; single men were viewed enviously as "swingers." As Peter Biskind and Barbara Ehrenreich put it, "Where there had been only marriage, there were now 'life-styles' featuring a bewildering multiplicity of relationships, all shored up by the seemingly inexhaustible affluence of the sixties."[29] These life styles now included living openly, or semiopenly, as gay.

While these developments seem to me largely positive—and absolutely vital for the emergence of any sort of "free space" for the development of a gay identity and life style—it would be silly to pretend that such changes are not without their casualties. Conservatives are quite right when they point out that the "sexually liberated" are not necessarily any happier than those who adhere to traditional norms. The real question is whether these norms would work for the people who reject them, or whether we need quite new ones. One of the great problems now facing us is the need to find new forms of relationships that better meet our conflicting needs for security and independence, stability and adventure, not to mention the needs of those upon whom our sexual lives impinge, above all children.

Why have these changes occurred? There is not merely a theoretical curiosity in asking this question; if we know what has lead to them we will find it easier to estimate how permanent they are likely to be. It seems to me that there are three crucial elements: the divorce of sexuality from procreation, made possible through improved methods of contraception; the changing role of women; and the increased inclusion of sexuality in the mechanisms of a consumption—rather than a production—oriented capitalism. All these are, of course, interrelated, and they seem to me ultimately a product of the shifts in the nature of modern capitalism, despite all the reservations one must always have about monocausal explanations.

According to Barry Adam, advanced capitalism includes four factors relevant to sexual organization: a decreased demand for reproduction (and attendant ease of contraception and abortion); the virtual disappearance of kinship (for example, the sort of family ties characterized in *The Godfather*) as a form of social organization; the declining importance of gender roles in determining the division of labor; and the relocation of courtship into special commercial establishments (bars, discotheques, etc.).[30] It is these factors that underlie the changing nature of the family and its declining centrality in modern life, not, as the conservatives claim, pornography, feminism, and overt homosexuality, all of which are equally the products of broader socioeconomic change. Just as the explosion of fast-food restaurants has undermined family meals and the growth of electronic games has replaced more traditional pastimes, so the growing scope of capitalism is intruding on our most private activities and indeed (as Bernard Tavernier suggested in his film *Deathwatch*) abolishing traditional ideas of privacy. We have become more and more accustomed to transience, impermanence, and what Beverley Hotchner calls "a throwaway lifestyle."[31] In such a life style recreational and uninvolved sex becomes increasingly acceptable.

Cultural values do not simply grow out of socioeconomic change, independent of historical factors. Nonetheless it is striking that the sorts of changes I have been discussing have occurred in almost all Western countries over the past decade. Thus in three societies with quite different historical, cultural, and political traditions—Australia, France, and Spain—one can see the virtual collapse of censorship since the end of the sixties. Of course there are individual peculiarities—in France the resignation of de Gaulle, in Australia the accession to power of a liberal customs minister, in Spain, most important of all, the death of Franco—but what is striking is how far all three societies reflect the same trends, trends that were equally at work in other Western countries. Since then there have been occasional reactions and clamp-downs, but there is no Western country today in which pornography is not much more freely available than was the case fifteen years ago. The idea that history alternates between "permissive" and "prudish" periods, as Gordon Rattray Taylor suggested in his book *Sex in History*, ignores the socioeconomic base of sexual regulation. (And, indeed, it overlooks the political variable, as the example of Franco's Spain suggests. It is no accident that all authoritarian societies, whether Argentina and South Africa or the Soviet Union and Cuba, are extremely puritanical sexually and, one should note, almost always strongly homophobic.)

As Western countries became societies of high consumption, ready credit, and rapid technological development, it was not surprising that the dominant sexual ideology of restraint and repression, which had been so functional during the early production-oriented development of capitalism, came under increasing attack. Restraint remains effective in countries undergoing rapid industrialization, and many Third World countries impose far more rigid morality than does the United States. The collapse of traditional values, whether in regard to sex, work, or authority, are in a sense the result of the very success of the capitalist societies these value systems had helped engender.

In his book Talese unwittingly indicates this through his almost total concentration on the way in which freer sexuality became a marketable commodity during the seventies, most particularly in the form of pornography and massage parlors. In both cases the market was largely male and the services provided almost entirely by women, a point, like the total disregard of homosexuality, that seems to concern neither Talese nor the journalists that turned the writing of his book into a news event. At the same time Talese's fascination with the career of Hugh Hefner, whose conspicuous consumption is described almost as much as the variety of his sexual partners, suggests that Talese is aware that the growth of "sexual freedom" is closely related to a consumption-oriented capitalism.

It is not merely that modern capitalism turns sex into a major commodity, both directly and indirectly, so that airlines, soap, and cars are all marketed by explicit sexual references. The values implied in modern capitalism have real implications for the way in which sexuality is expressed; the stress on hedonism and instant gratification makes old strictures seem less and less relevant. Those people who voted for Ronald Reagan in the hope he could lead America back to its traditional values will inevitably be disappointed, for there is a basic conflict between these values and those of consumer capitalism, which Reagan, himself a product of Hollywood, so strongly extolls.

This trend has been satirized masterfully by Stanislaw Lem in his story "Sexplosion," in which by the 1990s three corporations control sex, which:

> ... from a private amusement, a spectator sport, group gymnastics, a hobby, and a collector's market, turned into a philosophy of civilization. . . . The impersonal industry of the USA, having appropriated the situational wisdoms of east and west, took the fetters of the Middle Ages and made of them unchastity belts, harnessed art to the designing of sexercisers, incubunks, copulcots, push-button clitters, porn cones and phallophones, set in motion antiseptic assembly lines off of which began to roll sadomobiles, succubuses, sodomy sofas for the home and public gonorrarcades, and at the same time it established research institutes and science foundations to take up the fight to liberate sex from the servitude of the perpetuation of the species. Sex ceased to be a fashion for it had become a faith; the orgasm was regarded as a constant duty,

and its meters, with their red needles, took the place of telephones in the office and on the street.[32]

But not only new values are brought into being by socioeconomic structures; socioeconomic change has also helped produce a greater independence for women, several teenage and youth cultures, and a "new middle class," all of which are contributing to the decline of traditional sexual rigidities. It is this new class, made up of highly trained technicians, social welfare bureaucrats, computer operators, airline personnel, researchers, etc., that forms the troops of the "sexual revolution," and they include large numbers of women, both economically and sexually freer than ever before to choose how they live.

The influence of the growing independence of women on gains in tolerance for homosexuals is enormous. It is not necessary to subscribe to the argument that homophobia is itself the product of sexism to see that under modern conditions greater freedom for women and a breakdown in the rigidity of sex roles (the two are closely connected) has repercussions in allowing greater freedom for homosexuals, both women and men. Sexual repression has almost always affected women more than men; as women rebel against it, there is an effect on the whole range of coercive morality. The opponents of feminism are almost invariably homophobic as well, whether they be anti-ERA fundamentalists (one of the arguments frequently used against the ERA is that it would allow homosexual marriages) or the liberal intelligentsia, such as Norman Mailer and the New York literary establishment. (It is my hunch that the homophobes who talk to each other in the pages of *Commentary*, *Harper's*, etc. are basically men who were called sissies at school and are venting their anger on a safe target to prove their own masculinity.)

The sheer affluence of modern capitalism, however poorly distributed this affluence may be, fosters the growth of diverse patterns of consumption and allows people to escape from sexual restraints: not only the pill, pornography, massage parlors, and saunas but also antibiotics, cars, cheap motels, drive-in movies, and mind-expanding drugs all have played their part in the growth of a hedonistic sexual culture.

Modern consumer capitalism is producing new types of character structures often identified as narcissistic, a term that has become a code word for all the things social critics dislike about modern society. As Christopher Lasch put it:

Economic man himself has given way to the psychological man of our times—the final product of bourgeois individualism. The new narcissist is haunted not by guilt but by anxiety. He seeks not to inflict his own certainties on others but to find a meaning in life. Liberated from the suspicions of the past he doubts even the reality of his own existence. . . . His sexual attitudes are permissive rather than puritanical, even though his emancipation from ancient taboos brings him no sexual peace. . . . Acquisitive in the sense that his cravings have no limits, he does not accumulate goods and possessions against the future, in the manner of the acquisitive individualist of nineteenth century political economy, but demands immediate gratification and lives in a state of restless, perpetually unsatisfied desire.[33]

The stress on narcissism that Lasch, following analysts like Richard Sennett and Philip Slater,[34] identified as a central characteristic of contemporary society is clearly near, if not at the heart of, much of the new sexual morality. Lasch, being essentially a conservative, dislikes most contemporary attitudes and is troubled by a present characterized by "a casual promiscuity, a wary avoidance of emotional commitments, an attack on jealousy and possessiveness," and, above all, "the modern woman's increasingly insistent demands for sexual fulfilment."[35] That there are positive and genuinely liberating aspects to these developments seems not to occur to him.

Where Lasch's critique seems to me most acute is in its view of the contemporary ethos as one that promotes private pleasure at the expense of public life; the *Playboy* message, of which Talese seems so approving, is clearly one of "making it" within the existing system so as to enjoy both materialist and sexual rewards. There are echoes here of Sennett's view of the modern personality as essentially "narcissistic, protean (i.e., open to considerable fluctuations) and marketable," and his perception that "sexuality has been burdened with tasks of self-definition and self-summary which are inappropriate to the physical act of making love with another person."[36] Thus not only does modern capitalism create the socioeconomic conditions for the emergence of a homosexual identity, it creates the psychological ones as well. In short, the new homosexual could only emerge in the conditions created by modern capitalism.

Throughout this century there were always people prepared to flout social repressions and fight against them; the members of the early feminist and gay movements are an excellent example. When this challenge became widespread it was assumed that such challenges were necessarily going to undermine the existing social and economic order. A utopian belief in the revolutionary nature of freer sexuality was a mark of many of the movements of the late sixties, whether Yippies in the United States, anarchists in France, or Provos in Holland. In very different ways both Marcuse and some feminists pointed out that quite considerable relaxation of sexual restraints could occur in ways that would only strengthen the existing system. It does not seem to me accidental that the past decade, which has been marked by strong political conservatism in most Western countries, has also seen the sorts of changes in sexual morality I have discussed. In some ways, discos and singles bars are the contemporary equivalent of bread and circuses.

Nowhere are the apparent contradictions between freer sexuality as an act of revolution and as a new means of incorporating protest into the status quo more obvious than in the case of homosexuality and its definition, codification, regulation, and expression in modern capitalist societies. In a society where recreational sex is seen as a legitimate growth industry, and where even small cities have experienced a proliferation of sex shops, massage parlors, pornographic movie houses, and bars with topless waitresses, it becomes very difficult to justify prohibitions on similar establishments catering to homosexuals, and a judicious mix of corruption and large profits is almost always enough to keep open gay discos, saunas, backroom bars, and movie theaters. By and large, after all, they duplicate the straight scene, except that direct prostitution is less frequent. But this does not mean that there is genuine acceptance of the "homosexual life style," and anxiety over the changes in sexual mores and the increasing visibility of homosexuals that such changes have helped make possible often make us an attractive scapegoat. A gay man or woman who spends the weekend partying at the latest "in" disco may still arrive for work on Monday morning and be fired for being gay.

The connection between capitalism and the growth of the homosexual identity has been most strongly argued by Jeremy Seabrook, who seems to view almost all of contemporary gay life as attributable to the development of consumer capitalism:

> In fact, what they [homosexuals] are doing is carrying out the demands of changed economic conditions. It is the relaxation of traditional disciplines that allows them—even demands of them —that they be as they are. More than this, it gives great latitude for self-expression, permitting even revolutionary incantations, the

illusion of personal heroics. The gay community has been discovered in the early seventies in much the same way, and for the same reasons, that teenagers were discovered in the fifties. . . . Gay people are some of the most avid consumers of clothing, holidays, theatre and cinema, restaurant meals, cosmetics, as well as of household goods. And if there is an illusionary combat in the gay community's struggle for recognition, this can only strengthen the function which that community is required to serve. . . . If the consumer economy depends upon individuals consulting their needs and wants and then striving to fulfill them it is inevitable that a liberation in the area of sexual behavior should be set in train; and the crusading of gay groups can only occur in this context.[37]

Seabrook, indeed, comes close to arguing that we only exist because we form a commercial market. (It is interesting that he is writing of Britain, where the commercial gay world is both less lavish and less sexually permissive than in North America, or for that matter West Germany, Holland, or Australia.) In so doing he misses two points. The first is the importance of the political dimension in creating our identity, and the way in which this is a continuing struggle. Indeed heterosexism often means that the exploitation of the gay market is far less effective than it might be. (I have yet to read any mention of the Castro area in the U. S. Travel Service's handouts on San Francisco.) While changes in capitalism have certainly made possible the development of a particular form of homosexual identity, one should not assume that it has come into being without certain political choices and actions. Second, Seabrook, rather like Lasch, ignores the positive side of sexual consumerism. The new narcissistic hedonist whom they see as the prototype of modern man—and woman? . . . Seabrook largely ignores her—may well have less stability, certainty, and permanence to his life than before. But s/he is less trapped by tradition and by familial and social expectations, which were responsible for at least as much unhappiness as is contemporary narcissism. As Sennett has argued, "the less social relations appear embedded in a scheme of nature, of divine law, of organic necessity, the more people should be able to imagine themselves as creatures with a life apart from their social roles."[38]

One of the clearest examples of how changes in the nature of consumer capitalism have brought about real increases in freedom is the declining rigidity in sex role expectations, especially for women, that began with the countercultural movements of the sixties. However flawed these changes may have been, they could only occur under economic conditions that allowed women to break out of the largely dependent role they had occupied in the earlier stages of capitalism (as in most other forms of society), and they, in turn, made possible the emergence of the women's movement of the seventies. (Thus the present antifeminist backlash is undoubtedly related to the economic recession.) Similarly there is a double-edged effect to the increasingly blatant use of female sexuality in advertising, such as the Calvin Klein ads that feature Brooke Shields pouting: "Nothing comes between me and my Calvins." As feminists rightly complain, such advertising objectifies women and reinforces ideas that they exist to pander to male fantasies. On the other hand, they also imply that women are sexual creatures in their own right and hence challenge remaining puritanical norms that would deny this.

One of Seabrook's more acute observations is that the homosexual in some way pioneered the values and behavior that have become the norm in modern consumer society:

> The homosexual is no longer an outsider in the main flow of the culture. On the contrary, the homosexual has been a kind of pathfinder; a pioneer of the new kind of human being that has come into existence under the protective shelter of plenty. In one sense we have all become gay. The subculture of those homosexuals who dared to admit their membership of it originated in privileged areas of society—among the leisured and rich, who could buy themselves immunity from the moral obloquy that attended what was considered a dangerous deviancy. The subculture was well off, self-indulgent and reached only a minority of homosexual people. The tone was upper middle class with aristocratic leanings. It assimilated individuals from the lower reaches of society and more or less successfully colonized them. But because such people were leisured, because they were absolved from the need to raise a family and could divert their income to their own comfort and concern, the homosexual culture already showed incipiently many of the traits of what has come to be the consumer society.[39]

An excellent example of this is the vogue among gay men for self-improvement, both of the body and of the psyche. Gay women, while increasingly likely to be attracted to therapy, from revolutionary consciousness raising to invocations of traditional magic, seem less obsessed by the cult of the body and the search for eternal youth.

Indeed, gay men behave far more like traditional straight women. Thus gay men exemplify many of the characteristics of the "with it" American, especially the California variant. As Edmund White wrote of one man in San Francisco, a forty-two-year-old who kept himself young through exercise and meditation:

> Gerry is a twentieth century phenomenon. In the past, as George Orwell has reminded us, the bulk of humanity passed almost instantly from being adolescents (amorous, high-spirited, open to experience) into being toothless, downtrodden, self-sacrificing Mom and Dad. Only the aristocratic few escaped this sudden transition and prolonged the period of introspection, dalliance, egocentricity, physical beauty. Even so, this grace period ended in one's early thirties (after all, the Marschallin in *Der Rosenkavalier* is just thirty when she bids farewell to romance).
>
> In the United States, and especially among gay men, this period of adolescence is being extended for the first time in history into the forties, fifties, even sixties. It has become a way of life. Let me hasten to say that by "adolescence" I mean nothing derogatory; I am not asserting, as psychoanalysts once did, that homosexuals are "arrested" in their development, that they "refuse to grow up." Our so-called "immaturity" can be viewed just as easily as a prolonged and admirable resolve to stay attractive and susceptible to influence.[40]

I much prefer White's view of this to Seabrook's self-denigration. It is not the tendency of homosexual men to be concerned about their appearance that requires explanation, but rather the assumption of so many heterosexual men that women should be attracted to them no matter how they look. What is striking is that men like Gerry, who go to gyms and take up jogging, are increasingly common among straights. There is a fascinating anthropological detective story to be written on the way in which running shoes and shorts moved out of the gay ghettos to permeate mainstream middle-class America with what Blair Sabol called "phys. ed. fashion."[41]

* * * * * * *

As the seventies turned into the eighties, one of the crucial elements of contemporary American life became the symbolic role of changing attitudes toward sexuality in social and political debate. In 1979 Paul Cowan noted:

In most places I've gone—South Boston, Forest Hills, the white
ethnic neighborhoods of Chicago, the hollers of West Virginia,
fundamentalist, church-going communities in the ghettoes of Chicago and the Black-belt towns of Mississippi—political speakers
have been able to ignite far more passion by dwelling on cultural
questions that divide middle-class and working-class people—issues like abortion, busing, the E.R.A., back to basic education—
than they have by involving economic issues that unite them.[42]

There is something rather odd in suggesting that class divisions
occur on moral rather than political issues, and indeed Cowan is
outlining what Marxists would describe as a perfect example of false
consciousness. Irrational as it may seem, it is nonetheless true that
even during a time of economic recession such issues seemed to
arouse greater passions than those connected with the distribution
of wealth. As old values have come under attack, sexuality itself has
become an issue of increasing political importance. Issues such as
pornography, abortion, and homosexuality have all become highly
contentious, in part because they can be manipulated to become
symbols for a more profound debate, namely what sort of society
Americans want. In the battles surrounding the regulation of sexuality, one sees an argument over the very nature of society itself, an
argument exacerbated by that peculiar American tendency to vest
enormous emotional commitment in their sense of nationhood.

The backlash against "permissiveness," whether directed
against pornography, abortion, homosexuality, or the ERA, must be
understood as the attempts of a dying value system to repudiate the
new values brought about by the growth of a society of mass-con-
sumption. When there are increasing dislocations in social life people hunt for scapegoats, and insecurity about sexuality makes such
issues very attractive. I have already discussed the psychological roots
of homophobia. Its political salience is closely related to the specter
of social disintegration that has been growing in the United States
since the late sixties and that has been addressed, in different ways
and with different rhetoric, by three presidents, Nixon, Carter, and
Reagan. As Frances FitzGerald remarked, writing of the present
upsurge of fundamentalist Christianity and the New Right, "all the
great outbreaks of fundamentalist fervor in the past have been moti-
vated by a similar sense of crisis and cultural breakdown."[43]

Behind the specific antihomosexual rhetoric that became so
prominent in the late seventies is a more generalized fear of change
and a need for scapegoats to explain the vanishing certainties that

once seemed to exist. It is hardly possible for the right to blame the demands of expanding capitalism; it is far easier to locate an enemy, either external (such as communism, which was very useful in the early stages of the postwar boom and which Reagan is doing his best to revive) or internal (such as permissiveness, which is particularly attractive in a country torn between a puritan heritage and a hedonistic present). One need not be conspiratorial to recognize how useful such issues are to supporters of the status quo, who can thereby distract attention from such mundane questions as who owns and benefits from America's wealth.

This helps explain why it is so difficult to combat homophobia, for, rather like busing or opposition to the ERA, it is a code for a whole set of beliefs and values that, in the end, are not based on rational argument. When the Reverend Jerry Falwell, whose Moral Majority is one of the major components of the New Right, inveighs against "a minority of secular humanists and amoralists [who] are running this country and taking it straight to Hell,"[44] he is appealing both to a set of deeply held beliefs and to a desire—on which commentators on American life since Tocqueville have remarked—to blame all evils on a tangible enemy.

It is important to recognize just how threatening are the changes wrought by the "sexual revolution" of which men like Hunt and Talese write so approvingly. Most people, particularly those who are older or come from a more religious background, grew up committed to a high degree of sexual repression, albeit often unconscious. The changes in the past decades seemed to mock both their standards and the sacrifices they made for them; what was formerly condemned as immoral now became chic, and the media presented a barrage of images suggesting that other people thrived outside traditional restraints. What is bearable when it seems inescapable becomes intolerable when others do not share it, and the stress on sexual pleasure, the articles on female orgasms, swinging couples, and homosexual licence all added up to a clear message that traditional restraints had been undergone in vain.

The seventies, which to liberals could be seen as a period of revolution in life style and increased freedom, were for conservatives a threat to the very existence of the family, whose importance as a place of retreat is seen as all the greater in modern mass society, a haven, as Lasch put it, from a heartless world. (Perhaps a suspicion that even the family is not the haven it appears to be helps fuel attacks on those who, like homosexuals, seem to flout it.) Little wonder that so many people could be mobilized by evangelists and politicians against those whom they saw as threatening their system of values and beliefs, and that 1980 saw "moral" issues as major ones in a number of election campaigns.

But not only conservatives are experiencing unease because of "the sexual revolution"; Joseph Heller has caught perfectly the ambivalence of late seventies liberalism in the person of his character, Bruce Gold:

> Once, ten or fifteen years earlier, Gold had given testimony in defense of novels by Henry Miller and William Burroughs against charges of obscenity; now there were massage parlors and pornographic movies everywhere and newspapers and magazines on display that *were* obscene. The health club in the basement of the apartment house in which he had his studio had converted gradually into an elegant massage parlor; and his annual membership had been rudely terminated.[45]

Heller doesn't discuss homosexuals, but there have been enough articles of this tone in recent years to show that many liberals are in favor of civil rights as long as it doesn't mean they have to be aware of homosexuals around *them.*

Were, then, the conservatives right in their opposition to the new permissiveness—or, at least, in their insistence that small concessions would inevitably lead to a major decline in traditional standards? The answer is probably yes, except that what is a decline in standards for some is a lessening of oppression for others. Moreover it is not the change in values that creates social reaction as much as the ambivalence and confusion that surround the contemporary expression of sexuality. What the psychologists Eysenck and Wilson see as making for individual neurosis—a conflict between strong desires and equally strong inhibitions, a simultaneous feeling of attraction and revulsion[46]—also shapes current social attitudes toward sex. Philip Slater was surely right when he wrote that "erotic life in America is uniquely disturbed and self-conscious, matching our extraordinarily, culturally approved egoism and the unprecedented complexity of our social and technological existence."[47]

Most frightening is the way in which the frustrations and anger of so many people can so easily be converted into violence, to which homosexuals seem particularly vulnerable. It seems an American tradition that there is no major social change that is not accompanied by considerable violence, and the murders of Harvey Milk and San Francisco Mayor George Moscone in 1978 and the increase in beatings and killings in many cities echo earlier periods of change in America. While such violence is often perpetrated by people who are pathologically homophobic (as in the case of the man who fired a machine gun into the Ramrod Bar in the West Village and then told police that "homosexuals ruin everything"),[48] it is also true that fag baiting can be a product of general sociological trends rather than individual psychological ones; in their different ways both liberal and conservative homophobia act so as to make homosexuals a legitimate target on which to act out antisocial hostility.

It is often argued that "morality" is cyclical, and after the enormous relaxations of the past twenty years we can expect a period of greater rigidity and conformism. To some extent such an argument seems persuasive, but it ignores the extent to which socioeconomic changes produce cultural and psychological shifts that cannot be simply ignored. Homosexuals who have been politicized over the past decade, women who have come to demand more than the traditional role expectations allowed them, will not simply acquiesce in a return to the mores of the past. In the short run there may be some tightening of traditional restraints, but a return to the official morality of preconsumption capitalism is extremely unlikely. Indeed this was symbolized by the fact that when Reagan was elected president, an earlier divorce, a fact used against Stevenson in the fifties and Rockefeller in the early sixties, was almost universally accepted as irrelevant.

If there is to be a reassertion of antihomosexual pressure by the state, it will necessarily take new forms, ones that will probably accept many of the changes made in the definition of homosexuality over the past decade, and move on from there. It will take time, but existing antisodomy laws will be repealed, perhaps by judicial rather than political means, and even blatant discrimination will be prohibited, at least in theory. This will not necessarily mean full acceptance of either homosexuality or homosexuals. An illuminating example occurred in the Australian state of Victoria, where the conservative government effectively decriminalized homosexuality in 1980 but wrote into the legislation that "the Parliament does not intend by this Act to condone immorality" and under pressure amended its own legislation to prohibit "soliciting for immoral purposes."[49]

Evidence about the future is always unreliable, and one can suggest evidence both for increasing repression (particularly the growth of fundamentalist religions) and for slowly increasing tolerance (there is evidence that the majority of people who voted for Reagan did not necessarily endorse his views on social issues,[50] and

NBC polls suggest that support for gay rights increased between August 1980 and May 1981, despite the campaign of the Moral Majority).[51] The crucial question may be what consequences would follow a real reversal in the dominant ethos of consumer capitalism, as could conceivably come about if the prophets of inevitable scarcity, pollution, and growing economic decline are correct.

At first glance this would seem certain to change contemporary sexual mores, which are closely linked to high technology and consumption. On the other hand, any real decline in economic growth is likely to increase recognition of the need for zero population growth, which means an increasing separation between sex and procreation and a corresponding legitimization of homosexuality. As John Mitzel wrote, talking of Vidal's *Myra Breckinridge:*

> Myra understands the contradictions of our culture well enough to know that saving the species from overpopulation will only come by pitting this new necessity of sex realignment against the decadent social imperative of male prerogative.
> Control population.
> Take things in hand.
> Redesignate roles.
> Those are masculist notions associated with a Patriarchal culture. Yet to limit population means birth control, sterilization, free and accessible abortion, sexual awareness and open discussion. These are hallmarks of women's freedom in any society. If men can't subjugate women to be breeders of children, then their power is greatly diminished over the other sex.
> Queens of course are too self-involved to bother upholding a repressed order of personal-power relations. This self-involvement is the "narcissism" that shrinks find so contemptible in queens.[52]

The immediate political situation in the United States, as in a number of other Western countries, may not augur particularly well for homosexuals. In the long run, however, it is difficult to foresee any successful repression capable of undoing what has been achieved over the past decade.

*   *   *   *   *   *   *

The new freedom that consumer capitalism has made possible for homosexuals simultaneously allows for a new form of social control, more subtle and less violent than the old, but real nonetheless. I have already argued that in the seventies homosexuality was conceptualized and to some extent accepted as another life style, and it is easy to see how this is connected to the growth of a definable homosexual market. What is less obvious is the way in which this has become a new sort of restriction on individual freedom.

It is clearly ridiculous to argue that accepting a homosexual identity is itself a mark of oppression. Seabrook comes close to arguing this when he writes:

> Being gay, and becoming aware of being gay, may become a strong determinant on all future development; indeed, the only determinant, pervasive, exclusive, and all-enveloping. In this way, it is possible that many other potential areas of discovery may remain hidden, other talents smothered, and the whole evolution of the gay lifestyle subserves one permanent truth established at the centre of the individual consciousness: I am gay. It becomes an expanding awareness, opening out like a great tree in the shadow of which nothing else can survive; which spreads a sometimes sterile shadow; all other points of identity can be subordinated to it: economic, social, occupational, intellectual.[53]

Similarly Edward Sagarin has claimed that "to 'come out' and accept any identity is not freedom but a renunciation of freedom."[54] In both cases there seems to be a naively atomistic view of wo/man, which ignores how closely our sense of self-worth is bound up with identification with a group. (Indeed, outsiders sometimes express envy of the "community" possible for homosexuals.) What is limiting is the demand for orthodoxy, the belief that to be homosexual necessitates looking, speaking, and behaving in a certain way, whether this be effeminate, butch, macho, or lesbian-feminist.

In some ways this development is inevitable; the creation of community requires the erection of boundaries, however difficult this may be for individuals. Yet because the new homosexual identity is promoted so assiduously through the gay media and gay marketing, many people who accept a homosexual identity feel pressured to adopt outward signs and mannerisms with which they feel uncomfortable. Nonhomosexuals may feel equally excluded from styles that appeal to them.

The greatest restrictions of the new homosexual identity are felt by those whose sexuality is genuinely fluid, and who do not wish to be identified as homosexual, not because they see it as something of which to be ashamed (in my experience this is no more marked among bisexuals than among the exclusively homosexual), but because they do not feel the term accurately describes them. It would be a sad irony if the new affirmation of homosexuality as positive and valid were to lead to a tightening of boundaries and a new set of restrictions on human potential. On the whole this seems to me an unreal fear. As already suggested, the growth of a collective gay identity and consciousness can be seen as part of a trend in modern societies to combat the alienation and impersonality of urban industrial society by stressing bonds of community. In this sense the ethnic model *is* relevant (it is interesting that some people are beginning to speak of the "gay nation," and if this may seem artificial, so too did the concepts of a Czech or Romanian nation when these were first expressed in the last century). Putting on the key rings, denim, and handkerchief of the clone is an assertion of group identity, just as a black might grow an Afro hairstyle for the same reason.

The real change in the past decade has been a mass political and cultural movement through which gay women and men have defined themselves as a new minority. This development was only possible under modern consumer capitalism, which for all its injustices has created the conditions for greater freedom and diversity than are present in any other society yet known. For those of us who are socialists, this presents an important political dilemma, namely how to guard those qualities of capitalism that allow for individual diversity while jettisoning its inequities, exploitation, waste, and ugliness. I believe this can be done, and the social democratic societies of northern Europe offer the beginnings of a model for us; it is not, I suspect, accidental that these societies appear to be far less homophobic and violent than the United States.

NOTES

1   The Midler legend has produced a *roman à clef.* John Paul Hudson and Warren Wexler, *Superstar Murder?* (New York: Insider Press, 1976). Gay baths are also discussed in Michael Rumaker, *A Day and a Night at the Baths* (Bolinas, California: Grey Fox, 1979), Renaud Camus, *Tricks* (New York: St. Martin's Press, 1981), and are satirized in the film *Saturday Night at the Baths* (1975).

2   Robert Boyers, "The Ideology of the Steam-bath," *Times Literary Supplement,* May 30, 1980, p. 604, a review of Robert Martin's *The*

Homosexual Tradition in American Poetry (Austin: University of Texas Press, 1979).

3 Gay Talese, *Thy Neighbor's Wife* (New York: Doubleday, 1980), esp. Ch. 16.

4 Erica Jong, *Fear of Flying* (New York: Holt, Rinehart & Winston, 1973), p. 12.

5 Joseph Epstein, "Homo/Hetero: The Struggle for Sexual Identity," *Harper's,* September 1970, and Paul Cowan, review of Edmund White's *States of Desire,* in *New York Times Book Review,* February 3, 1980.

6 Michel Foucault, *The History of Sexuality* (New York: Vintage Books, 1980), pp. 7–8.

7 Henry Fairlie, "A Decade of Reaction," *New Republic,* January 6, 1979, p. 19.

8 Haynes Johnson, *In the Absence of Power* (New York: The Viking Press, 1980), p. 129.

9 Tom Wolfe, "The Sexed-Up, Doped-Up, Hedonistic Heaven of the Boom-Boom '70s," *Life,* December 1979.

10 See Jonathan Katz, *Gay American History* (New York: Thomas Y. Crowell, 1979), p. 50.

11 Jong, op. cit., p. 9.

12 Edmund White, *States of Desire* (New York: E. P. Dutton, 1980), p. 282.

13 Tom Wolfe, "The Boiler Room and the Computer," in *Mauve Gloves and Madmen, Cutter and Vine* (New York: Farrar Straus & Giroux, 1976), pp. 192–193.

14 Herbert Marcuse, *Eros and Civilization* (New York: Vintage Books, 1962), pp. 34–39.

15 Alexis de Tocqueville, *Democracy in America,* ed. by Andrew Hacker (New York: Washington Square Press, 1964), p. 243.

16 *The New York Times,* May 18, 1981.

17 *The New York Times,* June 17, 1981.

18 *Washington Post,* June 22, 1980.

19 G. Masnick and M. J. Bane, "The Nation's Families 1960–90," quoted in S. Ziemba, "The Vanishing U.S. Family," *Chicago Tribune,* June 8, 1980.

20 Ronald Kotulak, "American Family Disintegrates under Pressure of Divorce, Childlessness," *San Francisco Sunday Examiner and Chronicle,* May 3, 1981.

21 Morton Hunt, *Sexual Behavior in the 1970s* (Chicago: Playboy, 1974), pp. 9–13.

22   *The Village Voice,* August 6, 1980, p. 87.
23   Sam Kaplan, "Manhattan: For Young Singles, It's a Great Escape," *Los Angeles Times,* August 15, 1980.
24   John Kantner and Melvin Zelnick, "Sexual Experience of Young Unmarried Women in the U.S.," *Family Planning Perspectives,* Vol. IV No. 4, October 1972, pp. 9–19.
25   Edward Shorter, *The Making of the Modern Family* (New York: Basic Books, 1975), p. 114.
26   Hunt, op. cit., p. 65.
27   Molly Haskell, "Movies Ruined Me for Real Romance," *The Village Voice,* April 5, 1976, p. 65.
28   William Serrin, "That Oldest Business Is Getting the Newest Drive," *Australian Financial Review,* February 13, 1981.
29   Peter Biskind and Barbara Ehrenreich, "Machismo and Hollywood's Working Class," *Socialist Review,* No. 50/51, March–June 1980, p. 113.
30   Barry Adam, "What Has Marxism to Do with Sex Research?," paper presented to the Society for the Study of Social Problems, New York, 1980, pp. 11–12.
31   Beverley Hotchner, "Contemporary American Sex Shocks," in M. Cook and G. Wilson (eds.), *Love and Attraction* (London: Pergamon, 1979), p. 347.
32   Stanislaw Lem, *A Perfect Vacuum* (New York: Harcourt Brace Jovanovich, 1979), p. 42.
33   Christopher Lasch, *The Culture of Narcissism* (New York: W. W. Norton, 1978), p. xvi.
34   Richard Sennett, "Destructive Gemeinschaft," *Partisan Review* 43, No. 3 (1976), and *The Fall of Public Man* (New York: Random House, 1978); Philip Slater, *Footholds: Understanding the Shifting Sexual and Family Tensions in Our Culture* (New York: E. P. Dutton, 1977), Ch. 10.
35   Lasch, op. cit., p. 193.
36   Sennett, "Destructive Gemeinschaft," op. cit., pp. 352–353.
37   Jeremy Seabrook, *A Lasting Relationship* (London: Allen Lane, 1976), pp. 205–206.
38   Richard Sennett and Michel Foucault, *Sexuality and Solitude,* in *London Review of Books,* May 21–June 3, 1981, p. 3.
39   Seabrook, op. cit., pp. 64–65.
40   White, op. cit., p. 66.
41   Blair Sabol, "Jock Chic," *The Village Voice,* July 16, 1979, p. 33.
42   Paul Cowan, "Whose America Is This?," *The Village Voice,* April 2, 1979, p. 1.

43 Frances FitzGerald, "A Disciplined, Charging Army," *The New Yorker*, May 18, 1981.

44 *Time*, October 13, 1980.

45 Joseph Heller, *Good as Gold* (New York: Pocket Books, 1980), pp. 74–75.

46 H. J. Eysenck and G. Wilson, *The Psychology of Sex* (London: J. M. Dent, 1979), p. 63.

47 Slater, op. cit., p. 113.

48 Quoted by Andy Humm, "Anti-Gay Violence," *New York City News*, November 28, 1980.

49 See articles by Gary Jaynes and Adam Carr in *Gay Community News* (Melbourne), February 1981.

50 See David Broder, "Social Agenda Could Spoil the Party," *Washington Post*, December 10, 1980, and Adam Clymer, "Republicans' Elusive Prize," *The New York Times*, June 18, 1981.

51 Larry Bush, "The New Separatism," *Christopher Street*, August 1981, p. 14.

52 John Mitzel, *Myra and Gore* (Boston: Manifest Destiny, 1974), p. 28.

53 Seabrook, op. cit., p. 166.

54 Edward Sagarin, "The High Personal Cost of Wearing a Label," *Psychology Today*, March 1976, p. 28.

CHAPTER FOUR

The Movement
and Its Enemies

During the 1981 Lesbian/Gay Freedom Day Parade in San Francisco I was standing in front of a group of gay men on Market Street who groaned every time a political group marched by. "Why," they complained, "do they have to bring politics into everything?"

This should remind us that not everyone, not even every homosexual, sees homosexuality as political or accepts the need for a gay political movement. The 1970s, however, saw a major increase in both the political salience of homosexuality and the size and impact of the homosexual movement, so that in the United States, and to a lesser extent in most Western countries, we can now speak of the politicization of homosexuality as an accomplished fact.

There are a number of ways in which to understand the link between sexuality and politics. The simplest is to point out the role of the state in enforcing particular sexual moralities; there is virtually no established state that does not interfere, through both repressive laws and active policy (support for birth control programs, family allowances, sex education programs, etc.), with the sexual lives of its citizens. As Frank Mort put it:

> More generally, we should be aware that throughout the nineteenth and twentieth centuries the rule of law has occupied a central place in the construction and regulation of sexual and moral definitions—as much as it has in the sphere of capital-labor relations. Fresh legislation in the field of sexuality (such as the recent Bill on child pornography) or significant legal reversals (for example the *Gay News* trial of 1977) act as a sensitive register of the moral climate. The law occupies a quite particular relation to debates and struggles around sexuality, in that if a specific form of sexual practice is seen to break the law it crystalises and concretises what have previously been constructed as *moral* debates. The

breaking of legal barriers raises the potential threat of any action; illegal acts challenge the legal order and the social consensus on which it is based.[1]

In general authoritarian governments are particularly prone to interfere with sexual behavior, and John Boswell sees a major factor in the development of homophobia as "the rise of corporate states and institutions with the power and desire to regulate increasingly personal aspects of human life."[2] In this century totalitarian governments of both the right and the left have been excessively homophobic: in Nazi Germany homosexuals were sent to concentration camps; in Russia and China their existence is denied (if homosexuals persist in existing they are apparently severely punished); in Argentina and Chile the present military governments have unleashed extremely crude antigay persecution; in Iran the fundamentalist regime of Khomeini has ordered homosexuals stoned to death.

In America only recently has there been a recognition of the conflict between the liberal doctrine of individual rights, as set out in the Constitution, and the religious heritage of morality regulated through state interference. Over the past several decades the Supreme Court, in a series of cases dealing with contraception, abortion, pornography, etc., has tended to resolve the conflict in favor of the individual, although interestingly enough the Court has so far resisted any direct rejection of laws prohibiting homosexual behavior per se, even though such laws would seem to be clearly in violation of the concept of privacy held elsewhere by the Court to be protected by the Bill of Rights. Lower courts have, however, overruled antisodomy statutes in both New York and Pennsylvania. In the case of Pennsylvania the law involved was so broad that it prohibited "all sexual intercourse per os (mouth) or anus between human beings who are not husband and wife."[3]

But the role of the state in defining and regulating appropriate sexual behavior goes far deeper; through a whole range of activities, subsidies, regulations, proclamations, exhortations, etc. the state can promote certain forms of behavior and restrict others. Laws concerning marriage, adoption, immigration, taxation, inheritance, social welfare payments, and so on are all good examples of this capability. In modern liberal societies much regulation is accomplished through private or semiprivate institutions, such as the churches, the media, and the educational system; together they comprise a powerful network of ideological apparatuses that act so as to determine and enforce sexual orthodoxy. As the demands of consumer capitalism have led to considerable change in the sexual values promoted by at least sections of this network, there have emerged open divergences among these ideological arbiters over what is desirable and permissible.

Given these facts, there is a sense in which sexuality is inevitably shaped, at least in part, by politics, and because homosexuality has so clearly been singled out for condemnation, it is in many ways the clearest example of this. It is not just that until the 1960s most Western countries actually proscribed homosexual behavior; even in those countries, such as France, Belgium, and Italy, where the tradition of the Napoleonic Code meant that such laws did not exist, the state acted so as to restrict homosexual freedoms.[4] In those American states, still a minority, that have repealed the specific antisodomy laws invoked against private homosexual behavior, there remain frequent instances of police harassment against both lesbians and gay men and continued discrimination in all sorts of areas of governmental activity (such as immigration and the military). Most recently, and under pressure from the gay movement, the state has begun to play a positive role *vis-à-vis* homosexuality, through such measures as the antidiscrimination laws mentioned in Chapter 1. The gay movement has come increasingly to focus its attention on these, demanding state action to protect gay rights against both private and public discrimination and violence.

The reluctance of political scientists to examine the relationship between the state and social control of sexuality is in itself a symptom of the subtle efficiency of such control; because we are taught to think of sexuality as a private matter, we very easily overlook the systematic and constant intrusions of the state. Thus while most introductory American civics texts will discuss, for example, the role of the state in curtailing political dissent, very few texts will even mention how the operations of the state impinge on the day-to-day lives of homosexuals by curtailing diverse sexual behavior. Even sympathetic and radical writers, whose concern is to expose the extent of state repression, seem oblivious to the number of people whose lives are affected in this way.[5]

But the political dimension of sex extends beyond the direct interference of the state and its associated ideological apparatuses. As Kate Millett put it—and her book *Sexual Politics* was as important for the gay movement as it was for feminist:

> It may be imperative that we give some attention to defining a theory of politics which treats of power relationships on grounds

less conventional than those to which we are accustomed. I have therefore found it pertinent to define them on grounds of personal contact and interaction between members of well-defined and coherent groups: races, castes, classes and sexes. For it is precisely because certain groups have no representation in a number of recognized political structures that their position tends to be so stable, their oppression so continuous. . . . A disinterested examination of our system of sexual relationship must point out that the situation between the sexes now, and through history, is a case of that phenomenon Max Weber defined as "herrschaft," a relationship of dominance and subordination.[6]

The equivalent of such "herrschaft" as it applies to homosexuals is heterosexism, namely that ideological structure that assumes heterosexuality as the norm and homosexuality as deviant and, indeed, despicable.

The way in which we act out our sexuality is to a large extent socially and culturally determined, which is another way of saying it is the result of political constructs. The definition of homosexuals as a separate and identifiable category created the basis for a political movement, and the emergence of this categorization in the nineteenth century coincided with the beginnings of the early homosexual rights movement. As a result of this new way of looking at homosexuality, the state reacted to restrict and repress homosexuality, most noticeably through legislation in Germany (1871) and Britain (1885, ten years before the trials of Oscar Wilde),[7] and the first modern writings defending homosexual love were published by men such as Karl Ulrichs in Germany, Edward Carpenter in Britain, and Walt Whitman in the United States. It is worth noting that Karoly Benkert, the same man who coined the term "homosexual," was also a poineer of the early homosexual rights movement.[8]

As men and women came to accept the definition of themselves as different because of their sexuality, they also began to develop the analysis and the sense of community that opened the way for the first homosexual movements. This development was most marked in Germany, the only country before World War II to develop a large-scale homosexual movement. The crucial figure was Magnus Hirschfeld, who in 1897 formed the Scientific Humanitarian Committee. The committee sponsored considerable research and discussion of homosexuality, but its central campaign was to abolish the criminal laws against homosexual behavior, and to this end it organized a mass petition that won the support of many thousands of

Germans, including leading political, literary, and medical figures, and the Social Democratic Party.[9] Although the campaign was ultimately unsuccessful, in no other country was there anything equivalent to it until several decades later. (Similar groups in Holland and Britain, where Havelock Ellis and Edward Carpenter formed the Society for the Study of Sex Psychology in 1914, were much smaller and less influential.) In France, where the Napoleonic Code meant an absence of specific criminal sanctions, the 1920s saw a flowering of gay life, among both women and men (well recorded in Barbadette and Carassou's *Paris Gay 1925*), but no specifically political movement. In the United States a few individuals, of whom the best known was Emma Goldman, expressed support for the homosexual emancipation movement; in 1923, influenced by the German model, a Society for Human Rights was established in Chicago to "protect the interests of people who by reasons of mental and physical abnormalities are abused and hindered in the legal pursuit of happiness which is guaranteed them by the Declaration of Independence."[10] Police raids in 1925 effectively ended the society, and no further organization was established until after World War II.

In Europe as well, there was an almost total hiatus in homosexual rights activities during the thirties. Hirschfeld was forced into exile by the Nazis, and those activists who remained were rounded up and sent to concentration camps. That there was a major attempt in Nazi Germany to exterminate homosexuals is only now becoming generally known, largely through several recent books and Martin Sherman's play *Bent*.[11] Despite the evidence, there is still a widespread belief that there was a link between the Nazis and homosexuality, an implication found in the film version of *Cabaret* and Philip Dick's novel *The Man in the High Castle*. Just as the discussions of torture and persecution in contemporary Argentina rarely mention the extreme homophobia of the junta, so even today is there extraordinary resistance to any discussion of the Nazi case, and the West German government still refuses to compensate those who were in concentration camps because of their homosexuality.

The roots of the present gay movement were established in the late forties with the formation of homosexual groups in France, Switzerland, the Netherlands, and Scandinavia. In the United States the first postwar group was the 1948 Bachelors for Wallace. Something of the atmosphere of the times is caught in the words of a prospectus for this group, written in 1950 by Harry Hay, that called for "we, the androgynes of the world," to "demonstrate by our efforts that our physiological and psychological handicaps need be no deterrent in integrating 10% of the world's population towards the constructive social progress of mankind."[12] From this organization stemmed the original Mattachine Society, which as early as 1952 sent out a questionnaire to candidates for the Los Angeles City Council. Also in California a few early activists established One, Incorporated (which published the journal *One*, the victor in a Supreme Court case on obscenity in 1957), and the Daughters of Bilitis, the first lesbian political group in North America.

Although the 1960s saw a growth in homosexual movement activities—including the first gay political candidate (a drag entertainer, Jose Sarria, ran for city supervisor in San Francisco in 1961) —testimony before Congress (in which Frank Kameny of the Washington, D.C., Mattachine Society was the pioneer), an open lesbian presence in the newly formed National Organization for Women, and a number of conferences of homophile organizations,[13] it was only at the end of this decade that a sudden explosion of gay self-assertion produced the modern gay liberation movement. The years 1969 and 1970 mark an important dividing point in most Western countries, with the emergence of a much more militant and broadly based gay movement and the beginning of its real impact on society as a whole.

The underlying socioeconomic changes that made this development possible have been discussed in the previous chapter. To these we should add the impact of a general radicalization, particularly among the young, that occurred in most Western societies at the end of the sixties, and of which the black, antiwar, and countercultural movements in the United States and the May 1968 disturbances in France were the crucial events.[14] In English-speaking countries the new wave of feminism was a particularly important influence; this was less true in continental Europe, where Marxist, Freudian, and anarchist theories were better known and could more easily be adapted to the needs of the new wave of gay activism. Whatever the reasons, the period between 1968 and 1971 saw the emergence of the modern gay movement, characterized by a willingness to demand not just tolerance but total acceptance, and by a new militance in making these demands. This new wave is usually regarded as beginning with the street demonstrations in Greenwich Village at the end of June 1969, after the police raided the Stonewall Bar. The anniversary of that raid, and the resulting activity, is celebrated internationally as Gay Pride Day.

The few years that followed Stonewall saw the growth of a radical gay movement in a number of countries, a movement that rejected the existing organizations—such as the Mattachine Society and the Daughters of Bilitis in the United States, Arcadie in France, and the Homosexual Law Reform Society in Britain—as hopelessly accommodationist in both goals and methods. The radicalism of the early seventies, as expressed by the Gay Liberation Fronts in North America, Britain, and Australia and by groups like F.H.A.R. in France and FUORI in Italy, did not last very long; as there was a general decline of radical political activity, especially in English-speaking countries, during the seventies, so did onetime gay radicals either move into more conventional pressure-group politics or withdraw altogether. By the mid-seventies a new type of gay politics seemed to be establishing itself, above all and most successfully in the United States, where a number of gay activists started using the traditional forms of American minority-group politics to make their demands.

The most crucial development of the past decade has been the comparatively widespread politicization of homosexuals; the annual Gay Pride marches, above all those in San Francisco, are the largest mass demonstrations in the United States since the days of the anti-Vietnam rallies. The comment at the beginning of this chapter should remind us that there is a great disparity in the views of those who attend such marches. Yet if it is true—and it is—that in a heterosexist society any open affirmation of homosexuality is political, then we can speak of a mass homosexual movement of a sort unknown in any previous time.

As the movement has grown, it has also inevitably split over a number of issues and tactics. In general "the gay movement" is an umbrella term for a large variety of different organizations and groups that are often at loggerheads (as in disputes between lesbian-feminists and man/boy lovers, or between Marxists and gay Christians) and are able to come together only for specific events and to agree on only the very broadest of demands. It would be naive to expect otherwise; the diversity of the movement is testimony to the wide range of people it encompasses (and also to the fact that one's homosexuality cannot be a total identity, and that the gay movement is divided along lines of sex, class, and race). Nonetheless one finds every now and then an article or a television documentary that presents the false image of a united, centrally controlled movement embracing lesbian separatists, militant socialists, and gay business-men in a common front bent on destroying society.

Just because the affirmation of homosexuality is itself political, the movement can legitimately be viewed as including a whole range of groups and events that do not specifically view themselves as political. Nonetheless, the traditions of the early homosexual emancipation movement have continued today with the growth of a large range of local and national organizations aimed at affecting the political process to improve the position of homosexuals in American society.

As examples of the sorts of people, tactics, and goals involved in the gay political movement, let us look at two events, both associated with the 1980 Democratic Convention in New York City. Being an election year, 1980 saw considerable political activity; for gays what was notable was the presence of three openly gay delegates at the Republican Convention in Detroit, and more than seventy at the Democratic Convention the following month (estimates of the number vary slightly). The events surrounding these conventions are particularly revealing of the different strands that existed in the gay movement at the beginning of the 1980s.

*   *   *   *   *   *   *

In recent years the South Bronx has become the leading symbol of American urban decay, visited by presidential hopefuls, photographed by foreign journalists, and included in television documentaries on "the urban crisis." Untouched by all this attention, the South Bronx spreads across a large part of the borough, with its mile after mile of burnt-out buildings, slum tenements, deserted factories, small Puerto Rican and black businesses, chitlin stands, and pawnbrokers' shops side by side in an urban landscape that could be used to film the fall of Berlin. Like a putrescent wound it seems to constantly spread, each month extending another block further into Manhattan oblivious to half-hearted attempts at renewal.

It was in the South Bronx, most particularly at the spot President Carter visited in 1977 to declare his commitment to urban renewal, that a combination of radical political groups, largely Marxist in character and with a strong Hispanic flavor, decided to hold a counterconvention the weekend before the Democrats convened in Madison Square Garden to renominate the president. It was one of those searing hot weekends in New York when ice cream melts in your hands and all those people who are too poor to escape the city seem to be out on the streets carrying transistors; only a small number made their way uptown on the hot, noisy, urine-stinking subway to take part in the Charlotte Street convention.

Among them were about 100 gay women and men, gathered in earnest conclave under a canvas awning when I arrived at the site.

There was something of a time warp about the scene; these people resembled very closely the original members of the gay liberation movement whom I had known in New York in 1970. The women wore baggy green pants and loose tops; the men were bearded, but without the short hair and neatly trimmed moustaches of Christopher Street. The rhetoric, too, was reminiscent of those early days, filled with concern about consensus, about understanding each other's positions, about being politically correct.

It is tempting to parody the debate, which was largely concerned with a presentation that night by a lavender theater group of a cabaret performance in which several men would appear in drag. This had apparently concerned several vigilant feminists at other caucuses, and the gay group was meeting to determine its position (the upshot was that the gay group was highly supportive of the theater group, with lesbians doing most of the talking). Like the gay liberationists a decade before, these were people predominantly in their twenties, of mixed class backgrounds, with Hispanics and particularly blacks underrepresented. They found themselves in a difficult situation; some of the other groups at Charlotte Street were clearly homophobic, and in general the gay delegates were not taken seriously by the majority of those present. I had an uncomfortable sense of *déjà vu*, having already sat through much the same debates at the Black Panther-sponsored People's Convention in Washington in 1970. Clearly the gays' presence and the issues they were raising were important. At the same time they were not the issues that concerned most homosexuals, even most homosexual activists, in 1980.

That evening I had been invited to a party given by the lesbian and gay caucus at the Democratic Convention in a luxurious building overlooking the United Nations. Over seventy delegates at the convention were openly gay, and they were courted by both the Kennedy and the Carter forces during the week. That evening the guests of honor were Ted Kennedy and Bella Abzug, and at Kennedy's appearance a swarm of photographers, journalists, Secret Service men, and hangers-on swept through the apartment like a pack of army ants, forcing delegates and guests aside in their single-minded zeal to stay close to Kennedy.

The women and men who gathered in UN Plaza were very different from the gays up at Charlotte Street. These were a new brand of gay politicians, smart, affluent, at ease lobbying with members of Congress or being interviewed by *The New York Times.* The two biggest delegations came from California and Florida, where

political battles in the last few years (against the repeal of antidiscrimination legislation in Dade County in 1977 and against the
Briggs Amendment to fire teachers "sympathetic" to homosexuality
in 1978) had mobilized middle-class gays and turned them into
political activists. The California delegation included several people
from the Los Angeles area of considerable wealth and influence; the
guiding spirit of the Florida delegation was the owner of the Club
Baths.

The gay caucus included fewer women than men, had an un-
derrepresentation of blacks and Hispanics, and exuded a general air
of quiet competence that would give way during the week to the sort
of frenetic activity that marks such events. The caucus set up head-
quarters in the Statler Hilton, along with all the other special-inter-
est groups contained in the party; as you walked to their room from
the elevator you could sample free wines in the California hospitality
suite and notice the irony of having the pro-ERA and antiabortion
groups lodged in facing rooms.

The gay caucus was not particularly evident on the convention
floor (the platform committee had already accepted that sexual
preference should not be grounds for discrimination; asked about
this on television, President Carter, a born-again Baptist with a
strong sense of the need to hang on to his fellow evangelists down
south, admitted that he felt uncomfortable). Some gay banners were
held up during the fifty-minute jamboree that followed Kennedy's
emotional withdrawal speech; Mel Boozer, a black from the District
of Columbia, was placed in nomination for vice president, though
the fact received very little press coverage.

Despite the president's discomfort, the Carter people recognized the significance of the gay caucus and set out to woo it, with
a clumsiness that augured badly for their coming campaign. At the
initial meeting two Carter aides were required to address the caucus
immediately following Bobby Kennedy, Jr.; Bobby was still pressing
the flesh of his admirers as the Carter aides mounted the rostrum
looking like Mormon missionaries fallen among the sodomites.

Later in the week, worried by the possibility of gay defections
to independent candidate John Anderson, the Carter organization
sent a far more senior aide, Anne Wechsler, to address the caucus.
Her reception was generally extremely hostile; most of the gay delegates had been for Kennedy and they were unwilling to be mollified
in the name of party unity. Most interesting was the recognition of
a gay constituency that Wechsler's appearance represented. In her
speech she accepted that gays should be included in "the laundry

of minorities with access to the political process, a big step ward from 1976 when the Carter forces prevented any mention of gay rights in the Democratic platform and a huge one since R. E. L. Masters wrote in 1964 that "homophile backing would be, quite simply, a political kiss of death."[15]

Just as the distance between the South Bronx and Madison Square Garden mirrors the distance between the disadvantaged and the powerful in American life, so too do the two styles of gay activism. The people who came as delegates to the Democratic Convention were the new-style gay politicians who emerged as part of the growth of gay identity in the seventies, less concerned with the radical restructuring of sexuality and society than with winning equal rights within the ongoing system. Such people have benefited from a respectability won for the gay movement by the very radicals they dislike for giving the movement a bad name. (As Vito Russo has pointed out, moderate and feminist pressure to present an "appropriate" image of homosexuality in the annual Stonewall marches has often been directed against the very street transvestites whose actions are being commemorated.)[16] To the radicals at the convention in the South Bronx, such people have sold out to the illusion of respectability, an accusation that was to become much more bitter as the elections later that year made it clear that the limited acceptance achieved by the gay movement within the Democratic Party had come just at the time when that party no longer seemed the dominant force in American politics.

Before discussing the sorts of analyses and issues that divide the movement, let us examine what it is that a gay political movement can and should do. A gay movement can be seen as fulfilling four functions: defining a gay community and identity; establishing this identity and community as visible and legitimate within the broader society; winning specific demands for legal equality (usually abolition of antisodomy laws and inclusion within the ambit of antidiscrimination legislation); and challenging the general heterosexism of the society. At times there will be contradictions and conflicts arising out of these different strands.

The emergence of a gay identity and community was made possible by certain social and economic changes that have occurred over the past few decades. Ultimately, however, its creation is a political event. It was the emergence of the modern gay movement after 1969 and the associated publications, organizations, and activities that were largely responsible for the current assertion of gay identity, even if the most direct influence on many homosexuals came through the commercial scene.

The real change brought about by political activity was that homosexuals ceased thinking of themselves as individual victims and began to conceive of a gay community that was, as the early leaders of the Mattachine Society argued, a minority parallel to ethnic minorities. (Jim Kepner has recounted that this concept was seen as so radical in the fifties that it was attacked as a Communist cliché.)[17] One of the major ways in which the gay movement continues to affect individual homosexuals is by reassuring them that they are part of a larger group; even today, as a number of the interviews in the film *Word Is Out* make clear, many homosexuals think that they are "the only ones." Harry Hay's reminiscences of a Mattachine convention in 1953 capture some of the excitement and release that political activity can mean:

> On the second weekend in April 1953 the convention was called —and five hundred people showed up. . . . Can you imagine what that was like? This is the first time it's ever happened in the history of the United States. There we were, and you looked up and all of a sudden the room became vast—well, you know, *was there anyone in Los Angeles who wasn't Gay?* We'd never seen so many people. And in each other's presence you can't shut them up. This isn't the period when you hugged much yet—but nevertheless there was an awful lot of hugging going on during these two days.[18]

With more than this number of homosexuals assembling in hundreds of discos throughout America every weekend, the impact of such gatherings today might seem less, yet it is my experience that for most people the first gay conference, march, or demonstration still has a particular effect on the way in which they perceive themselves. It is through political action, in the broadest sense of that term, that we become aware of the possibility of shaping our own identity and demanding rights; the significance of the Stonewall riots was that they demonstrated that homosexuals could fight back against oppression. It was the growth of a gay political movement that in turn made possible so much of the flowering of gay culture over the ensuing decade; those members of marching bands and choruses who declare themselves nonpolitical are as much the products of Stonewall as are gay political caucuses. The construction of a sense of gay community is both the product of politics and, in turn, the prerequisite for continuing political activity.

Much of the focus of gay political activity is on homosexuals themselves, and it is hardly surprising that the stress on gay identity has been accompanied by a strong emphasis, above all in California, on the self-actualization ideologies of the 1970s. The Gay and Lesbian Lifestyles Expo mentioned in Chapter 1 included a host of workshops and talks about personal life problems, such as "Improving Communications in Gay and Lesbian Couples" and "Fifty Ways to Find a Lover." While this in part reflects the "me decade" and the self-centered preoccupations of the time, it also reflects the need to repair the psychic damage done by social oppression, discrimination, and stigmatization. There seems to be a clear link between the growth of a gay rights movement and the self-help style, with its stress on group therapy and personal growth (a good example would be the Advocate Experience, an extension of est-type therapy for lonely homosexuals): both the movement and the stress on therapy reflect that peculiarly American optimism about the possibilities of change within the existing system.

The gay movement is as much aimed at overcoming the internalized self-hatreds and doubts of homosexuals as it is at ending legal and social restrictions. Much of what respectable movement spokespersons see as unnecessarily flamboyant and provocative is valuable because it is an assertion by those involved of their right to be homosexual. Yet this poses a dilemma that is probably irresoluble; there is a tension between the creation of a sense of identity, which means stressing those things that set homosexuals apart from others, and the argument of the respectable movement that we deserve our rights because we are just like everyone else.

This tension is central to any discussion of the future of the gay movement. Over the past few years the basic assumption of most sections of the gay movement, except for the relatively few radical groups of the sort who attended the counterconvention in the South Bronx, has been that they speak for a legitimate minority that can expect to be granted full equality within the existing pluralist framework of American society. The radical assertion that this would be impossible without a major restructuring of American society has been heard less and less; with the relative success of pressure-group tactics, including lobbying and electoral intervention, and the resulting need to defend the gains made through such tactics (the beginning of the antigay backlash was Anita Bryant's campaign in 1977 to repeal an antidiscrimination ordinance in Miami), the civil rights model of gay politics seemed dominant.

Yet there is a need to distinguish between the winning of civil rights for homosexuals and the full acceptance of homosexuality and homosexual life styles. The former is clearly essential, and some very real gains have been made, such as the repeal of laws governing private sexual behavior, the repeal of city and state ordinances against job discrimination, changes in the administration of immigration laws, etc. Yet just as the black movement discovered that civil rights were a prerequisite for larger changes necessary to bring about real equality, so is it obvious that civil rights are not by themselves sufficient to win full acceptance for homosexuals. For blacks the cutting edge proved to be economic; for gays it is sexual. Support for homosexual civil rights is often accompanied by attacks on gay behavior that diverges from the official social norm. As Pat Califia wrote:

> We know that even if the Gay Rights National Lobby succeeds in passing a constitutional amendment that grants lesbians and gay men civil rights, the entire structure of state regulation of sex will remain intact. Prostitutes, lesbian and gay youth, pedophiles, tea-room cruisers, those of us who use or create pornography, those of us who do not have traditional gender identities, sadomasochists, and bathhouse patrons will still be vulnerable to police attack and street violence. We know this because even states like California which have consenting adults legislation continue to persecute and imprison members of these groups.[19]

Decriminalization of homosexuality in Canada has not prevented large-scale raids on bathhouses in both Montreal and Toronto, and even in San Francisco the city's official declaration of antidiscrimination measures has not prevented restrictions on adult bookshops and backroom bars. Comparatively few people today will argue that homosexuals should be imprisoned; far more will oppose open discussion of homosexuality in schools or try to refuse homosexual parents custody of their children.

There is a basic division within the gay movement between those people who argue that homosexuals can organize like other minorities and win their goals through the system, and those who contend that in a society permeated with heterosexism only a radical social transformation can achieve genuine equality and acceptance.

This division outlines two other sorts of disagreement, one over mass tactics versus elite organizing, and the other over separatism versus participation in a general radical coalition. What Edmund White characterized as a clash between assimilationists and radicals, and what John Mitzel describes as a conflict between the good gays and the bad gays, is a constant theme of gay politics, both in the United States and elsewhere.

The central conflict boils down to one between those who see gay liberation as part of a radical assault on existing social structures and seek to transform society, and those who see no reason to go beyond limited demands for gay rights within the ambit of the existing social framework. In a sense this is the same conflict that divided the early post-Stonewall movement and led to the splits in New York City between the Gay Liberation Front and the Gay Activists Alliance. Since then, however, the growth of the gay movement has produced a whole range of moderate political groups and leaders, such as those who attended the Democratic Convention, who had no real counterpart in these early organizations; there is a real gap between the good gays who wear suits and blouses to their meetings with mayors and members of congress and the bad gays who march with other radicals against Reagan's policies, even though some activists do both.

The evolution of the gay movement over the seventies paralleled to some extent the earlier evolution of the black movement, which is hardly surprising since both were shaped by a common American heritage and environment. In both cases the radical activists of the late sixties and early seventies responded to an earlier generation that they saw as too concerned with winning acceptance through proving its respectability; both groups experienced a short period when militant rhetoric and activism seemed to promise immediate gains (and when the media inflated the importance of a relatively small group of radicals, though gay militants never became "radical chic" in the same way as did the Black Panthers in their heyday). By the middle of the decade there was an apparent swing back to respectability, and men (and women) in suits replaced denim-clad radicals as the apparent leaders of both movements, even if in neither case were there undisputed national leaders with the charisma of a Martin Luther King or a Malcolm X or an Eldridge Cleaver.

Indeed, compared to the black movement, the gay movement in America has never really had such figures, despite the wide range of people who are generally recognized as spokespersons—pioneer movement figures such as Harry Hay, Frank Kameny, Morris Kite, Del Martin, and Phyllis Lyon; organization figures such as Jean O'Leary and Bruce Voeller, first chairpersons of the National Gay Task Force; elected officials such as Harry Britt in San Francisco, Elaine Noble in Massachusetts, and Karen Clark in Minnesota; writers such as Arthur Bell, Rita Mae Brown, Sally Gearhart, and Armistead Maupin; and entertainers such as Robin Tyler. Perhaps the closest to charismatic leaders yet to emerge are the Reverend Troy Perry, founder of the Metropolitan Community Church (M.C.C.), and, before his assassination, Harvey Milk.

Again compared to the black movement, there has never been any real national gay organization in the United States, and rarely the sort of national conferences that have occurred regularly in comparable societies such as Australia and Canada and that provide a focus for the movement as a whole. The National Gay Task Force (N.G.T.F.) has attempted to play this role, but the Task Force is a self-consciously elite organization whose advertising promotes it as the mouthpiece of financially and professionally successful middle-class homosexuals, and its claimed membership of 10,000 and annual budget of $350,000 are relatively unimpressive by the standards of national pressure groups. In 1981 a conference in Los Angeles sought to establish a more representative national organization, the National Organization of Lesbians and Gays (NOLAG), but so far this has had little impact.[20] Perhaps the closest there is to a grass-roots national organization is the network provided by the religious groups, in particular the M.C.C. These groups are the largest organized sector of the gay community, and like other religious groups they can draw on strong reserves of commitment and dedication. It is easy to assume that they will necessarily act as forces of moderation and respectability; the reality is more complex, and in many places the gay church is the only form of the gay movement that exists. (After the raids on the baths in Toronto in 1981, the M.C.C. pastor was one of the leaders of the protest.) In general, however, the gay churches have a conservative impact on the gay movement, often seeming more concerned with proving their respectability to other religious groups than with reaching nonreligious gays.

It is sometimes argued that the absence of any real national movement in a country as decentralized as the United States is less important than the strength of the gay movement at a grass-roots level. It was, in fact, a loose network of local organizations that produced the only real national activity of the gay movement to date, the October 1979 march on Washington that involved perhaps

100,000 people. Most of the political battles so far have been fought at a local and state level, though the Gay Rights National Lobby (G.R.N.L.), which maintains a full-time lobbyist in Washington, has been able to have some impact on Congress. At the beginning of 1982 G.R.N.L. spawned its own political action committee, the Human Rights Campaign Fund, which is undertaking large-scale fund-raising to support pro-gay candidates in congressional elections.

A more fundamental division is that between elite and mass politics as a means of winning gay rights. There is a strand in the gay movement that places great emphasis on access to politicians and backroom lobbying and is suspicious of mass action and demonstrations. (The N.G.T.F. only endorsed the march on Washington at the last moment.) Many of the delegates to the Democratic Convention seemed more interested in their ability to raise money for favored politicians than in their contacts with large numbers of gays; the best example of such an approach is perhaps the Los Angeles Municipal Elections Committee (MECLA), which is a group of wealthy gay business and professional people with sufficient clout to ensure the attendance of President Carter's mother and son at successive fund-raising dinners—one such dinner in October 1980 raised nearly $100,000[21]—and to use these resources to establish close ties with Governor Jerry Brown and other state politicians. (A lot of the support for Brown's presidential races came from people associated with MECLA.) Undoubtedly such contacts can pay off in certain limited ways and appointments; it is not accidental that California leads the nation in the number of open gays in appointed offices nor that the first openly gay judge in America, Stephen Lachs, sits in the Los Angeles Supreme Court.

Like other minority groups, the gay movement has been able to use the legal system to win certain concessions; there have been a number of cases involving discrimination in employment, in the military, and in immigration policy in which recourse to the courts has been successful. Aaron Fricke used this approach to take a male date to his school prom,[22] and the San Francisco Lesbian/Gay Freedom Day Committee in 1981 won an injunction from a United States District Court to prevent the Immigration Service from excluding aliens because of their homosexuality. Most important, the courts have been the means whereby antisodomy statutes in several states have been struck down. In the same way, gay participation in party politics has been instrumental in winning antidiscrimination ordinances in a number of major United States cities, including Atlanta, Boston, and Los Angeles. (In Miami, Wichita, and St. Paul, such ordinances were reversed in public referenda.) Lobbying at both the local and the national level through the G.R.N.L. and other gay groups is now a continuing activity of the gay movement. But one cannot counter an oppression based on irrational and complex fears and repressions in the same way as one lobbies for tariff reductions. An elitist, professional gay movement, even if able to win certain concessions from governments, fails in what is equally important, the generation of a sense of community and a belief that homosexuals can act against the forces that oppress us. In the struggle of any oppressed group, the process is as important as the goals, for it is through that process that a new sense of community and self-acceptance is forged.

The proliferation of gay political organizations over the past ten years has been accompanied by a decline in the use of terms such as "oppression" and "liberation" and their replacement by the language of "discrimination" and "civil rights," with the development in at least some states and cities of a sophisticated gay lobby able to use gay votes and money to influence politicians.[23] The techniques are less frequently demonstrations and "zaps," as in the early days of the modern movement; rather, the contemporary gay movement is following the style of traditional American pressure-group politics, working through sympathetic politicians and party organizations. Good examples are found in Florida, where the Florida Task Force supports a full-time lobbyist in the state capital, and in various Democratic gay political clubs, especially in California, where considerable attention is paid to endorsing candidates for office.

Not surprisingly, this development is discomforting to gay radicals. Arthur Evans, one of the founders of the Gay Activists Alliance in New York (ironically the pioneer of a militant civil rights strategy), wrote several years ago:

> Within the context of the gay movement, liberals have been very effective in changing laws and in changing attitudes on the part of some professionals. But gay liberalism has had little relevance for those of us who reject a middle-class lifestyle. At its worst, gay liberalism has encouraged gay men to mimic the behavior of upwardly-mobile straight professional types. This is the line pushed by David Goodstein, the millionaire owner of *The Advocate*, the leading organ of gay liberalism in the U.S.; Goodstein, who is proud of his hobby as a horse breeder, urges gay men to get "respectable" and to push on with the job of being assimilated into the American Dream. In effect he would have all of us

become Straight-Identified-Faggots (or STIFFS for short). A more subtle emphasis on professionalism and middle class values is found in the National Gay Task Force, the nation's leading gay liberal political group. NGTF greatly admires the ideal of the highly educated, middle class, professional gay person. It emphasizes the importance of a "professional approach" to gay liberation. NGTF runs itself internally on the model of a professional business organization. Interestingly, the phrase "Task Force" is a military-bureaucrat term, first being used by the U.S. Navy to denote a particular group of differing specialists under the leadership of one commander.[24]

It is easy to find examples of this push for respectability; a good one would be the inaugural meeting of the Gay Press Convention in New York, whose organizer Joe di Sabato argued: "One of the things that's always bothered me about the gay press is the hippie mentality it's had. This is 1980, not 1968."[25] In San Francisco the Concerned Republicans for Individual Rights has set out quite consciously to counter the image of activist gays as radical, and one finds similar moves in a number of the gay business groups.

The most important countertrend has been the organization of the gay community around specific campaigns. Here the two major examples are both found in California; the election of Harvey Milk as city supervisor in 1977 and the fight against the Briggs Initiative in 1978. In both cases the stress was on mobilizing and involving as many homosexuals as possible, on building alliances with other oppressed groups, and on asserting the need for real social change.

During the seventies when Harvey Milk battled both to establish a sense of gay community (he was a central figure in the development of the Castro Street area as a gay neighborhood) and to win city office, he clashed frequently with more conservative gay leaders whose strategy was to work closely through the structures of the Democratic Party. Milk was essentially a populist who sought to organize his own homosexual constituency and to form alliances with other groups (his links to some of the city's unions were a crucial element in his electoral success). It was his victory that first demonstrated that gay votes could be used as an effective basis for political campaigns, a lesson not lost on a number of straight big-city politicians throughout America. Milk's short career as city supervisor produced a rallying point for homosexual activism, particularly during the Briggs campaign.[26]

The battle over the Briggs Initiative was the largest electoral campaign ever conducted over questions of homosexual rights, and it has received remarkably little analysis. The initiative—to dismiss from California's schools all openly gay teachers as well as anyone who "advocates, solicits, imposes, encourages or promotes" homosexual activity—originally seemed likely to pass according to public opinion polls. How much its defeat was due to opposition from prominent media, religious, and political figures (including President Carter and former governor Reagan), and how much to intensive organization by the gay movement, is impossible to estimate. But one of the direct consequences of the campaign was an unparalleled politicization of the California gay community: as one of the organizers of the "No" campaign, Amber Hollibaugh, said:

> Gay people who'd never been political before took amazing risks; everybody took three steps further out of the closet; and we won in every single area of the state where we went and did work. We won because we came out, and the community was politicized. A huge number of gay organizations sprung up, it was a real flowering of the movement. . . . We won and we created a self-confident community . . . lesbians and gay men with a different level of respect for each other.[27]

Three weeks after the initiative was defeated by a 58–42 margin, Milk and Mayor George Moscone were shot by disgruntled former supervisor Dan White.

Since the shooting of Moscone and Milk, and the riots the following May when White was given the lightest possible sentence, gay politics in San Francisco have illustrated all the tensions already mentioned. Milk's successor, Harry Britt, has sought to continue the policies of radical alliances (he is active in the left of the Democratic Party) and argues for a type of cultural politics: "To me agitation around gay rights legislation has as much significance in terms of the process—calling legislators to account as to where they stand—as does the actual legislation itself."[28] To his left, groups like Solidarity argue for a politics of social transformation and links with feminist, Third World, and labor groups. To his right, the Concerned Republicans see no contradiction between supporting gay rights and Reaganite economic and foreign policies. Nor are such arguments purely theoretical, for there have been a number of disputes involving the unionization of gay businesses that have revealed the extent to which class conflict has the potential to divide the gay movement. In 1980 these divisions were dramatized during the San Francisco

Freedom Day Parade when there was a battle to include feminist and Third World speakers on the platform.

At the beginning of the eighties the gay movement was made up of a very large number of organizations throughout America, able to mobilize considerable numbers of people for specific events (above all the annual marches) but also lacking any real sense of direction or strategy for dealing with the attacks of the New Right. Between 1969 and 1980 the basic strategy of the movement had been one of coming out, of asserting homosexual visibility as a basis for demanding certain basic rights. The effectiveness of that strategy was demonstrated by the fact that it was precisely the open declaration of homosexuality that was most opposed by homophobes like Bryant and Briggs, who sought to link it with a threat to children. The defeat of the Briggs Initiative, and the withdrawal from active campaigning of Anita Bryant would seem to suggest that the gay movement dealt with these attacks successfully. But the right wing's victories in 1980 have produced a far more threatening situation, and one in which the gay movement finds itself divided over issues of sex, class, and race. Virginia Apuzzo's very pessimistic summary of the position is probably correct, although her starting point is different from mine:

> After ten years there is an unbecoming amount of evidence that we have not found an agenda, that we have not forged tools to get us an agenda, and that we are in danger of failing in our commitment to our own community as well as to all others with an investment in our participation in social change. . . . What we lack is the willingness within our movement to assess, to evaluate and to demand accountability.[29]

The starting point for such assessment and evaluation is probably the antigay backlash of the 1980s.

* * * * * * *

At the turn of the decade the major response to the gay movement seemed to be a mounting antigay backlash, not just from fundamentalists but also, and more disturbingly, from some liberals as well. For fundamentalist groups like Falwell's Moral Majority, homosexuality is one of a number of moral issues that together make up a package of "moral decline"; in the 1980 elections, support for gay rights was used against several politicians, most noticeably Senator Birch Bayh (Indiana). (Two Congressmen, both Republican, who had previously been arrested for homosexual "crimes" were up for reelection; only one, Representative Bauman of Maryland, was defeated. The Mississippi voters in Republican Hinson's constituency were apparently not sufficiently disturbed by his arrest to defeat him.) Smearing candidates as being "soft on queers"—or implying that they are themselves gay (as happened when Ed Koch first ran for mayor of New York)—is likely to persist in American politics into the foreseeable future.

The present wave of fundamentalist antigay pressure began in 1977, the year of Anita Bryant's Dade County campaign, of a national scare against "kiddie porn," and of the first attempt by Representative Larry McDonald (Georgia) to attach an antigay amendment to the appropriations for the Legal Services Corporation. This measure was adopted in subsequent years, while moves to extend federal protection to cover gay civil rights have not succeeded. In 1979 the lobby group Christian Voice, committed to a strong antigay stance, established itself in Washington, and Senator Laxalt, who was to become President Reagan's chief link to Congress, introduced the Family Protection Act, which claims "to counteract disruptive federal intervention into family life, and to encourage restoration of family unity, parental authority and a climate of traditional morality." To achieve this the act would strongly limit school desegregation, would prevent federal funding for any programs that tended to diminish "traditionally understood role differences between the sexes," and would remove all federal funds from "any public or private individual, group, foundation, commission, corporation, association or other entity which presents homosexuality, male or female, as an alternative lifestyle or suggests that it can be an acceptable lifestyle." This, according to the government's Congressional Research Service, would affect even Social Security and Medicaid programs.[30] The act was reintroduced in 1981 and has already gone through various modifications and amendments.

Opposition to homosexuality unites the various groups that make up the so-called Moral Majority and is more palatable to liberals than most of their other issues. Indeed a liberal backlash, while less obvious, has also been growing.

Several years ago Andrew Kopkind itemized the attacks on homosexual rights from such liberal media and political figures as Jeff Greenfield (in *The Village Voice*), Adam Walinsky (former aide to Robert Kennedy), Nicholas von Hoffman, and a former liberal, Norman Podhoretz, who saw homosexuality as being linked to appeasement in Britain in the thirties and in America today.[31] One would have thought the alleged homosexuality of such right-wing heroes as Joe McCarthy and J. Edgar Hoover would have been almost as embarrassing to Podhoretz as it is to most homosexual activists, but homosexuality is obviously a topic of considerable concern in the Podhoretz household; his wife, Midge Decter, added her attack in 1980.[32] To these Doug Ireland has added some more surprising examples, such as socialist Michael Harrington's denial of the issue as important, and *The New Yorker*'s refusal to carry an advertisement for *Christopher Street* magazine, particularly cruel since *Christopher Street* has been referred to as a gay clone of *The New Yorker*.[33] Perhaps most revealing is the fact that the Leadership Conference on Civil Rights has been unwilling to accept the N.G.T.F. as a member. (It first applied for membership in 1977.)[34]

To many liberals, homosexuals should be tolerated, should not be persecuted—and should remain invisible. There is a new uneasiness about the defiant visibility of the homosexual minority, caught very revealingly in a 1980 *Playboy* piece about San Francisco by Nora Gallagher:

> About a year ago I began to hear that word [faggot] again, a word seldom mentioned here for the previous five years. It was used, I noticed, by people who were liberal, who imagined themselves to be tolerant. It was used, when it was used discreetly at all, to refer to men in groups, men kissing and holding hands, men dressed alike.[35]

It is clear from Nora Gallagher's analysis that it is the open sexuality of gay men that most disturbs liberals: "What drives straights nuts is not love between men but sex between men."[36]

It is not just paranoia to see an upsurge of antigay violence accompanying this mood. In San Francisco, Los Angeles, Portland, and Houston there have been stories of growing street attacks on gays; in New York at the end of 1980 the massacre outside a West Village bar proved to be the first of a whole wave of antigay assaults. One might note, by the way, that much of this violence is a result of men deliberately seeking out gays to attack, despite the statement of two "experts" that male homosexuals experience such violence "as the result of their cruising behavior."[37] With a growing amount of social dislocation, a combination of fundamentalist hatred and liberal disinterest (gay beatings and murders get disproportionately little press attention) makes us particularly vulnerable.

The existence of such reactions illustrate that the struggle for homosexual liberation cannot be limited to legislative lobbying and intraparty intrigue; what is involved is an attempt to establish legitimacy in an area of life that is extremely personal and involves strong and irrational feelings. Thus the gay movement must be concerned not just with specific legal and electoral battles, but also with the far broader and more amorphous ways in which homophobia is maintained through a complex structure of institutions, values, and often unconscious prejudices. This has led some homosexuals to argue that the dominant approach toward gay politics of the seventies can produce only illusory gains, in effect no more than co-option into a basically homophobic system.[38]

Perhaps the clearest opposition to the dominant civil rights strategy comes from lesbian-feminists, whose view of sexism as an all-encompassing ideology of which heterosexism is only one part leads them to be critical of any belief in working through the system. Thus a number of lesbians are sceptical of the value of law reform and even of antidiscrimination ordinances, seeing them as both superficial and co-optive. Only a radical change in the basic sexist nature of Western society, they argue, will ensure real equality for homosexuals. While I have some sympathy with this view, it ignores both the enormous symbolism of legal changes and the importance of political mobilization; the experience of desegregation in the South should have demonstrated that changes in laws play a crucial part in changes in attitudes. This is why lesbians do have an immediate stake in the repeal of antisodomy laws, even where these laws are used only against male homosexuals, just as gay men have a direct stake in opposing restriction on abortion.

More convincing is the argument of some lesbian-feminists that gay men can, in fact, achieve most of what they want without having any real effect on the position of women. In an open letter to voters in the election that saw Harry Britt become a San Francisco supervisor, Sally Gearhart wrote:

> As a state and maybe as a nation, we'll see to it that gay people are not discriminated against in housing or employment while at the same time the ERA may fail to be ratified, thus perpetuating the lower economic and social status of women (fifteen or twenty percent of them lesbians); we may succeed in getting "homosexual acts" decriminalized in this country while every sixty seconds somewhere there will still be a woman being raped; we'll succeed in guaranteeing our first amendment rights so that the gay press's meatmarket and San Francisco's glory holes can continue to be

widely advertised while at the same time less and less protection will be given to battered women and children who are victims of precisely the kind of violence that anonymous sex perpetuates.[39]

Gearhart is particularly censorious of much of the gay male life style —I would question some of her assertions: most battering of women and children goes on within the home and has nothing to do with "anonymous sex"—and her position here illustrates some of the difficulties involved in cooperation between gay women and gay men. Many feminists who would not necessarily share her position on sexuality would nonetheless agree that a struggle for gay civil rights is not sufficient and leaves the basic structures of heterosexism unchallenged.

Lesbian separatism, as it was conceived in the early seventies, is now less important, for many lesbian separatists have become involved in specific campaigns with straight feminists and with gay men.[40] From the mid-seventies there emerged a new strand associated with mysticism and a celebration of what are seen as inherently female qualities, a strand associated with women like Mary Daly and, perhaps, Adrienne Rich. This new strand is more clearly antipolitical than the earlier lesbian separatism, which argued rather that lesbians needed to organize themselves as a basis for political alliances and intervention. There are, of course, many lesbians who maintain the need for social and cultural separatism, based on the very different needs and experiences of women and men, while accepting involvement with gay men in political activity.

The lesbian-feminist criticism of mainstream gay politics is similar in one respect to the Marxist one in that both argue for a major restructuring of society as a necessary prerequisite for gay liberation. (Liberation, of course, means different things to different people.) Marxists and feminists agree that concessions within the existing framework are not sufficient; they disagree on what the primary causes of homophobia are and what sort of changes are required. In some ways feminism is better equipped than Marxism to deal with these questions, for it seeks to analyze the basic psychological mechanisms that maintain conditions of inequality and insists as a fundamental part of its analysis that the personal is political.

The Marxist approach to homosexuality has generally veered between condemning it as a bourgeois deviation and assuming a vague civil rights position (now the policy of several Communist parties, as in Australia and Britain). In response, Marxist homosexuals have sought to develop a theory that would link the gay struggle to a broader-based class one, usually via connections with an analysis of gender roles and the function of the nuclear family. Such attempts often seem strained and fail to relate in any real way to the day-to-day experiences of most homosexuals; there is a real problem in that homosexuals, unlike women, experience their oppression least acutely in the economic sphere (even if the price of "making it" is often to remain closeted), which is one reason why Marxists often fail to understand the reality of homosexual oppression. I believe that a Marxist analysis is ultimately relevant to any movement concerned with social change, and some interesting attempts to use Marxism in gay theory have been made.[41] But despite the strong support from socialists like Edward Bernstein for the early homosexual rights movement, Marxist-based parties and organizations have so far not proved particularly supportive of the gay movement, especially in the United States where their rigidity is matched only by their inconsequence. Socialist groups within the gay movement—such as the Lavender Left, a loose network of feminists, socialists, and anarchists based largely on the East Coast—do, however, have the ability to affect the agenda and the ideological debate of the broader movement, and to counter the stress on individualism and life style of phenomena such as "the Advocate Experience."

A third alternative is that advanced by a new movement emerging among some gay men, largely based on the West Coast and known as the fairy movement. This strand first became visible in the summer of 1979 when under the aegis of Harry Hay, one of the founders of the original Mattachine Society, and several others, a Spiritual Conference for Radical Fairies was held in Arizona, followed by others in successive summers.[42] Its ideas are a strange mix of early seventies gay liberation, mysticism, and gay separatism, united by opposition to what is seen as the conformism and respectability of mainstream gay life. As Hay says: "The whole point about gay rights is an illusion, because when you come right down to it, we can buy a legislator but they can buy him back twice as fast—and they do."[43]

Insofar as the fairy movement stresses certain fundamental and allegedly inherent differences between gays and straights, it runs totally contrary to the neo-Freudian view of sexuality I have been arguing. Insofar as it stresses the need to develop a separate identity, it has much in common with the dominant gay culture, even though it dislikes the direction in which this is moving. Like both radical feminists and Marxists, the fairy movement sees conventional political tactics as ineffective except in very limited ways.

All these strands share a concern with the failure of the respectable civil rights strategy to challenge the way in which oppressive social norms are replicated in the "gay community," in particular sexism and racism. While the former issue is at least raised continuously through the critique of lesbians, the latter is largely ignored, although recently a number of groups of Black and White Men Together (B.W.M.T.) have formed to combat it and there are groups of Third World lesbians and gay Asians. In the winter of 1981 the New York group of B.W.M.T. filed a suit with the state Division of Human Rights and subsequently picketed a gay disco that allegedly discriminated against nonwhites. Such activities pose a real dilemma: a stress on racism, sexism, and class analysis of the sort radicals make is likely to limit the ability of the gay movement to mobilize support. At the same time, to ignore these factors is to win an "equality" that will only benefit white middle-class male homosexuals, and that leaves untouched the very real oppressions that exist among homosexuals for reasons other than sexuality.

There is something to be learned from all these critiques of mainstream politics, yet none seem to me sufficient to dispense with the creation of a powerful gay movement that intervenes in the political arena. For such a movement to be genuinely effective we need a vision of what sort of changes we seek; a strategy for mobilizing large numbers of homosexuals, both women and men, to work for this vision; and a theory of how to achieve such change, including a recognition of who our allies might be.

I have already suggested that civil rights is an important but inadequate goal for a gay movement. Ironically, it is the politicization of the gay community around civil rights issues that helps create new demands that the civil rights strategy is inadequate to meet, demands for the acceptance both of an open affirmation of sexuality and of homosexuality as valid. In some ways the civil rights strategy is most successful where homosexuals are largely invisible. Law reform in Great Britain was the work of respectable, establishmentarian groups that included a number of closeted homosexuals. Unfortunately, while they succeeded (in 1967) in decriminalizing homosexuality, they did little to change social attitudes, and Britain remains far more homophobic than most of Western Europe. (In recent years a number of widely publicized prosecutions for obscenity and "conspiracy to corrupt public morals" have illustrated this point.) In the United States this approach was exemplified in the trial of a number of sailors on the U.S.S. *Norton Sound* for alleged lesbianism in 1980; the women, unlike some other defendants in military trials (such as Sergeant Matlovich), refused to say whether they were lesbian or not and instead fought the issue on their right to privacy.[44] The problem with such a defense is that it implicitly admits that homosexuality *should* be grounds for dismissal. This whole question became relevant in the eighties when one of the codirectors of the N.G.T.F. argued that the best strategy for the gay movement was one of defending the "right to privacy." This formulation was widely rejected as being a prescription for closetry, and there is a widespread if unarticulated sense that the gay movement must go beyond this to a positive assertion of the legitimacy of homosexuality in public as well as private arenas (e.g., in education, in the media, etc.).

To achieve this requires a vision of change that goes beyond the idea of winning civil rights, a vision summed up by James Baldwin's memorable aphorism that blacks did not want integration into a burning house. Speaking of feminism, Linda Gordon has argued that it must do more than "try to get for women the rights John Locke said belonged to men. . . . There is another tradition in feminism, a critique of male-dominated hierarchical social organization, and a search for more egalitarian ways of constructing social relations. . . . It's been difficult in a capitalist culture to project a vision of new ways of people relating—meaning so-called alternatives to the family, as well as all kinds of projects and organizations."[45] More than most, the gay movement has reason to be concerned with the need for these new ways of managing everyday life and relationships.

To date the gay movement has been most successful in mobilizing support to meet clear attacks. Anita Bryant, John Briggs, and Jerry Falwell have all been very useful recruiters for the movement, and a visible enemy remains valuable for raising political consciousness. Excellent examples of this process would be the riots in San Francisco that followed Dan White's light sentence, and those in Toronto in early 1981 after police raids on the city's bathhouses. The problem with depending on our opponents to rally support is that it also allows them to determine our agenda. One of the most crucial steps that must be taken is to build on the anger aroused by specific antigay campaigns to construct a more permanent and inclusive movement.

While the present wave of attacks seems strongly aimed at gay men, with raids on bathhouses and other gay male gathering places, there is a particular need to create links between gay women and men. (The desire to maintain such links often leads to an insistence on equal representation of women and men in leadership positions, even where, as is often the case, there are many more men in a given organization.) Divisions in recent years over questions of public sex, pederasty, and pornography have created a sense among a number of activists that there is a necessary contradiction between gay men and feminists; this came to a head in the 1980 resolution of the National Organization of Women that sought to separate the pursuit of gay/lesbian rights from the defense of "pederasty, pornography, sadomasochism and public sex." The more respectable sections of the gay movement have also refused to take positions on these issues. Yet as many gay activists (including a number of women) have pointed out, it is precisely these issues that are being increasingly used by the right to attack *all* homosexuals.[46]

The growth of the very extensive gay culture and community that has already been discussed provides a potential base for creating a genuine mass movement that could challenge the new-found power of the right. The energy that one can find in literally hundreds of discos across the country is both very frustrating and extremely challenging; the single greatest task for the gay movement is to tap that energy and politicize the hundreds of thousands of women and men involved. This is, of course, a problem for all groups, particularly in a society in which, compared to many European countries, the level of political discourse is relatively unsophisticated and hostile to ideological analysis. There are particular problems for the gay movement.

Homosexuals make up the only minority whose primary oppression is their invisibility, and even today the majority of those whom you might see on Saturday night at the discos remain unwilling to come out publicly. It is always a big step to move from being part of a minority to undertaking some sort of political activity based on this group identity; for homosexuals there is an extra step in the process. We all know a number of homosexuals who feel it possible to be active in every cause but their own. The ability to pass as straight and the hedonistic life style available to many gays (men, at least) accentuates this.

A contributing problem is the general downplaying by the mass media of the gay movement; it is one of the ironies of our time that oppressed minorities must rely on the mass media to mobilize their own supporters, despite the creation of alternative communications networks. Just because one of the most common forms of oppression of homosexuals is to ignore them—what Christopher Isherwood referred to as "annihilation by blandness"—it has been extremely difficult to win adequate coverage for gay politics. Thus while the

1979 march on Washington was the largest American protest since the days of the antiwar movement, there was little reflection of the event in the mainstream news media (*The New York Times* put the story on its inside pages and a week later gave front-page coverage to fifty tenants who marched on Washington).[47] The sort of identification and politicization that such a march could have meant for homosexuals in Des Moines and Tallahassee was thereby greatly reduced.

The trickiest question for the gay movement is one of alliances, for this immediately raises questions about how far the movement should see itself as part of a broader radical front, as the left argues, and how far it should concentrate on building homosexual unity by downplaying potential divisions over issues of class, sex, and race. While there are probably connections between the oppression of homosexuals and that of other groups, these are by no means self-evident, nor is it enough to point out, true as it is, that many homosexuals are themselves poor and nonwhite. What can be demonstrated is that we have a common interest with other oppressed groups in challenging the monopoly of power—including the power to define what is "normal" and desirable—of the ruling white male heterosexual elite. The best form of alliances seems to me the construction of coalitions around specific issues by which most gay people can be shown to be affected; many of Reagan's budget cuts have been directly aimed at services used by the gay community (for example, funding of various programs under the aegis of gay community ventures), and the general redistribution of government spending away from the cities creates common interests between gays in urban neighborhoods and other city dwellers. Most clearly there are links between homosexuals and others who are being singled out for attack by the right; the battle to defend the right to abortion raises exactly the same questions about the role of the state in enforcing morality as do raids on bathhouses.

Ultimately liberation is indivisible; that is, we cannot expect a genuine sexual liberation, as distinct from co-option, in a society that remains repressive in other areas. At the same time radicals in the gay movement must be aware that plenty of their potential supporters in the gay world do not necessarily share the same political perspectives, and that much leftist rhetoric has the effect of turning off support from people who might in fact share a common concern, though not a common vocabulary.

To date the most effective construction of a solid mass movement that was able to mobilize homosexuals and to construct links between gay and other issues was achieved in Harvey Milk's political career in San Francisco. The problem is that in only a few large urban areas—certainly in Los Angeles, perhaps in New York, Washington, and Houston—is there the basis for this sort of politics. (In the 1981 mayoral elections in Houston the gay vote was considered an important factor in the victory of Kathryn Whitmire. The gay vote also played a role in Andrew Young's election as mayor of Atlanta.) Yet there is a need, as well, for a gay movement in small towns and cities (indeed, one of the most positive things to emerge in the creation of NOLAG was a rural caucus representing gays in precisely these areas). It is because of this that national and statewide networks are so important.

On the masthead of the Canadian paper *Body Politic* appear these words of the German gay activist, Kurt Hiller: "The liberation of homosexuals can only be the work of homosexuals themselves." This is undoubtedly true; the question is what form this work should take. In one sense all gay politics remains a variant on the original theme of coming out, the public assertion of homosexuality, as Richard Hall pointed out in an article on gay theater:

It is the instinctive understanding of the power of drama as the most accessible of the arts that has informed the gay movement from the beginning, and has led to the use of demonstrations, zaps and street theater to achieve our ends. The liberation day parades each June may be regarded as the culminating dramatic event of our year. They are dynamic expressions in space of the mimetic impulse, rich in costume, spectacle and signs, with a magical relation to reality and an absence of prepared texts. They are in fact the "precipitates of dreams" which Artaud describes as the true idea of a theater in his two manifestoes employing—as the parades do—ritual, masque, hieroglyphs and anarchy to reach viewers. The parades are the homophobe's nightmare come true —which probably explains the necessity of the police, whose function it is to neutralize the signs and symbols, to "frame" the street stage in order to keep it from bursting through to the onlookers. Our enemies understand the power and theatricality of these occasions, and frequently use film clips of the parades to convince legislators that civil rights for gay people should be defeated.[48]

The most successful political activities of the gay movement, from the early "zaps" of the Gay Activists Alliance against politicians, media, and psychiatrists[49] to the large-scale campaign against the Briggs Initiative have all understood that it is the mass self-assertion by homosexuals of their determination to win acceptance that is the most potent weapon, one that counts far more than quiet meetings with "sympathetic" politicians. The experience of the suffrage movement and the black civil rights movement should remind us that ultimately unpopular minorities take their rights by making a nuisance of themselves, not by politely asking for them.

* * * * * * *

This discussion of gay politics has largely been confined to North America, but there have been parallel though different developments in almost all Western countries. The differences are largely a reflection of different political cultures, which means that each gay movement tends to reflect the particularities of its society: tolerance of diversity in the Netherlands, a history of underground radicalism in Spain, greater ideological polarities in France.[50] Because of this the American gay movement is least useful as a model in the narrow political sense, even though as a cultural force it has had considerable influence (as shown in the international celebration of Stonewall Day). Even in Canada a different political system and tradition means that it is not possible to totally imitate tactics that work in the United States. The Canadian pattern does however most resemble the American, with strong pressure for antidiscrimination laws (already in effect in Quebec), with gay candidates in municipal and provincial elections,[51] and, ironically, with the emergence of a fundamentalist homophobic movement that itself calls on American examples (and has campaigned to prevent Toronto becoming "the San Francisco of the north").[52] But no other country has the sort of strong local government that allows for political gains at the city level of the American style; in Canada and Australia the crucial battles are at the provincial and state levels, and in most countries they must be national in scope.

While different paths have been followed by gay movements, the broader problems remain similar; even in Brazil I have heard gay activists debating them in remarkably familiar terms.[53] Probably the clearest distinction is between those countries in which the gay movement tends to function according to the pressure-group model, as in the United States, and those in which it is more inclined to see itself as part of a general radical movement, as in southern Europe. This is, of course, a very schematic generalization; in West Germany, where the movement has never reestablished its pre-Hitler strength, there are a number of activists who maintain the need for some sort of revolutionary stance, and in France the general ideological debate of the society is mirrored in an almost total split between the conservatives, who adhere to the long-established organization Arcadie, and the radicals, who since the collapse of F.H.A.R. in the early seventies have belonged to a number of short-lived groups and are now most important for their production of the newspaper *Le Gai Pied* and the journal *Masques.* (There was a resurgence of activity around the presidential elections of 1981, and François Mitterrand became the first French president to court a gay vote.)

In both Italy and Spain gay activism is clearly linked to the non-Communist left. The largest Italian group, FUORI, is an integral part of the Radical Party, which is opposed to both the ruling Christian Democrats and the opposition Communists—and on matters of personal freedom is often the sole opposition voice in Italy —and through the party it is able to influence the European as well as the Italian parliament. In Spain there are close links between various left-wing groups and the gay movement, particularly in Catalonia. Nor is the backlash restricted to North America; the fundamentalist position has echoes in all the English-speaking world, and there have been antigay attacks in both Britain and France, attacks linked to extreme right-wing groups (in Britain the National Front).

Probably only in the Netherlands have gay organizations achieved the legitimacy and recognition accorded them in the United States, and there the smallness and the centralization of the country mean that there is both an effective national movement and a very responsive national government. Dutch politicians have been prominent supporters of gay rights—and often the only ones—in international forums. In Holland laws are in effect that guarantee the rights of gay couples to state-subsidized housing, to residency permits (if one of the couple is a foreigner), and to welfare benefits; and Dutch homosexuals, unlike those in West Germany, are officially recognized as belonging to the groups persecuted under the Nazi occupation.

In 1973 a meeting in Coventry, England, established the International Gay Association (I.G.A.), which now has affiliates in twenty-one countries, largely in Western Europe, and at least since the Barcelona Conference in 1980 includes a fair number of lesbian groups. Its secretariat is in Dublin, an unlikely center for such a movement, from whence a complex international "message tree" reaches out across the Channel, across the Atlantic, and down to Australia and New Zealand. The I.G.A., which has begun to lobby international bodies such as Amnesty International and the World Health Organization, is seeking consultative status with the United Nations, and, perhaps most important, can provide support for campaigns in countries where there is really heavy repression—protest campaigns have been directed against the Greek, New Zealand, Soviet, and Iranian governments—and for embryonic and underground movements in countries such as Mexico, Colombia, and Cyprus where political conditions make organizing very difficult. So far the I.G.A. has had very low visibility in the United States, though a projected international march and protest at the United Nations might change this.

*   *   *   *   *   *   *

The growth of the gay movement and the corresponding response to it by the right have changed the shape of American politics to some extent over the past decade. As homosexuality, like other areas of sexuality, has become politicized, this has meant the intrusion of new issues, of new constituencies, and of new actors into political life. At least in the major urban areas, politicians have been forced to take account of the emerging gay vote; the polling of candidates, which began in California well before Stonewall, and the open search for gay votes, which took Bella Abzug into the Continental Baths in 1970, are now commonplace features of the political scene in most large American cities.

The present resolve of the New Right to use the political arena to impose a particular morality on American society would seem to ensure that this development will continue, and that homosexuality will increasingly operate both as an issue for political debate and as a basis for political activity. If a continued economic recession leads to gays' being scapegoated along with others who can be identified as moral deviants and degenerates, this will presumably increase the identification of homosexuals with each other and strengthen their political resolve. It may also help create a sense of solidarity with other victimized groups. But economic recession could also lead to politics' dividing more clearly along class lines, for there is increasing recognition that the real issues at stake are the division of not necessarily expanding resources. At the moment it appears as if the economic conservatives in America have allied themselves too firmly with traditional moralists for them to appeal to those homosexuals who may share their class interest. At the same time, comparatively few radicals have been prepared to recognize that protection of gay rights should rank high among their priorities for countering the shift to the right. Attacked by the right and ignored by liberals, the gay movement may manage to preserve a precarious unity and remain able, at least in the large cities, to assert certain initiatives. In many ways politics is the last area of human activity in which social change is reflected; ever since the election of Richard Nixon in 1968 the American electorate has been moving in a broad sense toward a repudiation of diversity and progressivism. Yet the impact of the emerging gay identity and community has been impossible to ignore, even in politics. Gay voters, gay lobbyists, gay candidates have become part of the fabric of American political life and yet another example of the homosexualization of American society.

NOTES

1   Frank Mort, "Sexuality: Regulation and Contestation," in Gay Left Collective: *Homosexuality: Power and Politics* (London: Allison & Busby, 1980), p. 41.
2   John Boswell, *Christianity, Social Tolerance, and Homosexuality* (Chicago: University of Chicago Press, 1980), p. 37.
3   *The Blade* (Washington, D.C.), June 12, 1980.
4   Guy Hocquenghem, *Homosexual Desire* (London: Allison & Busby, 1978), p. 51.
5   A recent example of such omission is Bertram Gross, *Friendly Fascism* (New York: M. Evans, 1980).
6   Kate Millett, *Sexual Politics* (New York: Doubleday, 1970), p. 24.
7   See Jeffrey Weeks, *Coming Out* (London: Quartet, 1977), Part II.
8   John Lauritsen and David Thorstad, *The Early Homosexual Rights Movement* (New York: Times Change Press, 1974), pp. 6–8.
9   Ibid.; see also James Steakley, *The Homosexual Emancipation Movement in Germany* (New York: Arno Press, 1975).
10 See Jonathan Katz, *Gay American History* (New York: Thomas Y. Crowell, 1976), pp. 385–397.
11 See, for example, Heinz Heger, *The Men with the Pink Triangle* (Boston: Alyson Publications, 1981); Rudiger Lautmann, *Seminar: Gesellschaft und Homosexualität* (Frankfurt: Suhrkamp, 1977); and "Gays and the Third Reich," a collection of articles compiled by Jerald Moldenhauer (Boston: Glad Day, n.d.).
12 Katz, op. cit., p. 410.
13 John d'Emilio, "Gay Politics, Gay Community," *Socialist Review*, No.

55, January/February 1981; Toby Marotta, *The Politics of Homosexuality* (Boston: Houghton Mifflin, 1981), Part I; Del Martin and Phyllis Lyon, *Lesbian/Woman* (New York: Bantam Books, 1972), Ch. 8.

14 On 1968 in France see Dominique Fernandez, *L'Étoile Rose* (Paris: Grasset, 1978). The impact in Italy is mentioned in Luciano Consoli, "The Homosexual Movement in Italy," *Gay Books Bulletin* (New York), Vol. 1, No. 1, Spring 1979.

15 R. E. L. Masters, *The Homosexual Revolution* (New York: Belmont, 1964), p. 152.

16 Vito Russo, "Still Outlaws," *Gay News* (London), No. 170, 1979, p. 17.

17 "Interview with Jim Kepner" in Rosa von Praunheim, *Army of Lovers* (London: Gay Men's Press, 1980), p. 40.

18 Katz, op. cit., p. 417.

19 Pat Califia, "Gay Rights, What's That?," *Front Line of Freedom* (San Francisco Lesbian/Gay Freedom Day Program, 1981), p. 68.

20 For an account of the conference see Scott Tucker, "Too Queer to Be Gay," *New York Native*, No. 13, June 1, 1981.

21 On MECLA see Edmund White, *States of Desire* (New York: E. P. Dutton, 1980), pp. 26–27.

22 See Aaron Fricke, *Reflections of a Rock Lobster* (Boston: Alyson Publications, 1981).

23 On the change in rhetoric see Craig Johnston, "From Movement to Community," *Gay Information* (Sydney), No. 5, Autumn 1981.

24 Arthur Evans, *Witchcraft and the Gay Counter Culture* (Boston: Fag Rag Books, 1978), p. 138.

25 Quoted by Vito Russo, "Gay Press-Men," *Soho News*, January 14, 1981.

26 See Randy Shilts, *The Mayor of Castro Street* (New York: St. Martin's Press, 1982); d'Emilio, op. cit.; A. E. Dreuilhe, *La Société Invertie* (Montreal: Flammarion, 1979).

27 This quotation was shown to me by Rob Epstein in San Francisco. Compare "Interview with Amber Hollibaugh," *Socialist Review*, No. 45, May/June 1979.

28 "Interview with Harry Britt," *The Advocate*, February 22, 1979.

29 Virginia Apuzzo, "Address to Kennedy Institute for Politics," *New York Native*, No. 2, December 1980, p. 8.

30 See Larry Bush and Richard Goldstein, "The Anti-Gay Backlash," *The Village Voice*, April 8, 1981, p. 10.

31 Andy Kopkind, "The Gay Rights Movement: Too Many Enemies," *Working Papers*, July/August 1978, p. 16.

[32] Midge Decter, "The Boys on the Beach," *Commentary*, September 1980. See comments in Gore Vidal, *"Some* Jews and *the* Gays," *The Nation*, November 14, 1981.

[33] Doug Ireland, "Open Season on Gays," *The Nation*, September 15, 1979, p. 207.

[34] Bush and Goldstein, op. cit., p. 12.

[35] Nora Gallagher, "The San Francisco Experience," *Playboy*, January 1980, p. 130.

[36] Michael Denneny, "Gay Manifesto for the 80's," *Christopher Street*, January 1981, p. 15.

[37] Marcel Saghir and Eli Robins, "Clinical Aspects of Female Homosexuality," Judd Marmor (ed.), *Homosexual Behavior* (New York: Basic Books, 1980), p. 290.

[38] See, for example, Michael Lynch, "The End of the 'Human Rights' Decade," *Body Politic*, No. 54, July 1979.

[39] Sally Gearhart, "An Open Letter to Voters in District 5 and San Francisco's Gay Community from Sally Gearhart," [mimeographed], (San Francisco, 1979).

[40] See Charlotte Bunch, "Learning from Lesbian Separatism," Karla Jay and Allen Young (eds.), *Lavender Culture* (New York: Jove/HBJ, 1979).

[41] See, for example, David Fernbach, *The Spiral Path* (Boston: Alyson Publications, 1981), and Barry Adam, *The Survival of Domination* (New York: Elsevier, 1978). See also some of the articles in Pam Mitchell (ed.), *Pink Triangles* (Boston: Alyson Publications, 1980).

[42] See Mark Thompson, "Desert Sanctuary's Spiritual Conference for Radical Fairies," *The Advocate*, November 15, 1979, and Robin Hardy, "Our Memories, Ourselves," *Body Politic*, No. 61, March 1980.

[43] Harry Hay and John Burnside, "A Call for Fairy Sanctuaries," *Vortex*, No. 1, Fall 1980.

[44] See Randy Shilts, "The Ship That Dare Not Speak Its Name," *The Village Voice*, September 24, 1980.

[45] Linda Gordon in "Holding Our Own Against a Conservative Tide," a round-table discussion with Lisa Cronin Whol, *Ms.*, June 1981, p. 53.

[46] See, for example, responses to the NOW Resolution in *Heresies*, No. 12, p. 93, and Scott Tucker, "The Counter Revolution," *Gay Community News*, February 21, 1981.

[47] David Rothenberg, "Homophobia at the New York Times," *New York Native*, No. 13, June 1, 1981. There is a somewhat different interpretation in Jeffrey Nelson, "Media Reaction to the 1979 Gay March on

Washington," in James Chesebro, *Gayspeak: Gay Male & Lesbian Communication* (New York: The Pilgrim Press, 1981).

48 Richard Hall, "The Elements of Gay Theater," *Gay Sunshine*, No. 36/37, Spring/Summer 1978, p. 16.

49 For the early "zaps" see Donn Teal, *The Gay Militants* (New York: Stein and Day, 1971). For those directed at the American Psychiatric Association see Ronald Bayer, *Homosexuality and American Psychiatry* (New York: Basic Books, 1981), pp. 115–117.

50 On the Netherlands see Page Grubb and Theo van der Meer, "Gayness in a Small Country," *Body Politic*, No. 53, June 1979; on Spain see Clara and Mariana Valverde, "Viva Gay," *Body Politic*, No. 47, October 1978, and Tim McCaskell, "Out in the Basque Country," *Body Politic*, No. 65, August 1980; on France see "Three Views of France," in Dennis Altman, *Coming Out in the Seventies* (Boston: Alyson Publications, 1981).

51 See articles on George Hislop's campaign for the Toronto City Council, *Body Politic*, No. 68, November 1980 and No. 69, December 1980/January 1981.

52 See Robin Hardy, "Toronto the Good versus San Francisco North," *The Advocate*, January 8, 1981.

53 See my "Down Rio Way," *Christopher Street*, April 1980.

CHAPTER FIVE

The Birth of
a Gay Culture

Whether there is such a thing as a "gay culture" or a "gay sensibility" has become a central preoccupation of the new gay intelligentsia, of whose existence at least there can be no doubt. Indeed the growing recognition of homosexuality—until a few years ago literary critics wrote tomes about Proust, Forster, Stein, and Whitman while totally ignoring their homosexuality—has made the question of culture a central preoccupation for those like Susan Sontag who believe that "Jews and homosexuals are the outstanding creative minorities in contemporary urban culture. Creative, that is, in the truest sense: they are creators of sensibilities. The two pioneering forces of modern sensibility are Jewish moral seriousness and homosexual aesthetics and irony."[1] This theme was echoed without acknowledgement eleven years later by George Steiner when he wrote: "Judaism and homosexuality (most intensely where they overlap, as in a Proust or a Wittgenstein) can be seen to have been the two main generators of the entire fabric and savor of urban modernity in the West."[2]

There are few questions as confusing as that of the existence and nature of "gay culture." When the *Soho News* posed the question it featured four images of food on the cover and captioned it, "Find the gay food." The answer was quiche and Perrier water, as any follower of the magazine *Christopher Street* would know, which illustrates the first step of the problem—culture is used both aesthetically and sociologically. Clearly there is a gay culture in the sense of certain aspects of life style found most commonly among at least some urban male homosexuals. (It is less certain that this life style is shared in any meaningful way by gay women.) It is more problematic whether there is a gay culture in the aesthetic sense that Sontag means when she speaks of "sensibilities."

There are at least four ways in which the term "gay culture" is used. The first is that of life style, which is becoming as important as class and ethnicity in defining identities in America. The second is by way of those aesthetic products, usually literature or representational art (realistic paintings, sculpture, and photographs) that clearly grow out of this gay life style. No one would dispute that plays like Doric Wilson's *A Perfect Relationship* or Jane Chambers's *Last Summer at Bluefish Cove*, the drawings of David Hockney, Judy Chicago's "The Dinner Party" (a ceramics exhibition), and the photographs of Arthur Tress are gay works. But even here there are ambiguous cases; the disco group the Village People is as much a product of the gay life style as are the photos of Tress or Robert Mapplethorpe, yet it is not marketed as such (and the group's movie, *Can't Stop the Music*, while full of gay references, was ostensibly superheterosexual).

Much more difficult to define are the two other ways in which the term "gay culture" is used. The first is the assumption that all art produced by "gay people" is part of "gay culture." At its crudest, this is the assumption made by Stephen Wright in his introduction to an anthology of short stories: "The homosexual writer I define as a writer who happens to be homosexual."[3] It might be argued that the distinction between being openly gay and being a closeted homosexual is the crucial one; thus John Perreault has written that "in some sense gay art is any art done by an openly gay man or lesbian,"[4] which at least escapes the claim that Tchaikovsky's Sixth Symphony is "gayer" than Brahms's Second. More often, however, once an artist is defined as homosexual, open or not, the assumption is that his or her art is part of "gay culture," even if the artist is dealing in areas of experience in which sexuality would seem to be irrelevant. This, not surprisingly, is annoying to artists who expect their work to be judged independently of their sexuality. "But of course," as Gore Vidal remarked, "the heterosexual dictatorship not only recognizes its enemies, but defines them in its own terms."[5]

One of the problems with defining gay culture by the homosexuality of the artist is that it excludes from the discussion of homosexual culture works whose theme but not whose creator is known to be gay; thus Balzac's Vautrin cycle or Thomas Mann's *Death in Venice* are presumably excluded, while Wittgenstein's works are not. Some of the difficulties are revealed if we take a play like Shakespeare's *Twelfth Night*, which can presumably be seen as either part of gay culture or not depending on whether we accept the claims that Shakespeare was gay, whether the director is, whether the cast is; in some circumstances, even whether the audience is.

One might get around the problem by concentrating on the work rather than on the creator (*Twelfth Night* is such a good example because it can be performed in ways that bring out strong homosexual implications that are not necessarily in the text). This leads us to the claim that "gay culture" is anything that expresses a "gay sensibility," and we are back to Sontag. Both these latter claims are very tricky ones that merely illustrate the fluidity of sexuality and the limits to which one can insist on clear-cut definitions. All sorts of claims are made for the "gay sensibility," the stupidest perhaps being that of Hemingway, who once said that Auden and Isherwood couldn't be homosexuals since he knew how homosexuals wrote, and they presumably failed the test.[6] Again it seems tempting to restrict ourselves to those people who identify themselves as openly gay, but to insist on this would be to exclude too many people, from Leonardo to Colette and Proust, whom most gays wish to claim as cultural progenitors.

Those who talk of a "gay sensibility" tend to confuse two quite distinct ideas; one, that such a sensibility is inherent in being homosexual and, two, that it is the response to the particular experience of homosexuality in a given milieu. The first argument seems to me clearly nonsense, but it surfaces from time to time, linked to the idea of an innate and immutable homosexuality. After all, if some people are born homosexuals, why not go on to argue that with this comes certain inherent insights, qualities, or sensitivities alien to others?

The second idea is more complex. At its simplest it argues that the homosexual sensibility is a product of being a minority. The French choreographer Roland Petit is quoted as saying: "Proust knew that other minorities have the same problem as gay people. He understood everything. Gay people are very sensitive; they have to be. That they are a minority makes them very much aware of everything going on around them. They must have eyes everywhere."[7] John Rechy goes a step further:

> For centuries homosexuals have been prosecuted and persecuted. The law tells us we're criminals and so we've become defiant outlaws. Psychologists demand we be sick and so we've become obsessed with physical beauty. Religion insists we're sinners and so we've become soulful sensualists. The result is the unique, sensual, feeling, elegant sensibility of the sexual outlaw.[8]

There is some parallel to this in psychoanalytic writings; Robert Stoller argues for a culture born of social conditions and is struck by the extent to which homosexual culture involves "clowning, mimicry, [and] caricature" as defense mechanisms.[9] Apart from all the definitional problems involved in determining who is homosexual—after all, "gay culture" may be as much the product of sublimation as of affirmation of one's homosexuality— there is the further problem of whether one can really find any common link between the "sensibilities" of, say, Gertrude Stein and Jean Genet, or Oscar Wilde and Carson McCullers, to use some of Rechy's examples. (This becomes even more problematic if one considers such undoubtedly gay writers as Edward Carpenter, who was a late nineteenth-century progenitor of the gay liberation movement, or writers of such limpidity as May Sarton and Christopher Isherwood.) The experience of being an outsider is clearly a central one, but it is also a very common one for artists; what must be established is that there is some way in which being an outsider *because* of one's homosexuality is the source of a particular vision shared by other homosexuals despite differences in nationality, language, and class.

I suspect Rechy's formula is only the first half of the answer: there must be a self-conscious homosexual identity for a common "sensibility" to emerge. Ironically, this is not the case in what is surely the least ambiguous sign of a "homosexual sensibility," namely an erotic interest in one's sex, whether expressed through art (Michelangelo and Leonardo da Vinci are only the best-known painters whose admiration for the male body seems clearly sexual in nature), or through literature (as in the writings of Genet and, in a very different way, Monique Wittig). This interest may often emerge despite the attempt of the artist to repress and censor her/himself as is the case in some of the writings of E. M. Forster.[10] Equally, a homosexual is likely to have a somewhat different perception of the other sex, although this can lead either to a greater empathy (as, again, the case of Forster illustrates) or to a certain disinterest (one does not look to lesbian artists for pictures of the male body).

Again, however, it is easiest to talk of a "homosexual vision" where it is clearly expressed in representational art, or homoerotic themes. Rechy is, of course, trying to go beyond this, to show how homosexuality informs a total view of the world, not just the depiction of sexuality and the human body, and it is here that there seems no universal homosexual culture (as there is in homoerotic drawings; we can respond quite easily to these even when they are produced in quite different cultures and epochs), but only the products of certain times and places. As Eric Bentley said:

> There is no single and constant form of the imagination or sensibility that is well defined by the word "homosexual," but, on the other hand, it does seem possible to apply the word with some degree of cogency to a certain type of imagination and sensibility within a certain period and within a certain geographical limit— "this is how homosexuals at a time X and a place Y do characteristically imagine and feel." What other word would come to mind of any reader of Ronald Firbank? Only homosexuals—in his time, using the English language—did camp it up that way. Of course, one must avoid using this argument in reverse; not all British homosexuals of the early twentieth century adopted that "lifestyle," were "camp followers."[11]

If we look at the claims usually advanced for the "homosexual sensibility," there are a number of distinct characteristics that can, perhaps, be linked to the dominant experience of being homosexual in modern urban societies. George Steiner characterizes the experience with terms like "solipsism" and "a strategy of opposition."[12] For Rechy there is a strong stress on sensuality, narcissism, and perhaps ambiguities (of Carson McCullers "the tenderness with the grotesquerie," of Visconti "the obsessions with inner disorder and madness, and visual order and composition"). For Sontag the sense of irony is accompanied by parody, theatricality, an emphasis on style. For Edmund White there is a "fascination with fantasy and ornamentation."[13] For Benjamin de Mott, whose 1969 essay remains a valuable discussion, there is a particular insight into emotions and human relations.[14] I suspect it is no accident that so many of our love songs are written by homosexuals—Cole Porter, Ivor Novello, Lawrence Hart, and a number of more contemporary figures whose homosexuality remains closeted. There can be no doubt of the impact of homosexual men on the Broadway musical.

With the possible exception of narcissism, which Rechy locates in both the prose style of Djuana Barnes and the alleged dominance by homosexuals of ballet, all these characteristics seem linked to the experience of concealment, which until the 1970s was the dominant experience for most homosexuals. As Sontag claimed, the aesthetic sensibility, the stress on style, is aimed at "neutralizing moral indignation, sponsoring playfulness."[15] In the same way ambiguity, parody, and fantasy are all ways of winning acceptance, and writing about one's experiences at times when only the very brave were prepared to be explicit. Maybe it is because of this that one finds a "homosexual sensibility" in the works of E. F. Benson but not P. G. Wodehouse, in *The Importance of Being Earnest* but not *School for Scandal.* In both the former cases there seems to be a subtext of references to homosexuality, whether in the character of Georgie in the *Lucia* books, or in Algernon's invention of "Bunburying." Concealment can make criticism of such works very difficult; if a writer's homosexuality is in some way essential to his/her art, and yet not something that s/he has disclosed, how does one discuss the work? (This becomes even more complex in the case of someone like Ivy Compton-Burnett, whose homosexuality was strongly repressed.)[16] I once had to refuse to review a film when it seemed to me the homosexuality of both writer and directer were crucial, yet neither wished this discussed publicly.

But there is a more direct way in which the need for concealment influenced the growth of a gay culture. Speaking of male homosexuals, Michael Feingold wrote:

> Homosexuals have had a hard time organizing as a political and cultural force, owing to the centuries of social stigma (still legally enforced in many parts of the U.S.) that obliged them to communicate indirectly, by signs. Cultural objects, items of dress, changing fashions in speech and gesture and even cologne became protective measures, ways of conveying a man's predilection that didn't put him in legal jeopardy or destroy his status in the eyes of the straight world.
>
> Given the concealment involved it was natural for male homosexual audiences to be attracted to art with a certain degree of flamboyance—repressed impulses return in a distorted or exaggerated form. What has happened with the dropping of many sexual barriers and public taboos over the last two decades is that these signs have been worn as badges of homosexuality instead of masks for it, like a fascist prison system taken over by revolutionaries for emergency housing.[17]

This is true of gay language, which is moving from an underground argot to a vocabulary that influences language in general. "The world of the homosexual," wrote Anthony Burgess, "has a complex language, brittle yet sometimes excrutiatingly precise, fashioned out of the clichés of the other world."[18] In fact homosexuals have used language both to conceal—Gertrude Stein's writing is only now being sexually decoded[19]—and to establish contact with others. A whole book, *The Queen's Vernacular*, is devoted to this language, and it deals only with words and phrases, leaving aside the equally crucial questions of tonality and emphasis, which is largely how homosexuals can recognize each other: "Certainly the person was gay," wrote Richard Amory in *Frost*. "In spite of the threatening tone, there was no mistaking that faintly lilting tang."[20]

Maybe one of the consequences of the new affirmation of homosexuality will be the end of a "sensibility" based on concealment, leaving only the most straightforward and unambiguous meaning of gay culture as valid. As White wrote:

> The new gay arts are flashier and simpler, more spontaneous, explicit, unmediated. . . . The new gay statements are unambiguous—the swoony mythology of *Dancer from the Dance*, the vitriolic satire of *Faggots*. Just as liberation has brought an end to the sly "double entendres" of gay talk, in the same way it has done away with some of the evasions of gay art. (That art at its best should be evasive and quirky is another question altogether.)[21]

One might suggest an over-schematic view at this point: traditional gay culture (that is, the culture associated with homosexuals, largely male, since the consolidation of our status in the late nineteenth century) is associated with survival; contemporary gay culture (that is, post-Stonewall) is about self-affirmation and assertion. In both cases there is a need to express a sense of community with other homosexuals and a view of the world based on the particular experience of being homosexual; as that experience is altered by changing self-perception, so too gay culture itself changes.

It is often argued, as Sontag suggests, that "camp," the best-known form of traditional male gay culture, is a particular way of dealing with oppression. In an article with the lovely title, "It's Being So Camp As Keeps Us Going," Richard Dyer wrote: "Fun and wit are their own justification, but camp fun has other merits too: it's a form of self-defense. Particularly in the past, the fact that gay men could so sharply and brightly make fun of themselves meant that the real awfulness of their situation could be kept at bay—they need not take things too seriously, need not let it get them down. Camp kept, and keeps, a lot of gay men going."[22]

But camp as the basis of a culture had certain problems; it

tended to become not merely a form of defense, but also an expression of self-hatred, or at least self-denigration. Dyer points to both sides of the phenomenon: the way in which "queens" both identify with and put down women, and the way in which the stress on style and beauty is both a statement against traditional masculine values and a way of trivializing homosexuals (who can be accepted as hairdressers or window dressers, that is, men doing jobs not important or serious enough for "real men"). The current preoccupation among gay men with asserting their masculinity is, in a sense, a rejection of this sort of culture. Moreover, camp tends to be extremely apolitical; wit, not politics, is seen as the panacea for social injustice. As a cultural style it often coexisted with extremely reactionary views.

A very nice example of camp and its persistence even within the new macho culture occurred during a party at one of Sydney's leather pubs the night of the wedding of Prince Charles. Immediately after the telecast of the ceremony, a drag version of the royal entourage entered, flanked by members of a local bike club in full leather regalia, and a drag queen presented awards to various celebrities of the bar scene. (It might also be noted that the pub was full of ardent royalists, and I was nearly hit for not expressing sufficient enthusiasm for the regal nuptials.) Since camp was the first genuine attempt by male homosexuals to find a form of cultural expression that would allow them an identity, a sense of community, and a way of dealing with external hostility, it is good to see it survive; although there is some hostility toward drag queens from elements of both the respectable gay male and the feminist movements, camp humor and style tends to reassert itself on occasions of celebration and adds an element of parody to the gay assertion of masculinity.

Both the macho gay man and the lesbian-feminist are embarrassed by the confusion in traditional homosexual culture between sex roles and homosexuality; at the popular level, at least, this seems to reinforce the idea that homosexuals are women in men's bodies, and vice versa. (This underlies the success of the French film *La Cage aux Folles*, although that film managed to use stereotypes in a remarkably clever and inoffensive way.) This has never been a simple matter; when old-style homosexual men and women come together they are as likely to act out traditional sex role expectations as they are to reverse them. I was very much struck by the fact that at the "Pol-olympics," an open-air sports carnival that is one of Sydney's traditional gay events, the women served the salads while the men carved the meats.

For lesbians the adoption of male characteristics and sometimes male appearance was a simple way of claiming privileges largely denied to women. For gay men the relationship was more complex, for in adopting female styles they in a sense renounced certain prerogatives while perhaps seeking others, such as the right to ornamentation and emotion, that Western and particularly Anglo-Saxon society has defined as feminine preoccupations. This is revealed in the idolization, by no means a thing of the past, of certain women singers and actors—Judy Garland, Bette Davis, Mae West, Barbra Streisand. (A Midler or Streisand concert today is likely to look like a denim-industry fashion show.)[23] Such women represent both the qualities that men are denied in this society and the defiance of traditional values, particularly through an assertion of sexuality, that have kept down both women and homosexuals. It is striking, as Michael Bronski points out, that gay men have no male cultural heroes, their idols being exclusively women.[24] There may also be strong elements of repressed heterosexuality at work here, although the reverse phenomenon does not appear among lesbians.

Drag queens act out this veneration of the strong woman who defies social expectations to assert herself; the popular model is often a Mae West or a Bette Midler. (Remember the scene in *The Rose* where Midler sings alongside her drag clones.) While drag is declining in the United States—according to Edmund White it remains important in the South and the "Royal Courts" of the West Coast —it is still very much apparent in Australia and New Zealand and in some southern European and South American countries; in Italy it is closely associated with some of the most radical liberationists.[25]

It would probably not be too fanciful to see the gay male interest in opera as an extension of both camp and the veneration of heroic women. Certain female opera singers, above all Maria Callas, take on the same mystique for gay men as do Garland and Streisand; moreover, since opera often centers on stories of tragic heroines *(Lucia di Lammermoor, Carmen, La Traviata, Madame Butterfly)*, there is the same projection of emotion and drama that existed at a Garland concert. Add to this the fantasy and artifice of opera, and it should hardly be surprising that it is an art form beloved of homosexuals. Ballet, too, in its traditional form, is an art that centers on the heroine, while allowing a display of the male body that elsewhere would seem pornographic. Opera and ballet are in many ways the upper-class, closeted equivalent of drag shows, as the Trockadero Ballet's send-ups make clear.[26]

The present declining interest in much of camp and drag culture is perhaps inevitable, given the need to assert a new sense of identity. It is not, by itself, this search for identity that is new. In rather extravagant terms Bryne Fone wrote of the new homosexual movements that emerged at the end of the last century: "Soon [they] became aware that there was more to being homosexual than sexuality alone, that as a group they possessed not only rights but a unique heritage and a unique point of view, an art, a literature, a life that was theirs and theirs alone, a usable past, a living present and, perhaps, a future free from fear."[27] It is only over the past decade that such sentiments have been held by more than a tiny minority; as mythology this view is becoming very important in the new gay culture. (By myth I mean what D. M. Thomas had in mind when he spoke of psychoanalysis as "a poetic, dramatic expression of a hidden truth,"[28] a set of ideas whose real importance is that people believe in them and act accordingly.)

The crucial question to be asked about the new gay culture in its broadest sense is whether the various developments of the past decade have created a genuine gay community, one held together not just by external hostility and commercial venues, but by self-created institutions and images. In this process matters of politics, psychology, and aesthetics blur together; indeed life style, political action, and cultural expression are often very similar, and there is a complex interrelationship between, say, the growth of the gay press, the gay political movement, gay counseling services, and what Karla Jay claims is the emergence of a "gay people."[29] With neither common territory nor common language, the most basic characteristics of nationality, to bind us together, the role of culture becomes particularly important.

Unlike traditional gay culture, the new culture publicly affirms rather than conceals our identity and confronts society with gay sexuality and demands for equal rights rather than seeking to win tolerance by "neutralizing moral indignation." The new gay culture is concerned not just with affirming the rights and the legitimacy of being homosexual; it is also, and equally, concerned with working out ways of living as a homosexual in a society that assumes happiness is predicated on the heterosexual family. As Edmund White wrote, "Once one discovers one is gay one must choose everything, from how to walk, dress and talk to where to live, with whom and on what terms."[30] All these choices are made by reference to gay cultural forms, one reason why homosexuals tend to be so conscious of matters of style and fashion.

Thus gay culture addresses itself to questions of who we are and how we should live: "For many of us reading about, say, David and Jonathan or seeing *The Killing of Sister George*, is one of the few ways of identifying with other homosexually inclined persons. Without that moment of identification no other political practice is possible."[31] Having so recognized ourselves, we rely on cultural forms, both social and aesthetic, to help show us how to live. Unlike other people, homosexuals cannot learn their life style from family, school, or church (though the growth of gay churches is part of the development of an all-embracing gay culture).

The creation of a minority that is based on voluntary choice rather than birth (for even if one accepts the hypothesis that one is "born" disposed to homosexuality, the adoption of a homosexual identity involves a series of choices) means that we are by necessity far more conscious of the symbols of identity than people who are part of an ethnic group from birth on. The willingness of so many gays to adopt prevalent dress styles—at the moment the ubiquitous clone look among men—is rather akin to the willingness of other social groups, such as hippies and bikers, to grow their hair or be tattooed in order to define themselves as part of a group.

The new gay culture and life style, like the old, confront questions about sexuality, sex roles, and relationships both sexual and nonsexual, but they do so much more directly; there is no longer a need for the evasions and irony of traditional camp, the baroque imagination of a Firbank, or the subtle undertones in the apparently straightforward prose of Gertrude Stein. (Dominique Fernandez has spelled out this transition in twentieth-century French writing, from the works of Mauriac, Montherlant, and Green to the contemporary writings of Genet, Wittig, and himself.)[32] In America Edmund White is an excellent symbol of this transformation. As a novelist, above all in *Nocturnes for the King of Naples*, he works through allusion and metaphor; as a social commentator, as in *States of Desire*, he articulates much of the new directness. At one point he identifies himself as culturally conservative and politically radical, his way of pointing to this contradiction.

Traditional gay culture accepted, at least on the surface, the basic norms of society and subverted them only through irony, fantasy, and ridicule. One might, for example, see a play like *The Importance of Being Earnest* as ridiculing many of the assumptions about heterosexual courtship and marriage, but this has hardly been obvious to the generations of amateur theatrical groups who have staged it, nor is it necessarily any more of a confrontation than the similar ridicule of social institutions in the contemporaneous works of Gilbert and Sullivan. The new gay culture, however, recognizes that there are certain crucial differences between homosexual and heterosexual life styles, most particularly, at least for gay men, a greater independence and social flexibility. Of course many lesbians, and not a few gay men, are involved in raising children; this is one reason for the limited degree of mutual understanding between gay women and gay men. Even so, lesbians too are more likely to reject the idea of monogamous coupling as the only possible form of relationship. Certainly the writings of the last few years suggest that the problems of nonexclusive relationships and sexuality are a common problem for both gay women and gay men.

There is a difference, however, in the way these issues are raised. Lesbian writers seem more attracted to fantasy and the invention of utopian models; gay men, to direct assertion of sexuality. "Gay sensibility sexualizes the world," wrote Seymour Kleinberg,[33] and as concealment has become less important, so sexuality has come to the fore. (There is a marvelous opportunity for a contemporary gay author to rewrite *The Picture of Dorian Gray* in the modern style.) While some women writers have been concerned with claiming a similar freedom for women to assert their sexuality, this has not been the dominant mode of lesbian writing; instead there has been a flood of science fiction/fantasy works, in which radically different modes of social organization are described. One finds this approach in many of the novels of Ursula K. Le Guin, in Joanna Russ's *The Female Man*, in Rochelle Singer's *The Demeter Flower*, in Marion Zimmer Bradley's *The Ruins of Isis*, and in Sally Gearhart's *The Wanderground*. All express the common theme of a world remade along feminist principles, in some cases with conceptions of sexuality very different from those now prevailing.

In many ways, as Richard Dyer has noted, the dominant tone of gay culture and life style is a middle-class one:[34] it is not that there are no working-class homosexuals, but rather that the absence of marriage and family ties makes social mobility easier. Again such mobility applies especially to men; under present socioeconomic conditions, to be a lesbian often means to surrender the possibility of social mobility through marriage. This claim has often been made on the basis of intuition, but there is some empirical evidence from studies in West Germany that "among homosexuals there is a mobility and a professional and social 'upward movement' unparalleled by any other group of the population."[35]

Moreover, it is also the case that the act of becoming homosexual, of taking on that particular identity, leads people to adopt certain values and forms of behavior that are largely middle class, at least as that term is generally understood. Perhaps no one any longer believes, as Bertha Harris wrote of Parisian lesbians of the twenties, that "the world, as they saw it, was quite naturally divided into rigid class systems, and into gay and straight; and in their extension of such logic, to be upper class at its finest was to be also gay. Even if she were raised by a washerwoman, as was the case with Romaine Brooks, her lesbianism gave her automatic rank as an artist: to be lesbian was at its finest to be also upper class."[36] But some such snobberies remain, sometimes coexisting with that *nostalgie de la boue* that leads affluent gays, both women and men, to deck themselves out in torn jeans and T-shirts to appear more proletarian and sexy.

There are, of course, working-class gay cultures (one finds them in a few bars in run-down areas of most large cities, as well as among certain occupational groups, such as women bus drivers), but by and large, while homosexuality exists to a considerable extent across all class lines, self-conscious homosexuality and thus a homosexual culture are much rarer outside an urban middle-class environment. The two major exceptions are, first, among hustlers and drag queens, in the world depicted in John Rechy's *City of Night* and some of the novels of Jean Genet, and second, among nonwhites. The world of the non–middle-class black and Hispanic homosexual, above all lesbian, remains largely uncharted. Moreover, class divisions and prejudices, while they clearly exist among homosexuals—they are central to Fassbinder's film *Fox and His Friends*—are often difficult to perceive, partly because there is more apparent mixing across class lines, and partly because the norms of the new gay culture, both the macho and the lesbian-feminist, make class divisions seemingly unimportant.

* * * * * * *

The new gay culture is, of course, considerable, and it is hard to cover its scope in a few pages. However, we can suggest certain characteristics—above all, I suspect, a preoccupation with realism (even in lesbian science fiction there is a reaction against traditional disguise and evasions) and with authenticity, especially of emotions. The new culture is often self-consciously political, as in films like *Word Is Out,* some of the early songs of Tom Robinson, and the plays of the English group Gay Sweatshop; it is always self-consciously open. No longer does the "gay sensibility" reveal itself through innuendo and coyness, as was true of a whole tradition from

Oscar Wilde to James Purdy, via such people as Carl van Vechten, Ivy Compton-Burnett, and Noel Coward.

The assertion of homosexuality and of the validity of homosexual sex and emotions shows itself in a whole string of confessional novels (*Rubyfruit Jungle, Sita, The Confessions of Danny Slocum,* etc.), in poetry (whether the lesbian-feminist poetry of Adrienne Rich, Judy Grahn, and Robin Morgan or the more explicitly erotic gay male poetry that is fostered by the San Francisco paper *Gay Sunshine*), in women's folk music and gay male theater, and in representational art and particularly in photography, which lends itself particularly well to realism.[37] Of course, the need to document gay life can lead to simplistic and schematic art—this was the case with such films as *Nighthawks* (Britain) and *Squeeze* (New Zealand) and with a great deal of gay theater—and, equally, the expectation that art should document and legitimize the gay life style can lead to all sorts of attacks on works not seen as sufficiently correct ideologically. (Thus the New York G.A.A. censured both *Faggots* and *Dancer from the Dance,* applying a logic that resembled Stalin's approach to art.) This is probably a characteristic common to all emergent cultures; I have heard similar debates about the need for realism among both American black and Australian dramatists. Ironically, among the most successful of the new out-front works have been novels like Patricia Nell Warren's *The Front Runner* and Marion Zimmer Bradley's *The Catch Trap;* there is a whole tradition, which includes Mary Renault and Patricia Highsmith, of women writers who have distanced themselves from homosexuality by writing positively about homosexual men.

The next stage in gay culture, and one that is more apparent in Europe than in the United States (where the urge to confess is ubiquitous), is to use openly homosexual references and experience to illustrate general human and social problems. This is particularly difficult at a time when the creation of a gay identity is paralleled by strong resistance outside the gay world to recognizing the universal relevance of such experiences. The dilemma is defined by James Monaco in relation to black films: "how to make a significant and fair contribution to the general culture while at the same time maintaining a separate and thriving Black identity. It's the same dilemma that has characterized Black American politics since the end of the Civil War: integration and separatism are both necessary, but seemingly mutually exclusive."[38]

Traditionally gay writers got around the problem by not writing predominantly of the gay experience—E. M. Forster gave up writing novels because he felt too restricted by this convention—or by disguising it, as did Melville, Proust, and even, perhaps, Somerset Maugham.[39] This has led critics to insist on seeing a play like *Who's Afraid of Virginia Woolf?* as being "really" about two gay couples, despite Albee's denials. Having largely abandoned such pretense— even though there are undoubtedly still writers, artists, and especially filmmakers who resist gay themes because treating them would force them to come out—the need is to establish that a play about two gay couples can say as much about relationships as one about straights. Examples of such attempts are found in two films, Fassbinder's *Fox and His Friends* and Brusati's *To Forget Venice*, neither of which seems to me as concerned with making a statement about homosexuality as they are about tackling other issues (class in the case of *Fox*, memory and aging in the case of *Venice*). Certainly these films are far removed from the products of Hollywood, which show homosexuals as victims, villains, and comics, but never as complex human figures. Not surprisingly, the great bulk of commercial films that assert a gay identity have come from outside the United States; in addition to those mentioned are *Der Konsequenz* (West Germany), *Taxi zum Klo* (West Germany), *Outrageous* (Canada), *Dear Boys* (Holland), and *Nous étions un seul homme* (France).

But culture is not limited to art works; there has been an explosion of gay culture in the broader sense over the past decade. Indeed, an examination of the gay press reveals that since the late seventies there has been a growing preoccupation with questions of life style, and an acceptance of the political implications of the creation of a new culture. The 1979 Sixth Annual Conference of the Gay Academic Union, held appropriately enough in Los Angeles (for California has always been the forerunner of new life styles, even if New York is the source of aesthetic fashion), was entitled, "The Challenge of the '80's: Our Changing Gay and Lesbian Culture," and while there were few papers in the traditional academic mold, there was a whole host of seminars and discussions on matters of relationships, life styles, spiritualism, etc.

While much of the stress of the gay political movement over the past few years has been to claim rights on the basis that homosexuals are just like everyone else, this is in part balanced by the stress on a separate life style that in some ways denies precisely the liberal assumption that all that separates gays and straights is the choice of sexual partner. One of the striking things about a gay cultural event, whether it be a performance by a gay women's chorus or the showing of a film like *Word Is Out* or *Greetings from Washington*, is the enthusiastic response to any sort of self-affirmation; as the banner in one Gay Pride march read, "When we celebrate it means our whole life is involved." Clearly the need for psychic restitution by people who have been constantly branded as immoral, sick, deviant, and so on can lead to its own chauvinism. The most extreme claims of this sort are often made in the name of a vague spiritualism; this is true of Sally Gearhart's novel *The Wanderground*, where women in an all-women's world possess certain qualities and empathies that nature denied to men, who are seen as naturally aggressive and destructive, but it is also true of the fairy movement, which makes the same sort of claims for gay men as against straight.

It is not surprising that in a country that has combined deep-seated and often violent homophobia with unrestrained commitment to materialist growth, the ideas of spiritual commitment and oneness with nature should appeal to those homosexuals anxious to disassociate themselves from the dominant culture. Unfortunately, this often leads to a quite unfounded assertion that gays are essentially different from straights, along with a rejection of the mainstream of gay life, which is seen as no more than a product of modern capitalism. In the words of Arthur Evans, one of the founders of the Gay Activists Alliance, who subsequently moved toward gay spiritualism:

> We look forward to creating a genuine Gay culture, one that is free from exploitation by bars, baths, and Gay business owners. We look forward to re-establishing women's mysteries and men's mysteries as the highest expression of collective Gay culture and sexuality. We look forward to regaining our ancient historical roles as medicine people, healers, prophets, shamans, and sorcerers. We look forward to an endless and fathomless process of *coming out* —as Gay people, as animals, as humans, as mysterious and powerful spirits that move through the life cycle of the cosmos.[40]

Even the majority of homosexuals, who are unlikely to claim any peculiar spiritual quality to their sexuality, are affected by the new assertion of a separate identity and culture. The growing sense of gay community has both political and socioeconomic elements. Most significant of all, argued Karla Jay, are the cultural factors:

> The culture that has grown since the Stonewall rebellion has been an important contribution (perhaps the most important) of the

current gay and lesbian movements. Legislative gains have been minimal. We have merely chipped away at silences and at social prejudice; we have gained but a few token open representatives in prestigious positions (although thousands more lurk in the closets!). But in the almost ten years since the Stonewall uprising we have created a culture and put fruitful energy into unearthing our heritage. That's a major achievement. Even if all the laws turn against us, if the so-called backlash of heterosexuals against "permissiveness" increases (although I personally don't believe there is a backlash, since I don't believe I've ever seen a frontlash—that is, any true acceptance) we will still have our songs to sing, our books to keep with us, our herstory to treasure in our hearts, and the knowledge that there is a common core uniting us as a people. We are a people who have always survived and always will survive.[41]

Jay goes on to argue that this "flowering of culture" has been particularly significant for lesbians, who did not enjoy even the token recognition allowed such gay male styles as camp. At the same time the interrelationship between lesbian and "wimmin's" culture makes a specifically *gay* female culture difficult to locate and means that many lesbians identify as and are seen as feminists rather than lesbians.

Jay has sought to develop a theory of the differences between gay male and gay female culture, based on the different nature of sexuality for the two sexes:

Male sexuality has a beginning (erection), middle (thrusting) and end (orgasm), and man has created all art in the image of his sexuality. However for women to orgasm is the beginning of another cycle of pleasure, excitement and ebbing, excitement and ebbing—seemingly without beginning or end. It is fitting that we have chosen to reflect *our* sexuality in our art forms.[42]

As examples she cites the music of Kay Gardner and the novels of Monique Wittig and Bertha Harris; of Harris's *Lover* she writes, "Her characters, like the female cycles of life . . . flow together. Her characters have no beginning, middles or ends, and her generations of women meld (no rigid, traditional, separate character traits for each individual)."[43] While I would like to see more development of the argument, it seems to me potentially crucial in understanding the differences between male and female life styles that seem to go far beyond different social and economic circumstances. (Much lesbian poetry could be fitted into Jay's analysis.) Maybe, too, the stress in lesbian culture on poetry and music is a reflection of female sexuality. "Music," wrote Chris Bearchell about the annual Michigan Womyn's Music Festival, "is the source of much of the magic that keeps us going."[44] Jay has hinted at a theme that is only now being developed in feminist discourse, namely the idea that there are innate differences between men and women that interact with social roles to produce quite different ways of perceiving the world. This is implied in the writings of the modern feminist fantasists and at a more analytic level has been explored by the French writer Hélène Cixous and the Australian Beatrice Faust.[45] If this supposition is correct, one implication is an inevitable divide between gay male and gay female culture—indeed, the dominance of male concepts of culture means that we may have difficulty even in recognizing some of the products of a woman-identified culture.

What is common to the new gay culture of both men and women is that it involves the creation of values and institutions that help make sense of the experience of being homosexual in a hostile world. While gay men are more likely to develop the sort of commercial enterprises associated with the sauna/disco culture already discussed, lesbians have been more attracted to the idea of self-conscious counter-institutions (the differences are real and are related to different assumptions about sexuality and sexual expression). One study of the lesbian-feminist network in San Francisco claims there are 2,000 to 5,000 women involved in a whole set of overlapping and interconnected institutions, including women's centers, dances, bookshops, coffee houses, bands, etc.[46] My observations of a seemingly similar, if smaller, world in Sydney suggests that such networks are much more likely than gay male networks to operate independently of the commercial scene. This cannot be accounted for by simply a difference in income—it is often cheaper to go to a bar or disco than to entertain at home—and these networks appear to involve a greater degree of communal intellectual and artistic activity. There are times when I, as a man, look at the lesbian community with a certain amount of envy.

There are, of course, some cultural areas in which gay women and gay men do come together. The Gay Academic Union, some gay bookstores, publications like *Gay Community News*, gay radio programs, and gay services centers are all examples of this. At the Los Angeles Gay and Lesbian Community Services Center, the largest and oldest such center in the world, there are a whole range of services and activities encompassing both women and men. The center grew out of the Gay Liberation Front and opened its first building in 1971; despite savage cuts due to Reagan's reduction of federal programs, it now operates on an annual budget of several million dollars, with the support of both state and local government, and employs some forty to fifty people, working on programs that cover employment, housing, health care, counseling, education, help for the disabled, and a large-scale alcohol-abuse program. The great success of the Los Angeles Center, and a reflection of the highly organized gay politics of southern California, is that considerable numbers of gay business and professional people have been persuaded to support an institution most of whose clients are people with whom the donors would normally have little social contact—"It's the rich subsidizing the radical dykes and the street queens," as one Angeleno put it.

One of the most important developments in the emergence of both gay culture and gay community has been the growth of a gay press; not surprisingly, gay movements often saw as one of their first priorities the creation of a gay magazine or paper. A woman known as Lisa Ben founded and ran a publication called *Vice Versa* between 1947 and 1948, and in the fifties small groups launched *The Ladder* (for women), *The Mattachine Review*, and *One* magazine; both *The Ladder* and *One* became for a time national magazines.[47] In Europe, *Der Kreis* was established in Switzerland in 1942 and was followed by papers in the Netherlands, Denmark, and France.[48] In the sixties various commercial publications, aimed almost exclusively at gay males, were founded; their descendents, such as *Blueboy* and *Mandate*, have become glossies on sale at local supermarkets. At the same time some commercial publications were themselves influenced by the movement to become forums for ideas and activity, as is true of both *The Advocate* (founded in 1967 as a movement paper) and *Gay News* in England. In a number of countries a regular newspaper is the central focus of the gay movement; papers such as *Body Politic* (Canada, founded in 1971), *Fuori* (Italy), *Lampiao* (Brazil), and *Le Gai Pied* (France) are all crucial to the development of gay politics in their respective countries. In the United States movement publications have had a more erratic history; with the demise of *The Lesbian Tide* in 1980 only *Fag Rag* (Boston) and *Gay Sunshine* (San Francisco) survive from the early days of gay liberation, and both appear infrequently.

The main sources for gay news coverage in the United States are now *Gay Community News*, a weekly publication from Boston,

THE BIRTH OF A GAY CULTURE

and *The Advocate,* which is published every two weeks in California. *Gay Community News* is much more movement-oriented and is produced by a collective with an equal number of women and men; *The Advocate* seems more clearly aimed at middle-class gay men and has a far greater emphasis on a high-consumption life style than does *Gay Community News.* With a circulation of 90,000 and a paid staff of thirty, *The Advocate* is the most important of the gay publications, and in recent years it has shown itself to be open to some of the more controversial (and noncommercial) trends in the gay world. Since early 1981 the *New York Native* has become another major source of news and comment, and there are probably half a dozen local papers of some importance, such as *The Blade* (Washington, D.C.), *Gay News* (Philadelphia), and *Gay Life* (Chicago), as well as literally hundreds of bar papers, primarily advertising media for the commercial scene.

Magazines like the lesbian *Dyke* or *The Furies,* or the male *Gay Sunshine,* play an important role in the development of gay culture and identity. The Washington collective that produced *The Furies* inspired a whole range of lesbian writing and music, including authors like Rita Mae Brown and Charlotte Bunch, singers like Meg Christian and Willie Tyson, lesbian businesses like Olivia Records and Woman Sound (audiosystems), while *Gay Sunshine* has been extremely innovative in encouraging poetry, in interviewing gay writers, and in exploring gay themes in other cultures, especially Latin America. In the same way *Le Gai Pied* established its literary reputation by publishing the last interview given by Sartre before his death and substantial studies of Barthes, Pasolini, and a number of French gay writers. The most important American gay literary magazine is *Christopher Street,* which was founded in New York in 1976 with the aim of being a first-class literary magazine and has become the main organ of an emerging gay literati.[49]

Equally important has been the development of gay publishing houses, such as Naiad, Persephone (both lesbian-feminist), Seahorse, Grey Fox, and Alyson. Even though there is a growing interest on the part of mainstream publishers in gay books—the paperback house, Avon, has a special catalogue of gay titles—a great deal of gay literature relies upon the small presses for publication. One should note, as well, the emergence of gay bookstores. The first, the Oscar Wilde Memorial Bookstore, was started in New York in 1967 with twenty-five titles; there are now at least ten such stores in the United States, as well as others in Montreal, Toronto, London, and Paris. Not only do they offer a remarkably wide range of relevant titles, but they are also often centers for cultural activities and readings and thus a focal point for much of the new culture. Their names—Lambda Rising, Giovanni's Room, Wilde-n-Stein—are an honor roll of gay culture.

At the grass-roots level perhaps the most significant developments are attempts to construct living arrangements that break down the isolation of modern urban society and provide an alternative to the nuclear family arrangements from which most homosexuals are excluded. Communal living has a particular appeal to gays, especially those who are raising children, because they feel unable to participate in the dominant family model of this society, and there have been numerous attempts to create such alternative living situations. Social and living networks that provide the sort of support often sought in the family are particularly strong among gay women, and they more than compensate for the much weaker commercial scene. More than gay men, lesbians stress the need to construct a new community at the level of living and sexual arrangements:

> We must move out of our old living patterns and into new ones. Those of us who believe in this concept must begin to build collectives where women are committed to other women on all levels—emotional, physical, economical and political. Monogamy can be cast aside; no one will "belong" to another. Instead of being shut off from each other in overpriced cubicles we can be together, sharing the shitwork as well as the highs . . . women-identified collectives are nothing less than the next step towards a Women's Revolution.[50]

*   *   *   *   *   *   *

"New York gays," wrote Edmund White, indulging in a certain amount of Gotham chauvinism, "are justifiably proud of their status as tastemakers for the rest of the country, at least the young and up-to-date segment of the population. Our clothes and haircuts and records and dance steps and decor—our restlessly evolving style—soon become theirs."[51] Others have made the same claim, though with less approval. R. E. Masters, who was blessed with the sort of conspiratorial mind that pop journalism thrives on, wrote in the early 1960s of efforts directed by the International Committee for Sex Equality, a largely paper organization then existing in Amsterdam, to "obtain favorable treatment of homosexual activities in the films, on the stage, and, to some extent, in literature," and to infiltrate the fashion industry, "said to have as its primary objective the defeminization of women through both unattractive styles and the creation of a stereotype of the chic woman as a flat-chested stick-figured near skeleton."[52] Gene Marine claimed at the end of that decade that "you can take almost any part of the world of culture and there it is, in bold lavender. Dance and interior design, fashion (women's *and* men's), music—especially outside the relatively virile jazz and rock fields—and music promotion, novels and poetry, little theater and magazines."[53] Even the 1980 *Hammond World Almanac,* a standard annual reference work, spoke enigmatically of "heterosexuality [being] in full retreat on the screen."[54]

The development of gay culture as part of the creation of a new gay minority has, in turn, had a major impact on the society that spawned it. It is not merely, as was the case of the periods when Masters and Marine were writing, that there were lots of homosexuals in creative areas. This by itself may have had some effect on who became fashionable (though the opposite was also true; both Paul Goodman and Gore Vidal have complained of being ignored by critics because they wrote of homosexuality) and even, perhaps, what works were performed (one of Europe's leading music festivals at Aix-en-Provence has long specialized in bel canto operas, allegedly due to the homosexuality of its directors); it does not, however, mean the sort of impact that is produced by openly gay artists. For that a politicized or at least a self-conscious homosexuality was needed, as Edward Lucie-Smith hints in his review of art in the 1970s:

> It is the gay subculture, not the Women's Movement, which has been a pioneer of fashion and which has imparted a particular tone to both homosexual and heterosexual lifestyles. This tone successfully combines two apparently incompatible elements—a freewheeling, live-for-the-day hedonism, and a claim to be avant-garde. Nevertheless it takes only a moment's thought to see how the two essentials are combined. Despite the fact that homosexual conduct, with certain restrictions, is legally permitted and therefore "visible" in North America and West Europe, it still carries with it a whiff of brimstone. Centuries of legal actions and of community disapproval are not to be got rid of so easily. This makes it easy for the homosexual artist to think of himself as a pioneer, exploring territory previously hidden to art.[55]

One of the implications of a self-conscious gay culture is that it often addresses itself primarily to gay people (Vito Russo has termed Rosa von Praunheim's film *It Is Not the Homosexual Who*

Is Perverse But the Society in Which He Lives a home movie for the gay movement).[56] Some lesbian writers and singers, in particular, insist that they are concerned only with a lesbian audience and reject claims for the universality of art as meaning, in Adrienne Rich's words, "a refusal to read and hear what I've actually written, to acknowledge what I am."[57] Such views can be seen as either a regrettable ghettoization of culture or as a necessary part of developing an identity and community. Clearly there is a certain value to the latter. But given the universality of homosexuality, if not of a gay identity, it would be a great pity if the larger culture were able to dismiss the products of the new gay writers, filmmakers, and artists as relevant only for those who already see themselves as part of the gay culture. There is already considerable resistance to accepting views of homosexuality that threaten the dominant heterosexism of our society; literary critics seem to prefer homosexual characters who are created by acknowledged heterosexuals, as in the case of Anthony Burgess's novel *Earthly Powers*.

The development over the past decade of a self-conscious gay culture sums up the paradox of the homosexualization of American life. On the one hand homosexuals are setting themselves apart and emphasizing the ways in which they are different from the heterosexual norm. On the other hand, their new openness makes a homosexual impact on culture in general far easier to recognize and discuss. Acceptance of the right to sexual diversity demands a general recognition that the development of a gay culture is a legitimate contribution to the general culture, just as the award of a Nobel Prize to Isaac Bashevis Singer, an American writing in Yiddish, represented a recognition of the legitimacy of ethnic diversity.

NOTES

[1] Susan Sontag, "Notes on 'Camp,' " in *Against Interpretation* (New York: Dell, 1969) pp. 291–292.

[2] George Steiner, "The Cleric of Treason," *The New Yorker*, December 8, 1980, p. 180.

[3] Stephen Wright, *Different: An Anthology of Homosexual Short Stories* (New York: Bantam Books, 1974), p. ix.

[4] John Perreault, "Lesbian Lessons," *Soho News*, September 10, 1980, p. 57.

[5] "Interview with Gore Vidal," *Christopher Street*, January 1978, p. 10.

6   Quoted in Jonathan Fryer, *Isherwood* (London: New English Library, 1977), p. 226.

7   *The Advocate,* November 27, 1980, p. 44.

8   John Rechy, *The Sexual Outlaw* (New York: Grove Press, 1977), pp. 193–194.

9   Robert Stoller, *Perversion: The Erotic Form of Hatred* (New York: Pantheon Books, 1976), pp. 200–202.

10   See my discussion of Forster in *Coming Out in the Seventies,* (Boston: Alyson Publications, 1981), pp. 162–171.

11   Eric Bentley, "We Are in History," George Stambolian and Elaine Marks, eds., *Homosexualities and French Literature* (Ithaca, N.Y.: Cornell University Press, 1979), p. 122.

12   George Steiner, *On Difficulty and Other Essays* (New York: Oxford University Press, 1978), pp. 116–117.

13   Edmund White, "Of Course, There Is a Gay Literary Culture," *Soho News,* June 25, 1980, p. 18.

14   Benjamin de Mott, "But He's a Homosexual . . . ," in *Supergrow* (New York: Delta Books, 1970), p. 25.

15   Sontag, op. cit., p. 292.

16   See the discussion by Jane Rule in *Lesbian Images* (New York: Pocket Books, 1976).

17   Michael Feingold in *The Village Voice,* June 14, 1980, p. 77.

18   Anthony Burgess, *Earthly Powers* (London: Hutchinson, 1980), p. 10.

19   See James Mellow, *Charmed Circle* (New York: Praeger, 1974), p. 134; and Lillian Faderman, *Surpassing the Love of Men* (New York: William Morrow, 1981), pp. 400–405.

20   Richard Amory, *Frost* (New York: Freeway Press, 1973), p. 173.

21   Edmund White, *States of Desire* (New York: E. P. Dutton, 1980), p. 257.

22   Richard Dyer, "It's Being So Camp As Keeps Us Going," *Body Politic,* September 1977, p. 11.

23   See John Stapleton, "Streisand," *Klick* (Melbourne), January 1981.

24   Michael Bronski, "Judy Garland and Others," Karla Jay and Allen Young, eds., *Lavender Culture* (New York: Jove/HBJ, 1979).

25   See Mario Mieli, *Homosexuality and Liberation* (London: Gay Men's Press, 1980), esp. Ch. 7.

26   See "Beaning the Banal Mr. Barnes," *Christopher Street,* January 1977, p. 3.

27   *The Advocate,* February 8, 1979.

28   D. M. Thomas, *The White Hotel* (New York: The Viking Press, 1981), author's note, unpaginated.

29   Karla Jay, "No Man's Land," in *Lavender Culture,* p. 50.

30 White, *States of Desire*, op. cit., p.16.
31 Derek Cohen and Richard Dyer, "The Politics of Gay Culture," Gay Left Collective, *Homosexuality: Power and Politics* (London: Allison & Busby, 1980), p. 172.
32 Interview in *Masques*, No. 7, Winter 1980/1981, p. 31.
33 Seymour Kleinberg, *Alienated Affections* (New York: St. Martin's Press, 1980), p. 45.
34 Richard Dyer, "Gays & Class," *Gay Left*, No. 3, Autumn 1976, p. 15.
35 Reimut Reiche and Martin Dannecker, "Male Homosexuality in West Germany—A Sociological Investigation," *Journal of Sex Research*, Vol. 13, No. 1, February 1977, p. 48.
36 Bertha Harris, "The More Profound Nationality of Their Lesbianism," P. Birkby et al. eds., *Amazon Expedition: A Lesbian Feminist Anthology* (New York: Times Change Press, 1973), p. 79.
37 See Allen Ellenzweig, "The Homosexual Aesthetic," *American Photographer*, Vol. 5, No. 2, August 1980.
38 James Monaco, *American Film Now* (New York: Oxford University Press, 1979), p. 193.
39 This is argued in Ted Morgan, *Somerset Maugham* (London: Jonathan Cape, 1980), pp. 41–42.
40 Arthur Evans, *Witchcraft and the Gay Counterculture* (Boston: Fag Rag Books, 1978), pp. 154–155.
41 Jay, op. cit., pp. 50–51.
42 Ibid., p. 56.
43 Ibid.
44 Chris Bearchell, "Michigan," *Body Politic*, No. 58, November 1979, p. 31.
45 See Hélène Cixous, "Rethinking Differences," George Stambolian and Elaine Marks, eds., op. cit.; Beatrice Faust, *Women, Sex and Pornography* (New York: Macmillan, 1980).
46 See Deborah Wolf, *The Lesbian Community* (Berkeley: University of California Press, 1979).
47 See Alan Winter, "The Gay Press," mimeographed, Austin, Texas, n.d., Ch.1. The role of Lisa Ben and her paper is discussed in an interview with W. Dorr Legg by Brad Mulroy in *Vortex* (San Francisco), Vol.1, No.3, Summer 1981.
48 For the influence of *Der Kreis* (Zurich) on American gay writing see Samuel Steward, *Chapters from an Autobiography* (San Francisco: Grey Fox, 1981), Ch. 7.
49 See my (somewhat tongue-in-cheek) "A Moveable Brunch: The Fag Lit Mafia," *Soho News*, November 19, 1980.

50 Rita Mae Brown, "Living with Other Women," *Women* (New York), Vol. 2, No. 2, Winter 1971, p. 34.

51 White, *States of Desire*, op. cit., p. 259.

52 R. E. L. Masters, *The Homosexual Revolution* (New York: Belmont, 1964), p. 49.

53 de Mott, op. cit., p. 18.

54 Stephen Handzo, "Films," *Hammond World Almanac 1980* (Maplewood, N. J.: Hammond Almanac, 1979), p. 857.

55 Edward Lucie-Smith, "The Gay Seventies?," *Books and Bookmen*, February 1980, p. 7.

56 Vito Russo, *The Celluloid Closet* (New York: Harper & Row, 1981), p. 204.

57 "An Interview with Adrienne Rich," Part II, *Conditions: Two*, Fall 1977, p. 58.

CHAPTER SIX

Sexual Freedom and the End of Romance

It is in the interconnected areas of sexuality and relationships that gays have the greatest impact on social mores, and where one can speak most accurately of the "homosexualization" of modern society. No longer can gay behavior be seen as unrelated to the sexual norms and anxieties of society as a whole; and as traditional norms of sexual behavior and relationships collapse, it is homosexuals who are prospecting the frontiers of new possibilities. The growing preoccupation of society as a whole with sex, the collapse of old beliefs and standards, means that the very outlaw status of the homosexual makes him or her a model of new possibilities that have meaning for others.

Nowhere is this clearer than in the definition of personal relationships. The Western idea of marriage, a product of both economic reality and religious ideology, assumes that only in a lifelong partnership can and should sex be fully expressed; the history of the bourgeois novel revolves around the creation, maintenance, and escape from the restraints of such partnerships. Because of far-reaching social changes, this form of organizing sexuality is disappearing as a universal norm, yet few people are sure what might replace it. The search to reconcile unlimited sexual freedom and the emotional security of committed relationships is no longer a peculiarly homosexual problem; it is a growing dilemma for a large part of the population, especially the affluent, well-educated "new middle class."

The increasing visibility of homosexuals also contributes to the growing general discussion and acceptance of sexuality, even if such visibility can also trigger considerable hostility. This is not confined to males; lesbians have played a very significant role in heightening awareness of female sexuality especially through the women's movement.

Acceptance of homosexuality involves an acceptance of sexuality that is unfortunately rare in American society; as already suggested, this implies an end to both the quite extraordinary repressions and the expectations with which this society surrounds sex. As homosexuals have come out and a subject once considered unfit for public discussion has become a media staple (however badly it may be reported), the homosexual becomes a scapegoat for general sexual fears and frustrations. The single strongest characteristic linked with homosexuality in the popular imagination is the idea of unrestrained sexuality, and the fear and loathing that we conjure up is often the fear and loathing of sex itself. This image of homosexuals as exclusively sexual beings takes many forms—the frequent use of lesbianism in male-oriented pornography (and the just-as-frequent hints of it in "respectable" films), the press's obsession with stories of homosexual promiscuity and orgies, and the hysteria about homosexual child molesters (which ignores all the evidence that the great majority of child molestation is of little girls by heterosexual men: one study found that 90 percent of all reported molestations are by adult males on female minors, 75 to 85 percent of the victims being relatives or friends of the molestor).[1] To the respectable integrationists these images are seen as both incorrect and damaging. To some radicals—John Rechy and Guy Hocquenghem are good examples— at least some of them are seen as the basis for a genuine assault on dominant social norms.

Three aspects of gay sexuality seem particularly vulnerable to attack—its promiscuity, its publicness, and its "kinkiness." As is so often the case, these images are largely restricted to male homosexuals, although they often carry over into the stigma experienced by lesbians, undoubtedly a factor in the way in which sexuality has become a potentially crucial dividing line between gay women and gay men.

What evidence exists suggests that gay men do not necessarily have more sex than straights but that we have it with a far greater variety of partners. Indeed, Ken Popert, drawing on the studies of Kinsey, has argued that gays are comparatively deprived:

> In our lives promiscuity, far from an expression of license, is a strategy of naked need. At first this assertion may seem silly, for it flies in the face of a view, widespread among gay men and assiduously propagated by glossy gay consumer magazines, that our sex lives are a manifestation of liberated sexuality, that we enjoy dimensions of sexual freedom unknown to straights. . . . The facts, in so far as they have been reliably ascertained, say some-

thing else . . . daily sex is a reality for one married man in four, but for only one gay man in 20.[2]

Popert's figures are based on a study which is now more than thirty years old, but they are supported by Jay and Young's *The Gay Report*. This book, based on a survey of some 5,000 gay women and men and published in 1979, is the most accurate and revealing study of gay sexuality we have, and I will have frequent occasion to quote it, despite the self-evident problem that its sample is not—and could not be—in any sense representative.[3] In regard to Popert's point, Jay and Young find that of their survey only 10 percent of the men and 4 percent of the women have sex daily; on the other hand, among both gay women and gay men sex at least once a week is the experience of about 60 percent.[4]

More interesting is the finding that among the men in their survey over 50 percent had at least ten different partners in the past year—and 3 percent claimed over fifty; among women the figures fell dramatically, with only 4 percent mentioning ten or more partners in the past year. (Over a "lifetime," however, 38 percent of the women responding claimed to have exceeded ten partners, as did 84 percent of the men.)[5] By the conventional expectations of most straights, even in a time of "liberated" sex, gay men's experiences differ quite markedly.

Clearly the reality of homosexual "promiscuity" is very different for women and men. Moreover it is the way in which gay men, but again not gay women, meet their sexual partners that most separates them from straights, though even here the differences are less than one might imagine. According to Jay and Young, men are most likely to meet through friends, at bars, and at parties; work and school account for fewer meetings and beaches and baths for more than would be the case for heterosexuals (they all rate about equal); for women bars are less important, social and political groups more (but this may be a reflection of the differing samples for each sex). There are no real equivalents to male meeting places such as baths, parks, movie theaters, and toilets, although these rate comparatively low as meeting places, even among gay men.

Nonetheless it is the ever-present *possibility* of meeting men in such places (less than half the sample had "never" met anyone in parks, streets, or beaches) that sets male homosexuals apart. Gay men spend much of their time cruising, unlike straight men who seem more likely to be just watching. Many of us are constantly alert to the possibility of sex, and often in search of it, whether on foot, in cars, on bikes, even (for the rich) on jet-set expeditions to Amsterdam and Morocco. There is a literature of cruising: the detective story of that name by Gerald Walker (basis for the unfortunate film *Cruising*), a rather voyeuristic study by Laud Humphreys with the wonderful title *Tearoom Trade*, a brilliant novelette by Guy Hocquenghem called *Oiseau de la Nuit* that became the fourth episode in the French film *La Race d'Ep*, and above all the novels of John Rechy. Both the popular image and the self-image of male homosexuals stresses the hunt for sex; for many the male homosexual represents depersonalized, anonymous sex in which no names or even words are exchanged.

The reality is more complex; encounters at the baths, in parks, even in public toilets can lead to long-lasting relationships and intimate friendships, and "promiscuity," in the sense of having a large number of sexual partners, need not mean an absence of serious and committed relationships. The dictionary meaning of promiscuity implies a lack of discrimination that is not necessarily the case. Indeed anyone who watches a gay bar or cruising area for a while is likely to be struck by how few people do make sexual contact, which, if anything, suggests more discrimination than the situation seems to warrant. What seems clear is that there is in the gay male world a strong stress on sexual adventure, which is not seen as necessarily incompatible with relationships. There are, of course, men who only seek out instant sexual encounters and refuse any other contact. In a surprising number of cases such men are likely to be those who refuse to acknowledge any sort of gay identity.[6] The crucial point, true also for a number of gay women, is that gay relationships are not based upon an assumption of monogamy.[7] Until recently most homosexual men and women sought to duplicate traditional heterosexual marriage in the search for the perfect partner with whom to settle down in lifelong bliss. Such an attitude pervades novels such as Radclyffe Hall's *The Well of Loneliness*. It is only recently that homosexuals have felt sufficient confidence to assert that this is not necessarily an appropriate model. "Nor do I regret," wrote the Canadian novelist Jane Rule,

> that there was nothing of conventional pairing in that first relationship, which required of me, instead of jealous exclusiveness, real generosity and love for someone else's husband and children. It confirmed for me very early the value of loving, the awareness of sex as one of the languages for loving rather than either an identity or an act of possession. To be a lover was no more a lable,

under those circumstances, than to be a daughter or sister or friend, responsibilities and pleasures I have not, even now, devalued in order to own and be owned by another person. Cleaving is an activity which should be left to snails for cleaning ponds and aquariums. Multiplicity of relationships does not create the number of conflicts the morality tales of our culture would have us believe, if the basis of each relationship is the autonomy of the self and the freedom of the other.[8]

Or as Bruce Voeller, often identified with the more conservative wing of the gay movement, put it:

We should put an end to our embarrassment about transcending monogamy, for by moving beyond it we have also transcended the possessiveness and jealousy adopted from traditional heterosexual relationships in which males "own" women, who are in turn dependent. By openly and honestly incorporating recreational sex into our relationships we have tapped a rich quarry of "resistance," that essential quality needed for rewarding, ongoing sexuality in a relationship such as described by C. A. Tripp in *The Homosexual Matrix*.[9]

What so many discussions of gay sexuality have missed is that there is no necessary connection between sexual freedom and emotional commitment, that the idea of monogamy and love are quite distinct and are only confused because of certain social pressures.

* * * * * * *

The rise of gay identity and assertion has meant a corresponding assertion of homosexual sex as good and valid in itself. Unlike heterosexual relations, sex between those of the same sex cannot lead to procreation, nor is it based on the assumption that one partner is necessarily subordinate to the other. (Such assumptions may, of course, be parodied in some forms of butch/femme role playing.) Thus the affirmation of gay sex is quite unambiguously an affirmation of sexuality that is sanctified by neither religion nor the state. This applies even more forcibly in the case of gay women, just because society has been reluctant to concede that women have any sexual feelings at all; that women can experience sexual fulfillment with each other is still seen by many men as an insult and by many women as an impossibility. Growing openness and awareness of homosexuality is likely to have a perceptible effect, albeit subtle, on the general perception of sexuality, making for the acceptance of broader and more diverse forms.

As part of the new self-affirmation, homosexuals have had to combat the idea, often held only semiconsciously, that theirs is somehow an inferior form of sexuality. I have little doubt that this is an important obstacle in many gay relationships, and it may help explain why many gay men constantly seek validation through new partners. There is no way to really compare the sexual experiences of those who are homosexual and those who are heterosexual; it seems to me impossible to generalize from the evidence of those who are bisexual except on a purely behavioral level. Masters and Johnson have provided some evidence (although from a very distorted sample) that homosexuals are by and large more accomplished in and take more pleasure in sex than heterosexuals. Both among their male and female couples they found more relaxation, more involvement, more "exchange of pleasure at all levels of sexual excitation," more communication.[10] This is particularly marked when compared with the experience of women in heterosexual intercourse, the point that so enraged male commentators when it was made by Shere Hite. Homosexuals, both women and men, were even found to have "a more active and diverse fantasy patterning than their heterosexual counterparts."

This is especially striking when one considers that the homosexuals whom Masters and Johnson surveyed engaged in a very restricted range of sexual activity. Most importantly, very little notice was taken of anal intercourse, which they presented as of minor interest to male homosexuals. This is, however, completely contradicted both by Jay and Young's findings and by the evidence from V.D. clinics with a large gay clientele. Moreover Masters and Johnson seem on very shaky ground when they do talk about anal intercourse, completely ignoring, for example, the specific pleasure engendered by stimulation of the prostate which is only experienced by men.

Masters and Johnson are really quite naive when it comes to the details of homosexual sex; they could profitably spend a couple of nights in a St. Louis sauna. Thus they argue that homosexual sex is essentially of a "my turn, your turn" nature as compared with the "our turn" nature of heterosexual coitus, ignoring the "mutual orgasmic potential" (their expression) of mutual cunnilingus and fellatio. What, after all, is "sixty-nineing" if not an "our turn" activity? Be that as it may, they have provided, as Martin Duberman remarked "the most substantial case for gay chauvinism ever made."[11] As an antidote to the suspicion that homosexuals are missing out on something—expressed, most crudely, in the classic remark that "all lesbians need is a good man"—their research is very valuable.

It is impossible, even with the sort of evidence one can compile from Kinsey, Jay and Young, Masters and Johnson, and other such surveys to say very much about changes in gay sexuality, in particular to say whether the developing sense of identity and self-worth among gays has affected sexual behavior. *Prima facie*, one would expect this to be the case; to prove the point would require evidence of a type that is almost impossible to discover.

Thus to argue that there have been behavioral changes requires considerable reliance on my own observations, which clearly biases the discussion toward men, and on the hints thrown out in gay writing. It does seem agreed by almost all commentators that rigid role playing has declined dramatically; the old stereotypes of "active" and "passive" have become meaningless. As a character in Paul Monette's *Taking Care of Mrs. Carroll* mused:

> But you see that you are over 45 in this way too, when the young
> outsex you. I come from a time when you fucked or you got
> fucked, you didn't do both. But the boys I meet go back and forth.
> A bullet of amyl nitrite swings from a chain around their necks,
> and nothing the flesh is weak enough to want appals them.[12]

Older American male homosexuals agree that there has been a marked rise in anal as against oral sex and mutual masturbation over the past decade. This is significant because the anus has always been the most despised and denied of all erogenous zones;[13] while Jay and Young cannot provide historical comparisons they do suggest that only relatively few gay men never fuck. (Bell and Weinberg in their survey of homosexuals in San Francisco suggest that older men are more likely than younger men to concentrate on fellatio, though they are wary of concluding that this means any overall shift in mores.)[14] The old inhibitions about anal sex, especially about being fucked (still seen in macho cultures as equating oneself with a woman) would seem to have largely disappeared, though one still finds echoes of it, both among "real men" and among some who see fucking as too close a copy of the heterosexual model.[15]

Among women there is no one taboo of equivalent force; indeed, the absence of the real fear that many men feel about being taken anally is probably an important factor in making men more rigid than women in their attitudes toward homosexuality. It is not only that the diffuse nature of sexual experience for women, who seem less genitally centered than men, makes lesbianism less threatening, there is also the real factor that a woman is less likely to think of rape with another woman, while the reverse is the case for men. On the other hand, the increasing recognition of the importance of the clitoris and clitoral orgasm has certainly played a role in lesbian sexuality,[16] and there has been, as well, a marked decline in butch/bitch role playing. For both sexes, homosexual sex is becoming more a matter of equal action and equal response.

*   *   *   *   *   *   *

In being part of the word "gay" weary lesbians have spent untold hours explaining to Middle America that lesbians do not worry about venereal disease, do not have sex in public bathrooms, do not seduce small boys, do not go to the baths for flings, do not regularly cruise Castro Street, and do not want to go to the barricades fighting for the lowering of the age of consent for sexual acts.[17]

Sally Gearhart is undoubtedly expressing the feelings of a number of gay women, whose vision of sexual liberation is far removed from that of some gay men (but not of all gay men, nor indeed all gay women, as Pat Califia has made clear).[18] It is a view reflected in the 1980 resolution of the National Organization of Women to support lesbian issues while condemning pederasty, pornography, sadomasochism, and public sex as matters of "exploitation, violence or invasion of privacy" and not issues of "sexual preference/orientation." When these questions were debated at the founding conference of NOLAG in 1981, they almost split the organization, and although the sexual libertarian motion was brought by two lesbian delegates, a number of women insisted on posing the debate in female/male terms.[19]

Gearhart's list covers a wide range; it is very unlikely that the same man would both seduce small boys and engage in orgies in baths or public bathrooms. By lumping together all these phenomena she is appealing to a conservative stereotype that sees any sex outside stable, long-lasting relationships as somehow inferior (although as a feminist she might concede that there is more genuine consent in much of the sex that she dislikes than there is within many marriages, and as someone concerned with the rights of children she might reflect on the fact that they, as much as their adult lovers, are oppressed by notions of an age of consent).

Apart from the particular case of sex with nonadults—and most such sex involves teenagers rather than "young boys"—what is really at issue is the acceptance of sex as valid even when it takes place outside the context of a long-lasting emotional relationship. Beyond this there is a further point that underlies the attitudes Gearhart represents, namely the feeling that such "promiscuity" is associated with an apparent upsurge in a wide range of activities loosely typed as sadomasochistic (or just "kinky"). These range from dressing up in leather, which may tell us nothing about the sexual proclivities of the person involved, to the genuine use of whips, ropes, and even torture. For most feminists, and not a few gay men, this sort of sexual behavior suggests total alienation in which fantasies are acted out upon other bodies in the same detached manner in which one might manipulate a video game. It is worth exploring the development among a minority of gay men—albeit the most blatant and reported minority—of a seeming cult of sexual experimentation, the constant search for more drugs, more bodies, another orifice, satirized in Larry Kramer's *Faggots*.

That only a minority of gay men live in the world described in novels such as *Faggots*, or Richard Hall's *The Butterscotch Prince*, is born out not just by my observations but by the figures from Jay and Young. Only a relatively small number of their sample have ever been involved in sadomasochism, bondage, or fist fucking or have used drugs other than alcohol or marijuana during sex. (Even amyl nitrite or "poppers" were used by only 21 percent "somewhat" frequently.[20]) Nonetheless the image of "groovy" sex, involving a willingness to get into all of these, has taken on its own momentum and become a standard to which numbers of gay men feel pressured to conform. Indeed, the controversy over the film *Cruising* occurred largely because of the fear on the part of many militants that the world it depicted, with its backroom bars and sadomasochistic sex, would be seen as representative of *all* homosexuals.[21] Given the way media stereotyping works, this was not an unreasonable fear, but there was also an element in the protests of wishing to hide from discussion one element of gay life that clearly exists.

Here we return to the images of gay life as involving promiscuous, public, and kinky sex. To some extent this is, of course, true, although all three terms are so loaded that it is difficult to discuss them rationally. It is perhaps truest in the case of public sex, a term often applied to sex in bathhouses and backroom bars, which are, in fact, places that often impose rigid conditions for entrance. Where sex does take place in public areas, as in parks or beaches or deserted buildings, it is almost always the case that nonhomosexuals would have to go to considerable trouble to find themselves in a position to observe and, presumably, to be offended. In fact one can quite legitimately argue that places such as the Rambles in Central Park, the Meat Rack on Fire Island, or Land's End in San Francisco have become a part of gay space, and that there is as much reason to protect them for such use as there is to close Fifth Avenue to traffic for the St. Patrick's Day Parade.

The invocation of terms such as "promiscuity," "public," "kinky," etc. represents a basic attempt to restrict any expression of gay sexuality to a model based on heterosexual morality, and to oppose this restriction is to move beyond liberal tolerance to an acceptance of genuine diversity. At the same time this does not prevent discussion and analysis of the dynamics involved in such sexuality; all I would ask is that those who adopt moral postures about other people's sexual behavior try to provide a rational basis for their judgments. I would have considerable sympathy, for example, with someone who expressed concern over the high dependence upon alcohol and drugs of many people in some gay subcultures, because of the demonstrably harmful effects of such stimulants.

The clearest example of the dilemma for the respectable gay movement in an emerging stress on gay life style is the extent to which that life style, at least for men, revolves around unorthodox expressions of sexuality, which in turn are increasingly being invoked to attack gays. Of this, Edmund White wrote:

> One explanation of this style would hold that homosexuality is inherently "neurotic" and that in a permissive atmosphere the neurosis is sending forth its most garish flowers. A second explanation might assert that the subjugation of gays has been so prolonged and punitive that it has left us deformed; in the aftermath we are expressing the rage and the impersonality and the panic we've absorbed from the dominant culture. Our violent sex is the sign of that rage, deflected from its true object (heterosexual repressiveness) and misdirected against ourselves. Our promiscuity is, according to this view, merely an extension of the furtiveness we were forced to resort to in the alien and hostile world of the past (the historic past and our individual past). By this interpretation we would consider the current notion of hot sex in New York to be a mere transition, a new recuperation of old oppression, and we would expect this period to be followed by a sweeter, calmer

one in which romance and intimacy and sustained partnership
between lovers would emerge again.[22]

Yet like White I have reservations about the judgments underlying such arguments. What I think *is* true of the sort of male gay
sex acted out in the backroom bars of large cities is that it involves
a great deal of fantasy and ritual, and that the feelings it expresses
are common to all men in Western society (if seemingly less so
among women), but heterosexual men must for the most part find
other arenas in which to express them.

It is a cliché to observe that American society is violent, competitive, and guilt-ridden about sexuality. Yet clichés are, unfortunately, usually true. Gay men have more opportunity than straight
men to act out through sexual fantasy the frustrations and fantasies
engendered by social pressure; they do not, I suspect, experience
them to any greater degree than do straights. Indeed, the beating
up of fags by straight men is often a similar way of dealing with these
frustrations, and one with far graver consequences than anything
that goes on in the Mineshaft or on Folsom Street.

But why do women seem so much less in need of this kind of
release? At this stage I doubt that we can say how far the reasons
are biological and how far social; while most psychologists argue that
women are less attracted to sadomasochism and "impersonal" sex
than are men,[23] there is some evidence that women do experience
similar feelings more than is usually admitted. (It seems to me that
sexuality is so much a matter of social construction that we must be
very sceptical of *any* assumptions about innate differences in such
matters.) One straight woman, describing her visit (dressed as a
man) to the New York bar The Anvil, recounts how much she was
turned on by the ambiance of fist fucking, urination, and pornography.[24] Pat Califia's account of sadomasochism among lesbians in
The Advocate, and the emergence of a lesbian s-and-m group in the
Bay Area, led both women and men to reevaluate their glib assertions that lesbians aren't turned on by sadomasochism.[25]

One can barely overemphasize the difference between male
and female socialization about sex. As Ellen Willis put it:

It is impossible to understand female—or for that matter male—
sexuality without acknowledging the impact of growing up in a
culture that despite its surface permissiveness is deeply anti-sexual.
A distorted, negative view of sex is basic to patriarchal psychology;
since girls learn to regard their genitals as a badge of inferiority,

boys to equate theirs with dominance and aggression, sexual pleasure gets tangled up with sadistic and masochistic feelings and
hostility between the sexes. At the same time, both sexes have a
powerful emotional investment in traditional masculine and feminine behavior because they associate it with their sexual identities
and with sex itself.[26]

This shows up in arguments about pornography, where a strange
alliance has emerged between some feminists and moral conservatives, two groups who are adamantly opposed on almost all other
issues. Pornography takes quite different forms when it is directed
at women rather than men; indeed, as Beatrice Faust points out,
much female pornography is not even recognized as such by men.
This probably explains why feminists are so willing to condemn
pornography that seems harmless to men, and why even gay male
pornography (in which no women appear) is seen as objectionable.[27]
I am less sure, as Faust seems to argue, that these differences are
innate. Certainly no one would dispute that different attitudes toward sexuality are a product of the interplay between culture and
biology; the problem is the relative weight of the two factors. As
Willis suggests, socialization is a very powerful factor in explaining
the gap between male and female responses of the type Gearhart
discusses. One might note that, in contradiction to the stand of
feminists like Millett, there is an implicit return in some more recent
feminist arguments to the Freudian belief that "anatomy is destiny."
Oddly enough, there is relatively little stress on the fundamental
difference that intercourse for women can result in pregnancy,
though one might make the argument that this is the basis for an
innate tendency of women to regard sex more seriously than men.

In its broadest sense it is certainly true that many more gay men
than women seek out "casual," "impersonal," and "anonymous" sex
(all these words have loaded and largely inaccurate connotations). It
is common to point to this as an example of the alienation of
homosexuals, inherent in our condition according to homophobic
psychologists, a product of oppression according to our apologists.
The latter view, for example, is argued strongly by Martin Hoffman,
a pioneer in combating the "disease" view of homosexuality, who
wrote, "To put the matter in its *most* simple terms, the reason that
males who are homosexually inclined cannot form stable relations
with each other is that society does not want them to."[28] For some
reason a society in which "swinging" and massage parlors are becoming widely accepted remains both titillated and affronted by the idea

of sex at beaches or parks and can only see them as proving the "instability" of homosexuals.

But perhaps the reverse is true, and we should view this sort of sex as a healthy affirmation of both sexuality and human contact, with very little effect on whether one maintains "meaningful relationships" or not. Once sex is desacralized and separated from its procreative function, it becomes evident that there is no reason to regard it as a form of behavior set apart from all others. If it is regarded as legitimate to have a "meaningful" discussion with someone one meets on a voyage and will never see again, why cannot it be equally meaningful to have a fuck with someone in similar circumstances? Sex has a number of possibilities, of which procreation and emotional bonding are only a part; while moralists have largely abandoned the former as the major justification for sex, the attempt to validate sexuality in terms of the latter causes considerable havoc. For sex can also serve as a means of experiencing pleasure, of finding an escape (far less harmful than most of its substitutes, such as alcohol and drugs), and of creating intense contact with those with whom one does not wish—or is not in a position to have—any sort of longer relationship.

The true alienation of the contemporary homosexual has nothing to do with his (occasionally her) sexual adventures, but rather it is reflected in the lack of any personal contact, sexual or otherwise, that is often true in bars and discos. Such lack of contact is even more strongly experienced by those isolated women and men who, because of fear, social pressures, self-hatred, and ignorance, are unable to find others. Among those men you might find in search of sex in thousands of cruising grounds across the country, there will be a small number unable to relate to others on any level other than immediate genital gratification; there will be many more who have a whole range of emotional relationships in their lives but want the excitement and gratification of a new and/or temporary sex partner.

Few of us can fully accept this; we carry around with us the whole set of assumptions with which society seeks to limit and regulate sexuality. Thus to take part in sexual adventures in a park or the baths is seen as somehow second-best, although there is a tradition of gay writing from Whitman on that seeks to come to terms with this sort of sexuality. It is even less acceptable for women, which makes Rita Mae Brown's comments—written after she spent some time in a New York sauna disguised as a man (and thus started a trend that has attracted a number of women writers)—all the more interesting:

Despite changing attitudes towards sex, we can't create our version of the baths because, for most of us, sex for the sake of sex is still wrong—whether you are a heterosexual woman or a lesbian. . . . Sex still calls up awesome emotions, the old tyrannies of romance. We scramble to invest sex with love, and we call men dogs because they've been taught to separate the two. If a woman manages to distinguish between sex and love and her need for both she's "fast," as my grandma used to say, whether she is straight or gay. . . . Yes, I do want a Xanadu. I want the option of random sex with no emotional commitment when I need sheer physical relief: erotic freedom. . . . Xanadu is not a lurid dream, it's the desire of a woman to have options. Like men we should have choices: deep long-term relationships, the baths, short-term affairs. And those choices are not mutually exclusive.[29]

Yet perhaps it is true that someone who, whether male or female, has come to accept himself or herself as homosexual has broken through at least one of the major barriers with which sexuality is surrounded. It is my hunch that it is this that makes gays freer to break other barriers and, as White suggested, to help others do the same. It is this, of course, that most frightens conservatives. As Charles Shively wrote in the preface to *Meat* (a collection of first-person accounts of sexual adventures): "We live loosely; we know nothing lasts because there will always be something more. We embody our dreams."[30] Perhaps the real secret is the extent to which we embody everyone's dreams.

*   *   *   *   *   *   *

The move toward redefining homosexuality as a life style rather than a deviance has meant a greater interest by sociologists and journalists in gay relations. Indeed, spurred by the ideological belief that long-lasting relationships are a necessary part of a happy and fulfilled life (a prejudice I must admit to sharing), researchers have fallen over themselves to demonstrate that homosexuals are, indeed, capable of such relationships. Thus an advertisement for *The Mendola Report: A New Look at Gay Couples* proclaims: "This proves conclusively that homosexual relations are similar in nearly every respect to heterosexual relations."[31]

Mendola is not very concerned by the increasing questioning of the assumptions that lie behind marriage (she describes herself as being involved in a lesbian marriage). It is hardly surprising that homosexuals have largely taken for granted the model offered by heterosexual marriage—it has been, for most of us, the only model around—without necessarily reflecting on the particular social conditions (the economic and psychological dependence of women on men, the need to create an environment for child rearing) that created it. At a time when the idea of lifelong marriage is under severe strain, when as Toffler has argued "the odds against [its] success may prove overwhelming,"[32] the model becomes particularly inappropriate.

Without entering into the enormous literature of the recent debate on marriage, it seems fair to say that the institution is in crisis for at least three reasons: the rate of social change, which means an increasing likelihood of partners' growing apart from each other relatively quickly; the growing pressures for sexual experimentation; and the breakdown of rigid sex roles, which by subordinating most wives to their husbands had allowed marriages to survive. It seems probable that the strains of a partnership in which neither partner is prepared to subordinate his or her interests to the other nor is ready to accept lifelong monogamy are on the whole better dealt with by homosexuals than heterosexuals.

Love is barely affected by sexual preference; the emotions associated with "being in love" do not vary much whether the loved one is of the opposite or the same sex, a child, or, indeed, a parrot. Once love is reciprocated and a relationship commences, the differences become crucial. For while love may exist on a purely spiritual and emotional plane, a relationship is a profoundly social event, and one shaped by all sorts of open and covert social and economic pressures. Forster's hope in *Maurice* of taking to the greenwood to escape the realities of social pressure is hardly, as the novel itself makes clear, a very realistic solution.

As a generalization, but one that is supported by the evidence from Jay and Young and other such surveys,[33] it seems clear that homosexual relationships are considerably less likely than heterosexual ones to involve financial dependence, living together (only about half the women and men in Jay and Young's survey who claimed lovers lived with them), or monogamy. Clearly these factors are in turn related to the absence of the kind of social support enjoyed by heterosexual relationships and, in most cases, of children. Even though many homosexuals have children, and these children live with their gay parents relatively often,[34] they clearly cannot be the offspring of their parent's lovers, although very close bonds may develop between lover and children. In all these ways homosexual relationships, even very long-lasting and committed ones, are less like the idealized norm of marriage than some gay conservatives like to claim.

While the idea that all lesbians seek totally monogamous relationships while all gay men reject monogamy is clearly a myth, it does seem clear that among gay men a long-lasting *monogamous* relationship is almost unknown. Indeed both gay women and gay men tend to be involved in what might be called multiple relationships, though of somewhat different kinds. For many lesbians, especially those affected by feminist precepts, the very exaggeration of this paragraph by Charlotte Waters sums it up:

> Once upon a time Deardra loved Carol. Deardra also loved Margo, Toni and Kathy, but was just coming out of a primary relationship with Jan and so didn't want to get into anything heavy with anyone. Carol loved Deardra and also Margo and sometimes Renalda, but she didn't give a hang about Toni and she hated Kathy's guts. Actually, Carol loved Deardra best, but Deardra wasn't into loving anyone best and claimed she was equally non-committed to them all.[35]

For gay men a parallel case is described by Edmund White:

> The gay male couple inhabiting the seventies is composed of two men who love each other, share the same friends and interests and fuck each other almost inadvertently once every six months during a particularly stoned, impromptu three-way. The rest of the time they get laid with strangers in a context that bears the stylistic marks and some of the reality of s-and-m.[36]

Both these descriptions are caricatures, but they do catch one of the features common to a great many gay relationships, namely a degree of fluidity that allows for considerable variety and autonomy. What often appears to straight critics as an obsession with sex is more accurately a preoccupation with constructing relationships that can meet our needs for both security and independence, commitment and variety.

A great deal of the gay writing of the past decade has been concerned, both explicitly and implicitly, with the construction of new relationships: just to cite Kate Millett's *Sita*, Michael Denneny's *Lovers*, Marie-Claire Blais's *Nights in the Underground* (subtitled *An Exploration of Love*), plays like Robert Patrick's *T-shirts* and Jane Chambers's *Last Summer at Bluefish Cove* makes the point. Again there is a difference between female and male writing; much lesbian writing has been concerned with the development of nonpossessive multiple relationships (which underlies Sally Gearhart's fantasies in *The Wanderground* or Monique Wittig's *Les Guérillères*), while gay men seem caught between the two myths of finding everlasting true love and happiness in the same person and constant excitement through sexual adventures. These myths are not as incompatible as one might think; much of the tension present in contemporary male gay writing stems from the attempt to reconcile the traditional image of romantic love and the reality of present-day sexuality, with its demands for constant variety and performance.

The most explicit discussion of the problem is *Faggots*, a Rabelaisian account of contemporary New York fag life that disguises a serious discussion of sexual ethics. Larry Kramer is, in fact, a traditional romantic who believes in monogamous coupling[37] and is upset by its disappearance in the world of fast sex, drugs, and Fire Island—"Our sexual fantasies are ruining us," says one character,[38] speaking (it would seem) for Kramer himself—but his novel poses, nonetheless, very real questions. It is, I suspect, a quite unrealistic novel in its desires, but not necessarily a homophobic one; Kramer just wants the sort of relationship that is less and less possible even outside the rarified world of Fire Island.

Kramer is, however, fairly exceptional; in practice most gay males accept that fidelity to a relationship is not to be measured in sexual terms. A large-scale study of gay male couples in San Diego concluded that every couple together more than five years had outside sexual contacts as a recognized part of the relationship. As David McWhirter and Andrew Mattison put it: "We never heard the word 'cheating' or 'faithful' applied to outside sex, even though outside relationships caused pain. And many couples reported that sex outside the relationship enhanced or reinvigorated the sexual contact when they were back with their partner."[39]

Just because there *are* no real social sanctions to support gay couples (indeed, it is often easier to remain closeted if one is not in a relationship) and no clear role definitions as to who should do what, it is easier for gay couples to experiment with unusual arrangements, and to maintain relationships that allow more flexibility and freedom than the norm. The absence of gay marriage (except among a very small group who have used gay churches for such purposes) means that it is easier for homosexuals to develop other ways of living than conventional coupledom; there has been considerable discussion, in the new gay writings, of the advantages and disadvantages of a whole range of possible living and sexual arrangements.

In their study of homosexuals in San Francisco Bell and Weinberg did find a number of men in "closed couple" relationships and concluded they were happier than those in "open couple" ones. However, an examination of their definitions reveals that the difference is not a simple one of monogamy versus promiscuity; having defined "closed couples" as those in which the partners "tend to look to each other rather than to outsiders for sexual and interpersonal satisfactions,"[40] it is not very difficult to "prove" that people in such relationships are more satisfied with them. For all its protestations of tolerance and understanding, Bell and Weinberg's book is heavily influenced by conventional assumptions about relationships and happiness.

It is my hunch that the illusion of love is more important for homosexual couples than for heterosexual ones, because without it there is much less reason to persist with the relationship, and this becomes truer as the overt gay world grows and there is less fear of never meeting anyone else. At the same time, while homosexuals may well have more illusions than do straights about love, they also have fewer illusions about permanence (I still remember my shock when one of my lovers said to me, early in our affair, "When we finish . . . ," and I recognized the chance of his being right). In a study of lesbian couples Donna Tanner noted that, despite the fact that the majority of women had been involved in at least one previous "paramarriage," several respondents considered their relationship a long-term commitment: they exchanged rings and provided for their partners in case of death through insurance policies and wills. On the other hand, while most of these relationships were monogamous, there was also an acceptance of the possible end of the relationship that differed from the marriage model. "I guess," said one woman, "we are of the mind that we should make it go as long as it goes, and when it stops going we should be reasonable enough to say that it is over and move on."[41]

Both lack of marriage and exclusion from the heterosexual world of conventional families tend to make friendship all the more important for homosexuals; while sociologists in recent years have shown some interest in gay coupling, they have tended to completely miss the significance of friendship among both gay women and gay men. Over the years numbers of people have said to me that they place more importance on their friends than on their lovers, and what many gay lives miss in terms of permanent relationships is more than compensated for by friendship networks, which often become de facto families. (Emily Sisley has described one such network in her story, "The Novel Writers.") Former lovers often are drawn into such networks, so that many gays are surrounded by a rich network of friends (often originally sexual partners) and past and present lovers, which can be far more supportive than are most nuclear families.

I don't want to appear to deny the negative side of gay relationships; it does seem, at least among male homosexuals, that there is often a real fear of commitment and a quite unrealistic level of expectations that dooms many men to never finding a satisfactory relationship. While it is tempting to claim that this reveals something about inherent differences either between gays and straights or between women and men, I suspect it is largely a reflection of social pressures; the low level of self-esteem among many homosexuals hardly helps in establishing the mutual trust and tolerance on which relationships must be based. Nonetheless there is much in the gay experience of relationships that is of more general relevance. It is not just that gay relationships are a threat to the dominant family structures that conservatives are desperately trying to bolster up. (This theme is found in much gay writing; John Rechy sees acceptance of homosexuality as leading to a questioning of "not heterosexuality itself, no, but the stagnant conformity of much of his tribal society.")[42] The attempts of homosexuals to create new forms of relationships can also be seen as part of a more general search to resolve universal problems. Under present conditions no one can be very sure of having solved the problem of how best to order one's personal life.

* * * * * * *

There has been considerable discussion over the past decade about the ethics and politics of sadomasochistic sex, pederasty, and transvestism. All are perceived as fringe elements of the gay scene and as potential embarrassments to the more "respectable" movement. Equally, all represent to the gay world what homosexuality as a whole signifies to the straight, namely a part of our sexuality that has been repressed and that is often painful to confront.

The greatest theoretical difficulties seem to me to lie in the issues raised by s-and-m. The point of this discussion is not to prescribe other people's behavior, but rather to come to terms with it. It is perfectly possible to make moral and aesthetic judgments about sexuality without believing that such judgments should be forced on others. In recent years this issue has generated very considerable debate within the gay movement, which seems to have fallen for the line that s-and-m is almost exclusively a concern of gay men. In fact, to a greater or lesser extent sadomasochism, both in the sense of inflicting and seeking pain and that of dominance and subordination between sexual partners, is probably an integral part of all sexuality, especially male sexuality. As Freud wrote:

> The sexuality of most male human beings contains an element of *aggressiveness*—a desire to subjugate; the biological significance of it seems to lie in the need for overcoming the resistance of the sexual object by means other than the process of wooing. Thus sadism would correspond to an aggressive component of the sexual instinct which has become independent and exaggerated and, by displacement, has usurped the leading position.[43]

As for masochism, Freud saw it as:

> an extension of sadism turned round upon the subject's own self, which thus, to begin with, takes the place of the sexual object. Clinical analysis of extreme cases of masochistic perversion show that a great number of factors (such as the castration complex and the sense of guilt) have combined to exaggerate and fixate the original passive sexual attitude.[44]

Now while Freud's basic premises may well be true and certainly explain the potential to link sex with pain, punishment, and domination, they hardly explain why sadomasochism, bondage and domination, fist fucking, and sexual play with piss and shit should have become so important in the sexual "liberation" of the past ten years, nor why they are so closely associated with male homosexuality. There is evidence that s-and-m and other such activities are also increasing among heterosexuals,[45] but they are so much more hidden that it is difficult to be certain. Symbolically s-and-m has come to be linked with male homosexuality in the eighties as firmly as effeminacy and an attack on gender roles was in the sixties and early seventies, and hence it must be dealt with seriously as part of the overall impact of the new gay consciousness on society; it is, indeed, often used as a way of "proving" the decadence of homosexuality. No one who read this extract from "Voice Choices" in *The Village Voice* could have missed the implicit slur:

The announcement for this exhibit [by Philip Masnick] shows a bent-over nude with a carnation sticking out his anus. This show —picturing ropes, chains, handcuffs, jock strap sniffing and an apparently painful perversion involving a fist and some Crisco— speaks to a limited audience and has no redeeming artistic value. It is noteworthy only because it's presented at a gallery that once was the most promising avant-garde showcase in New York. It's distressing to watch this gallery sink into a slime pit.[46]

The literature on s-and-m suggests a wide variety of reasons for its apparent increase. The simplest, and one that I am sure plays a part, is that the growing visibility of such sexuality allows many people to act out what were previously only fantasies and in turn allows others to develop fantasies they could barely have conceived before. What does seem clear is that there is a strong degree of ritual and theater in such sex, in which the roles played out are often more important than the actual physical acts. As Sontag wrote:

Sadomasochistic sex is more theatrical than any other. When sexuality depends so much on its being "staged," sex (like politics) becomes choreography. Regulars of sadomasochistic sex are expert costumers and choreographers; they are performers in the professional sense. And in a drama that is all the more exciting because it is forbidden to ordinary people. "What is purely realistic, slice of life," Leni Riefenstahl said, "what is average, quotidian, doesn't interest me." Crossing over from sadomasochistic fantasies, which are common enough, into action itself carries with it the thrill of transgression, blasphemy, entry into the kind of defiling experience that "nice" and "civilized" people can never have.[47]

What seems equally true is that there is a relationship between sex of this kind and the broader social environment, and it is not an accident that sadomasochism is most apparent at times and in places of moral and social upheaval, whether it is Rome during its decline, Berlin in the twenties, or New York today.

I should note, too, that the sexual expression of sadomasochism is only a small part of what some writers such as Erich Fromm mean by these terms.[48] Indeed I am increasingly uneasy with the term as it is used to apply to a wide range of sexual practices, from wearing leather to seeking and applying enemas; as already suggested, costume, ritual, and language (which Edmund White, in particular, sees as central)[49] are the common denominator. What I have seen of *heterosexual* s-and-m pornography makes it clear that the fantasies often involve a hatred of women that is quite frightening—but it would be wrong to assume, therefore, that all s-and-m involves misogyny and/or self-hate.

Both apologists and critics of the present vogue of s-and-m agree that it is an acting out of the aggressions to which Freud referred. Carried to its extreme, it becomes quite literally an enactment of Freud's death wish, as in Terry Andrews's *The Story of Harold*, where one character seeks to be burnt to death by his lover. For an observer like John Rechy, s-and-m represents an acting out of self-hatred, where men dress as the cops who persecute them and punish themselves, either directly or through others, for their homosexuality. Given the strong religious culture of America and the peculiar sadomasochistic nature of Christianity, with its base in the particularly gory execution of Christ, the psychological mechanisms are not difficult to understand. Religion has always offered real possibilities for the sublimation of sadomasochism and sometimes for its acting out, as in the vogue for self-chastisement. There has long been a particular attraction to homosexuals about the pomp and ceremony of Catholicism and High Church Anglicanism; in some ways backroom bars like the Mineshaft have become the contemporary equivalent of the cathedral.

Yet what may appear to be a clear case of self-hatred—for example, a man lying in a bathtub and being pissed on by half a dozen seemingly bored spectators—is almost certainly more complicated. Behind the ritual of much of this sort of sex there is a return to the forbidden pleasures of childhood: not only the play with urine and feces, but the fascination with beating and slapping (so much the staple of nineteenth-century upper-class British s-and-m).

Both self-hatred and Freud's repetition principle (the need to reenact all sorts of repressed memories and fantasies) are involved. Undoubtedly, too, the greater freedom to act out sexual fantasies means that what was previously repressed, denied, channeled elsewhere, is now much more open. There is, too, something of a need to find new frontiers: if anal intercourse has lost its capacity to shock (and not only among homosexuals; Bertolucci confronted that taboo in *Last Tango in Paris*), then use the fist. At least *that* proves one's masculinity (though perhaps not, since Pat Califia points out that women, too, engage in fist fucking). For many of those into the s-and-m scene, the motivation seems to be a constant heightening of sensations, a search for new experiences, which is no more than a response on the sexual level to the dominant ideology of modern consumerism. Thus the average age in backroom bars and "heavy" baths is around the early forties; we don't yet know whether this is because this generation bears the scars of self-oppression or because it is just bored after twenty years of "ordinary" sex. Sontag points to the ambiguity of seeing s-and-m as the search for heightened emotions:

> According to Reich, the masochist's taste for pain does not spring from a love of pain but from the hope of procuring, by means of pain, a strong sensation; those handicapped by emotional or sensory analgesia only prefer pain to not feeling anything at all. But there is another explanation of why people seek pain, diametrically opposed to Reich's, that also seems pertinent: that they seek it not to feel more but to feel less.[50]

Ultimately, sexuality can only be understood within its social context. Edmund White hinted at this in a discussion of sadomasochism:

> The anger and brutality that the child glimpses in his duplicitous parents, that the boss senses in his wisecracking employees, that the middle class attributes to working people—this anger and brutality are exorcized in s-and-m. Sex becomes an act born of the repetition compulsion, an Aristotelian drama with its unities of time, place and situation, and its definition of character through action; the drama recapitulates the incoherent and far more frightening violence of our society.[51]

If White is right, as I suspect he is, we can best make sense of what is happening to sexuality in terms of the collapse of traditional values or authority. Or, to cite Sontag again, "the explanation for Nazi Germany becoming a sexual turn-on is not merely an expression of self-hatred," but also "a response to an oppressive freedom of choice in sex (and possibly in other matters), to an unbearable degree of individuality."[52] What is crucial in this sort of sex is the ritual, the order, the discipline, and not the pain or its infliction.

It may seem ironic that it is gay men who are reacting thus to a collapse of traditional authority and moral absolutes when they would seem to have the most to gain from this collapse (as Sontag herself earlier suggested in her "Notes on Camp"). But the oppressed are not immune to the attraction of clear rules that define their status; when the rules become as ambiguous as they are today, people will look for a new set of certainties and rituals. This may explain why s-and-m seems largely confined to Protestant societies; in Catholic societies there are other rituals and ways to handle these needs. By and large gay men do not seem attracted to the right-wing political movements that provide these certainties for so many (although there is clearly a link between repressed homosexuality and the attraction of such movements, as Sartre demonstrated in his story "The Childhood of a Leader"). The ability to express certain needs for punishment, discipline, and power through sexual play seems to limit the need to enact it in political and military ways.

The s-and-m scene, indeed the whole male gay sex scene, becomes a way of dealing with the violence, madness, and injustice of the bigger world. Outsiders see fear, humiliation, and degradation in saunas, backroom bars, and leather clubs. They fail to see that here lies the possibility of catharsis (a term used by Califia in her discussion of s-and-m), of acting out the sense of pain and injustice that modern society engenders in us. This would explain why most studies suggest that men involved in s-and-m are likely to be personally gentle, liberal, and of above-average education.[53]

Apologists for s-and-m claim for it a therapeutic social role; an early expression of this view is found in a 1972 article in the now defunct paper *Come Out:*

> A theatrical representation of violence, such as a boxing match, is not going to increase real violence in the world but if anything will tend to *decrease* it by providing a harmless, controlled outlet; and the more such symbolic representations exist the more whatever S-M drives we might have (1) become raised from the subconscious to the conscious level where we can deal with them and (2) are satisfied by being expressed in some way within us, purged out of us (Aristotle's theory). How much more so in the case of an actual S-M relationship between two consenting people; by performing a ritual of dominance and submission, that is as ideally suited to their mutual needs as they can arrange, they not only more precisely satisfy these needs, but they also achieve an understanding of the difference between such a voluntary and ideal relationship, and the confused mess of involuntary oppression-garbage that we see around us. Such clear-cut S-M relationships therefore tend to prevent exploitation and oppression of imperialistic cultures.[54]

One might add to this that between two gay men there are not the in-built power imbalances that exist between a woman and a man in a heterosexual relationship, and that s-and-m rituals become a way of creating but also of limiting such power relations. Certainly among couples who are into this sort of sex there does not appear to be the sort of clear-cut role demarcation that is sometimes found among more conventional homosexuals.

Such arguments are persuasive only if it can be demonstrated both that we do have aggressive instincts that must be acted out and that acting them out through the ritual and fantasies of sexuality prevents their being expressed more directly in nonplayful violence. (It might be argued, after all, that such play only increases the appetite for aggression.) Freud's claim that men, at least, have such instincts is a theme that is echoed in much contemporary literature. It is suggested in Ernest Callenbach's utopian novel *Ecotopia*, in which Callenbach predicates mock gladiatorial combats as a way of dealing with it, and in a more specifically homosexual sense it is an underlying theme in much of Samuel Delaney's science fiction (*Dahlgren* and *Tales of Nevèrÿon*, for example). Certainly there is no evidence that gay men who play-act s-and-m rituals have any desire to enact them on any other than consenting partners, and plenty of evidence exists that sexual repression *does* fuel very real and brutal violence.

It has indeed been claimed that far from blunting the moral sense, which would be one of my fears about s-and-m, it heightens it. Speaking for men involved in such sex, Ian Young wrote: "There does seem to be a close connection between our interest in dominance/submission psychodrama and our opposition to political power and injustice . . . S & M involves a sort of imaginary or dramatic power—exciting where the real power in the world is tedious and squalid."[55] Those concerned with the growth of s-and-m sex should reflect on the very much more brutal violence that is meted out by police and military, who are often upholding rigid codes of sexual morality.

If all these claims are correct there is, I suspect, one remaining valid objection that the literature of s-and-m has failed to fully answer, and that is the extent to which—if sadomasochism is the expression of a largely unconscious degree of self-hatred (greatly increased in the case of gay men by internalized social prejudices) —its expression only reinforces such feelings. While it is true that s-and-m is almost always consensual and that rape by self-acknowl-edged homosexuals is very rare—though male rape by those who deny their homosexuality is, of course, quite widespread—we must ask about the nature of consent. If such sex is often an expression of self-hatred, which is certainly the way it is commonly depicted in s-and-m pornography, then is it possible to speak of consent as if it were a simple matter? Does someone who seeks to be whipped or fisted (possibly with severe consequences to his health) because he has an unconscious need to be punished really pose no moral question?

If the above speculations are correct, we must ask why particular forms of s-and-m are so much more apparent among gay men than among straights. The simple answer is that just because it is a predominantly male desire, homosexuals can satisfy it through sexual play in a way largely unavailable to heterosexuals, who often resort to prostitutes for sadomasochistic sex. However, things are less simple than this, for there are women, both gay and straight, who engage in s-and-m sex, and it is my hunch that the differences are more of style; that is, s-and-m is very common among heterosexuals, but not in the institutionalized and ritualized forms found in the male gay world. Rather it is built into a large number of sexual transactions (who does not know of women who stay with men who beat them up?). Freudians would claim that such masochism is particularly "feminine," recognizing both constitutional and social causes.

Once again we are back to the question of whether there are biological as well as cultural differences between women and men: do women so internalize their frustrations and aggression that these cannot be acted out through s-and-m rituals, or is there some inherent difference between men and women that makes women less aggressive? This is one of the few areas in which psychoanalysts, ethologists, and some feminists can agree. Whether the proof is sought in genetics, hormones, or an ill-defined "female spirit," they all argue that women are "naturally" less attracted to this sort of behavior. When Pat Califia attacked this assumption she horrified many readers, not least for her declaration that "I identify more strongly as a sado-masochist than as a lesbian."[56]

How far the aggressions that underlie s-and-m are universal, and how far particularly masculine, must remain a matter for conjecture. The growing prominence of s-and-m in the gay world (reflected, for example, in a particularly gory s-and-m scene in Patricia Nell Warren's *The Beauty Queen*, where the religious connotations are underlined) poses a crucial question that goes far beyond the needs of gay men. Erich Fromm argues that sadism (and by extension, masochism) is inevitable as long as societies are structured around exploitation and power. If so, it is surely preferable that it be acted out in backroom bars than through the authoritarian institutions of the modern state. The straight world has a great deal to learn from the leather bars of the gay.

*   *   *   *   *   *   *

Just as the gay world plays out the general sexual fears and fantasies about sadomasochism (which William Friedkin probably sensed when he decided to film *Cruising* and unfortunately for him could never properly articulate), so too broader social anxieties and fantasies about children's sexuality are projected onto gays. This fact has become the crux of much current debate about homosexuality; it was no accident that the Bryant campaign in Florida in 1977 was known as "Save Our Children."

I have already stressed that the great bulk of sexual abuse of children is of little girls by older men, and that the most common form of pederasty involves timid men and teenage boys, already sexually mature, who are clearly in control of the situation. Nonetheless the myth of homosexuals as child abusers persists; as Ian Young wrote:

It is interesting that European society evolved three frightening myths to stigmatize the three groups it most ostracized and that each of these myths involved a threat to children directly connected with the particular deviation of the group. The Jews were religious heretics; therefore they were said to kill Christian children for use in their religious rituals. The gypsies were social deviants whose vagabond life was mistrusted; therefore they were said to kidnap non-gypsy children and take them away to distant places, raising them as their own. The homosexuals were sexual deviants and so were, and are, said to sexually attack children. The myths are powerful, relying on people's deep and ambivalent fear for their offspring. No amount of hard statistics or reasoned sociological analysis has the power of such myths. And of course, the myths are manipulated—by Mary Whitehouse, by the press, by the police, and in at least one instance by children themselves. Earlier this year several boys at an English church school accused their teacher, a Church of England clergyman, of sexually assaulting them. They maintained their story right into the witness box, where, fortunately, an able defense counsel was able to trip one of them up. It turned out the boys had invented the whole thing after reading of such cases in the newspapers. Their aim was to get rid of a teacher who they felt was too tough in marking their test papers.[57]

In the last few years there have been a number of well-publicized moves against "pederasts." In addition to the Bryant campaign one can cite the raids in Boston in 1977 against an alleged child pornography ring, leading both to widespread arrests and to the first public organization of man/boy lovers in the United States (this later became the North American Man Boy Lovers Association or NAM-BLA); the prosecution in Ontario of *Body Politic* for its article "Men Loving Boys Loving Men" (the paper was acquitted but the provincial government successfully appealed the verdict); the Briggs Amendment in California and the introduction of the Family Protection Act; and, in Britain, the campaign against the Paedophile Information Exchange, which has resulted in several court cases and considerable media hysteria.[58] Allegations of homosexual molestation, seduction, and corruption of children are becoming the cutting edge where lines are being drawn.

If one examines the attacks on pedophilia it becomes clear that they are largely disguised attacks on homosexuality; it is as if, since 1977, the moral conservatives have recognized that it is here that homosexuals are most vulnerable, not because they are child molesters but rather because of the fears that such allegations arouse. Those who campaign to "save our children" refuse to come to terms with two facts: children, as Freud demonstrated, are sexual beings, and modern consumer capitalism exploits this consciously and consistently, and in the great majority of cases in an exclusively male-oriented and heterosexual way. The way in which advertising is making increasing use of the sexuality of pubescent girls has been widely remarked and is reflected in the movie industry (which so far has not been able to deal honestly with even adult homosexuality). Brooke Shields became a star by playing a sexually precocious twelve-year-old in *Pretty Baby*, which, while certainly causing controversy, did not generate the sort of enraged reaction that would have been accorded a film that showed a *boy* seducing Keith Carradine. (*Pretty Baby* followed other films, such as *Night Moves* and *Taxi Driver*, that featured sex between girls and older men, and preceded others, such as *Foxes* and *Little Darlings*, in which teenage girls compete to lose their virginity.)

There are two separate issues here: the sexuality of children, and the power relations implied in adult/child sex. One could quite

logically defend the right of children to engage in sexual experimentation and activity, both heterosexual and homosexual, among themselves, while criticizing adult/child sex as inevitably wrong because
of the imbalance of power and maturity between the two. One
might also argue that since no one advocates preventing all interaction between children and adults, it is making too much of sex to
argue that this relationship alone should be prohibited. Indeed, the
real violence perpetrated on children in our society is very rarely
sexual, and the staunchest defenders of children against such "molestation" often happily support political and economic programs
that condemn thousands of children to malnutrition; inadequate
housing, schooling, and medical care; and environmental poisoning.
Apart, perhaps, from those who campaign for the "rights of the
unborn," there are few people as hypocritical as those who agitate
to "protect our children."

     Their strength is based on the fact that they appeal to a number
of strongly held and irrational beliefs, all of them strongest when
"child molestation" can be linked to homosexuality. The idea of
adult/child sex is threatening on at least three levels: it suggests that
children are, in fact, sexual beings (particularly threatening to those
who are ambivalent about their own sexuality); it suggests that they
are capable of both heterosexual and homosexual response (most of
the "boys" involved in man/boy love appear to become predominantly heterosexual as they age—proof, indeed, of the flexibility of
sexual response); and it threatens the power of parents over their
children, which is the reality of adult/child relationships in this
society. This last point is recognized in a number of "primitive"
societies in which part of the initiation of teenagers into the broader
society involves sex with adults (often homosexual, as among Australian aborigines).[59] There is a slight echo of this point in the belief
among some Europeans that an older woman should initiate boys
into sex—girls of course, must remain virgins—which combines with
the need to retain parental control in the incest of Bertolucci's *Luna*
or Louis Malle's *Murmur of the Heart*. As Sylvère Lotringer wrote:

> The pedophile appears all the more threatening to parents in that
> he liberates in the child a potential for love and pleasure necessar-
> ily stifled by the confusion within the family of adult roles and
> parental status. The child's desire for adults is met by the stranger
> —child seducer, abductor and alleged molestor. Since the child's
> guilt strongly contributes to maintaining his parents' authority
> over his life, a desire freed from guilt and repression is immediately

felt as a threat to the family order. I suspect a good deal of the parents' sheer panic over the issue of pedophilia lies here.[60]

If sexuality were free from the sorts of pressures that exist in our society—it would be utopian to argue for *no* social pressures on the regulation of sexuality—I suspect child/adult sex would be fairly common, though not perhaps as common as sex among children themselves. That few women appear to be involved in such sex probably has more to do with conditioning than with innate sexual differences; there is no evidence that girls are less curious and experimental about sex than boys, nor that women do not find the young attractive. It may also reflect the possibility that for many women sexual desire is often sublimated into mothering, which, if it is true, also helps explain the extreme hostility of many women to discussion of child/adult sexual relations.

Feminists argue that the basic question is power, not sexuality. As Judith Coburn put it:

> It is impossible to imagine an equal relationship between a child and an adult—particularly since its most common configuration is that of an adult male, often a relative, with a female child. Children are inexperienced, easily impressed, malleable. A child often has sexual feelings that can be manipulated by an adult whom the child loves, fears or respects. A seductive child may not understand the implications of his or her own behavior; to a child, flirting may not be sexual, it may just be mimicking Mommy.[61]

This is, at first, an attractive proposition. Yet I suspect the power relations in child/adult sex (and I am obviously not speaking here of situations of clear coercion; there is almost universal agreement that these should be proscribed) are much more ambiguous than in almost all other relationships between adults and children. Nearly all the accounts of man/boy love with which I am familiar stress the extent to which the boys manipulate the situation.[62] In an atmosphere in which any discussion of child/adult sex was not greeted with dismay and demands for revenge, the child's autonomy would be all the greater. The images of coerced incest that feminists conjure up and that have considerable basis in fact are not arguments against adult/child sex, but rather against the ideology and social arrangements that make children so powerless in all areas, arrangements which the moralists would only strengthen.

Coburn's fears seem more appropriate in cases of man/girl

relations than in those involving men and boys or women and children, which seems, in turn, largely a reflection of social differences between the sexes (although the example of *Lolita* should remind us that the power relationships even between men and girls are more ambivalent than the feminist critique recognizes). But it is not only for this reason that man/boy love cannot be discussed as if it were indistinguishable from other forms of adult/child sex. For pederasty involves a double taboo, children and homosexuality, and hence it is doubly threatening. Ironically, in many societies the most accepted form of homosexuality has been precisely that involving older men and boys. This Socratic vision of homosexuality, with its notion of the education of a younger man by an older man, is a powerful part of the European imagery of homosexuality—note the relationship between Diaghilev and Nijinsky, *Death in Venice*, and the novels of Tony Duvert in France and Pier Paolo Pasolini in Italy—as opposed to the American vision of a Whitmanesque democracy between men. Indeed, one expert on Greek homosexuality, J. Z. Eglinton, has even argued that pederasty could well be the solution to some of the social problems of youth, rather than being itself a social problem.[63]

Over the past few years the issue of man/boy love has become a divisive one in the gay movement, not only in the United States but also in Britain, Canada, and France (where there is a strong tradition of viewing homosexuality in this way, and where more seems to have been written on the subject than in any other Western society).[64] It was debate over this question that split the planning of the 1980 Gay Pride march in New York, and it is one of a number of issues that tends to set gay women apart from at least some gay men. Our enemies have been able to use the issue as a way of controlling and defining homosexuality, and the emotions it arouses are frightening (many gay activists will say that while they support the abolition of all "age of consent" laws, to say so publicly is too dangerous). I sat through a debate on the question in which one woman threatened to shoot a man who defended man/boy love by invoking his own experiences. No other aspect of sexual behavior except perhaps abortion conjures up such fears and fantasies, or produces such hysteria.

*   *   *   *   *   *   *

The various debates on sexuality that are dividing the gay movement and society as a whole suggest that the sexual arena remains one in which all sorts of fears, hatreds, and phobias are acted out, often because of semiconscious manipulation by the media and the politically ambitious. Again it is necessary to reiterate that what lies behind this is an extraordinary overemphasis on and reification of sex; as Jeffrey Weeks wrote:

> Moral purity is seizing the initiative because progressive thought is losing its grip, and because it is implicated in the same imagery of sex as puritanism; [it] is, indeed, a mirror image. At the heart of the phenomenon is that peculiar feature of western thought, the simultaneous elevation and terror of sex, which finds its strongest embodiment in the puritan imagination, but which liberal thought has confirmed. The road away from moral authoritarianism lies not with the elevation of King Sex, whether in the sacred form of puritanism or in the profane form of permissiveness, but in his dethronement.[65]

Thus the crucial questions posed by sadomasochism are not whether it is good or bad or even a sign of decadence that men fist and piss on each other, but how such activities are related to the frightening degree of violence in this society, violence in which the gay practitioners of s-and-m are strikingly absent. The crucial questions posed by man/boy love are not whether boys are being corrupted, but what is the overall position of children in our society, and why are so many forced to run away from home and to survive through prostitution and pornography. The crucial questions posed by transvestism/sexualism ask how far our conventional sex roles restrict and repress individuals, both women and men.

Over the past decade there have been considerable changes in both sexual behavior and sexual values. Among the most striking of these is the tendency for more heterosexuals to behave according to the conventional stereotype of the homosexual, to engage in numbers of short-lived sexual adventures either in place of or alongside long-term relationships. There have even developed heterosexual equivalents of gay saunas (perhaps the best known, Plato's Retreat, inherited the premises of the Continental Baths), and the whole proliferation of the "swinging singles" scene suggests that promiscuity and "impersonal sex" are determined more by social possibilities than by inherent differences between homosexuals and heterosexuals, or even between men and women. As George Whitmore put it, "The myths usually assigned to the gay world have been assigned now to the singles world."[66]

American society today is suffering from an enormous national neurosis about sex, brought about by the conflicting messages from traditional teachings and the constant barrage of advertising extolling hedonism and sexual adventure. As sexuality becomes more open but also more problematic, homosexuals become both a scapegoat and a model; our very redefinition as a discrete minority, with a distinctive life style, makes us available as an object on which society's anxieties about sex can be vented. It is much easier for those who feel anxious and guilty about their sexual feelings to focus their anxieties on a specific group that can be defined as "the other."

The positive side of this is that, because homosexuals are unable to organize our sexuality and relationships in totally conventional ways, we are perhaps better able to discover ways of resolving these questions that are workable under current social conditions. The irresoluable dilemma of the moral conservatives is that sexuality cannot be separated from other areas of life, and hence the pressures for constant change, experimentation, and hedonism that are generated by the dominant socioeconomic order inevitably affect our sexual lives. It is in this sense that one can speak of the "homosexualization" of society, and that what is happening in the gay world is of relevance to others.

NOTES

1   *Child Abuse and Neglect: The Problem and Its Management,* Dept. of Health, Education and Welfare Publication (OHD) 75.30073. See also A.C.L.U. Gay Rights Committee, *Sexual Child Abuse: A Contemporary Family Problem* (Los Angeles, 1977).
2   "Between the Lines," *Body Politic,* No. 67, October 1980, p. 7.
3   See my review in *Christopher Street,* October 1979. There is further evidence in Alan Bell and Martin Weinberg, *Homosexualities* (New York: Simon and Schuster, 1978), and Jim Spada, *The Spada Report* (New York: New American Library, 1979).
4   Karla Jay and Allen Young, *The Gay Report* (New York: Summit Books, 1979), p. 161.
5   Ibid., pp. 248–289 and 324.
6   See Laud Humphreys, *Tearoom Trade* (Hawthorne, N.Y.: Aldine Publishing Co., 1975), esp. Ch. 6.
7   This is argued in Letitia Anne Peplau, "What Homosexuals Want in Relationships," *Psychology Today,* March 1981.
8   Jane Rule, *Lesbian Images* (New York: Doubleday, 1975), p. 5.

9   Bruce Voeller, "Stonewall Anniversary," *The Advocate,* July 12, 1979.

10 William Masters and Virginia Johnson, *Homosexuality in Perspective* (Boston: Little, Brown, 1979), esp. Ch. 5.

11 Martin Duberman, review of *Homosexuality in Perspective,* in *The New Republic,* June 16, 1979, pp. 27–28.

12 Paul Monette, *Taking Care of Mrs. Carroll* (New York: Avon Books, 1978), p. 57.

13 See Guy Hocquenghem, *Homosexual Desire* (London: Allison & Busby, 1978), Ch. 4.

14 Bell and Weinberg, op. cit., p. 111.

15 An example of this is Steve Wolf, "The New Gay Party Line," *Christopher Street,* September 1980.

16 Jay and Young, *The Gay Report,* op. cit., p. 385.

17 Sally Gearhart, "An Open Letter to Voters in District 5 and San Francisco's Gay Community from Sally Gearhart," [mimeographed] (San Francisco, 1979).

18 See, for example, Pat Califia, "What Is 'Gay Liberation'?," *The Advocate,* June 25, 1981.

19 Scott Tucker, "Too Queer to Be Gay," *New York Native,* No. 13, June 1, 1981.

20 Jay and Young, *The Gay Report,* op. cit., pp. 497, 555.

21 On the controversy over *Cruising* see Scott Tucker et al., "Sex, Death and Free Speech," *Body Politic,* No. 58, November 1979.

22 Edmund White, *States of Desire* (New York: E. P. Dutton, 1980), p. 279.

23 See, for example, Chris Gosselin and Glenn Wilson, *Sexual Variations* (New York: Simon and Schuster, 1980), pp. 158–159.

24 Janice Arthur, "Behind Closed Doors," *Christopher Street,* March 1977.

25 Pat Califia, "A Secret Side of Lesbian Sexuality," *The Advocate,* December 27, 1979.

26 Ellen Willis, "The Family: Love It or Leave It," *The Village Voice,* September 17, 1979, p. 35.

27 For an example of this see Andrea Dworkin, *Pornography: Men Possessing Women* (New York: Perigee Books, 1981), esp. pp. 36–45.

28 Martin Hoffman, *The Gay World* (New York: Basic Books, 1968), p. 176.

29 Rita Mae Brown, "Queen for a Day: A Stranger in Paradise," in Karla Jay and Allen Young, *Lavender Culture* (New York: Jove/HBJ, 1979), p. 76.

30 Charles Shively in Boyd McDonald, ed., *Meat* (San Francisco: Gay Sunshine Press, 1981), pp. 7–8.

31 *Gay Community News,* October 18, 1980, p. 7.
32 Alvin Toffler, *Future Shock* (New York: Random House, 1970), p. 221.
33 See Mary Mendola, *The Mendola Report* (New York: Crown Publishers, 1980); Reimut Reiche and Martin Dannecker, "Male Homosexuality in West Germany."
34 Jay and Young, *The Gay Report,* op. cit., pp. 79–81, 133–136.
35 Chocolate Waters, "Lesbian Fable," *Christopher Street,* March 1977, p. 60.
36 White, *States of Desire,* op. cit., p. 267.
37 See interview with Bob Chesley, "It's Hard to Walk Away from a Good Blowjob," *Gaysweek* (New York), January 1, 1979.
38 Larry Kramer, *Faggots* (New York: Random House, 1978), p. 42.
39 See Scott Anderson's interview with David McWhirter and Andrew Mattison, *The Advocate,* February 7, 1980, p. 20.
40 Bell and Weinberg, op. cit., p. 132.
41 Donna Tanner, *The Lesbian Couple* (Lexington, Mass.: Lexington Books, 1978), p. 78.
42 John Rechy, *The Sexual Outlaw* (New York: Grove Press, 1977), p. 200.
43 Sigmund Freud, *Three Essays on the Theory of Sexuality* (London: Hogarth Press, 1962), pp. 23–24.
44 Ibid., p. 24.
45 See Morton Hunt, *Sexual Behavior in the 1970's* (Chicago: Playboy Press, 1974), pp. 327–330, and Gerald and Caroline Green, *S-M: The Last Taboo* (New York: Grove Press, 1974).
46 "Voice Choices," *The Village Voice,* May 12, 1979.
47 Susan Sontag, "Fascinating Fascism," *New York Review of Books,* February 6, 1975, p. 29.
48 See Erich Fromm, *The Anatomy of Human Destructiveness* (New York: Holt, Rinehart & Winston, 1973), esp. Ch. 11.
49 See Edmund White, "Sado Masochism," *New Times,* January 8, 1979.
50 Susan Sontag, *On Photography* (New York: Farrar Straus & Giroux, 1978), p. 40.
51 White, "Sado Masochism," op. cit., p. 60.
52 Sontag, "Fascinating Fascism," op. cit., p. 29.
53 This is claimed by White, who discusses a study in progress by Edward Gregersen; see White, "Sado Masochism," op. cit., p. 58.
54 "Larry S.," "S and M and the Revolution," *Come Out* (New York), Winter 1972.
55 "Forum on Sadomasochism," *Lavender Culture,* op. cit., p. 104.
56 Califia, op. cit., p. 19.

57 Ian Young, "Politick and Paradox in England," *The Advocate*, December 25, 1980, p. 18.

58 On these events see John Mitzel, *The Boston Sex Scandal* (Boston: Glad Day Books, 1980); Gerald Hannon, "Men Loving Boys Loving Men," *Body Politic*, No. 39, December 1977/January 1978 and subsequent reports of the trials (Nos. 51, 54); Gay Left Collective, "Happy Families? Paedophilia Examined," and Jamie Gough, "Childhood Sexuality and Paedophilia," in Pam Mitchell, ed., *Pink Triangles* (Boston: Alyson Publications, 1980); and Tom O'Carroll, *Paedophilia: The Radical Case* (London: Peter Owen, 1980).

59 See, for example, Robert Brain, *Rites Black & White* (Melbourne: Penguin Books, 1979), Ch. 10.

60 Sylvère Lotringer, "Editorial: Dirty Old Minds," *Semiotext(e)*, Summer 1980, p. 4.

61 Judith Coburn, "Trafficking in Innocence," *New Times*, January 8, 1979, p. 71.

62 See, for example, Hannon, op. cit.

63 Quoted by Gerald Jones, "Current Literature in Child-Adult Sexual Behavior," *NAMBLA Journal*, No. 3, 1980, p. 11.

64 See, for example, René Schérer, *Emile Perverti* (Paris: Laffort, 1974); René Schérer and Guy Hocquenghem, "Co-Ire: Album Systématique de l'Enfance," *Recherches* (Paris), No. 22, May 1976; "Fous d'Enfance," *Recherches*, No. 37, April 1979; J. L. Pinard-Legry and B. Lapouge, *L'Enfant et le Pédéraste* (Paris: Editions du Seuil, 1980).

65 Jeffrey Weeks, "The Rise and Fall of Permissiveness," *Spectator* (London), March 17, 1979, p. 17.

66 George Whitmore, "Living Alone," in Karla Jay and Allen Young, eds., *After You're Out* (New York: Pyramid, 1975), p. 59.

CHAPTER SEVEN

A Personal Conclusion

I wrote my first book, *Homosexual: Oppression and Liberation*, exactly ten years before finishing this one. In the intervening period a great deal has happened, both to me and to the gay movement. Neither of us anticipated how the seventies would turn out nor how the eighties would begin. A comparison of the indexes of the two books shows some of these changes; ten years ago the most often cited names were James Baldwin, Norman O. Brown, Eldridge Cleaver, Jean Genet, Paul Goodman, Christopher Isherwood, Norman Mailer, Herbert Marcuse, Kate Millett, and Gore Vidal. Apart from Millett, these all belong to generations older than mine; in the ensuing ten years, the creation of a new gay community and culture has been largely the work of my contemporaries, some of whose names are mentioned in this book.

There are also, it should be noted, references to very many more women writers in the present work. Perhaps my biggest single problem in writing this book has been to include women, not just as an afterthought but as an integral part of the analysis. The very process of constructing the new gay identity has tended to separate the experiences of gay women and gay men, making this a difficult task. Yet to state that only women are capable of writing about women seems to me too easy a way out. This does not mean that a gay man should write about gay women in the same way as would a woman. As Rosemary Pringle suggested: "Rather than tacking lesbians onto the gay world, we need to draw on the lesbian experience to *interpret* the gay world more generally, to help us make sense of the contradictions implicit in the identity of gay males, and of the resistance of most heterosexual men, including those on the Left, to gay critiques of masculinity and of sexuality in general."[1]

The changes of the past decade have not, of course, been quite what we expected. My first book was written at a time when radical change, at least in the United States, seemed far more possible than it does now—at the end of the sixties there was a spate of writings about the possibility of revolution in America—and when the new gay liberation movement seemed part of the agenda for the transformation of Western society. The war in Vietnam was already in decline, there was mounting opposition to President Nixon (this was before both the McGovern debacle of 1972 and the scandals of Watergate), and conventional wisdom asserted that Ronald Reagan was far too right wing ever to become a serious contender for the presidency.

Looking back over the past ten years, I am struck by a number of developments. The first is the enormous growth of gay self-assertion and affirmation, which is the basis for much of this present book. Whether this takes the form of openly gay legislators, gay marching bands and parades, or a proliferation of all-male discos and lesbian music festivals, the variety of gay life today far exceeds what most of us could imagine in 1969 and 1970.

But much of what has happened would also have seemed undesirable to us in the early days of the new gay movement. We did not expect, by and large, that the growth of gay pride would be accompanied by a growing separation between men and women, gays and straights. We did not foresee the extent to which much of the new gay culture, especially for men, would be no more than the development of a new market based on the provision of luxurious entertainment and commercial cruising grounds. In New York I danced in 1971 at gay liberation dances at Columbia University, in 1981 at The Saint disco, and that change is symbolic of much larger developments. We certainly did not imagine the extent to which our new visibility would lead to the antigay campaigns that began in the late seventies and have been taken up so vigorously by the Moral Majority.

In retrospect there was a naiveté to early gay liberation that explains why many of us are ambivalent about the changes of the past decade. I have walked through several of the present gay ghettos with people whose gay politics date back to the Stonewall era and seen them react with a mixture of pride and distress to the way things are. On the whole I see as positive the sort of change like that in the Castro, through which an old Irish neighborhood with some hippy overtones became the most celebrated gay neighborhood in the world. At the same time I am aware that many people in the ghettos feel a pressure for conformity that can become a new form of repression. Such reactions probably underestimate the extent to which the psychic damage done to homosexuals by generations of social stigma can be reversed without the acceptance of a certain amount of separatism.

If my first book suffered from an excess of optimism in its belief that gay assertion would lead to social acceptance, it is easy today to veer to the other extreme and speak darkly of coming repression that will consign us all to concentration camps (a theme of novels such as Paul Welles's *Project Lambda* and Alabama Birdstone's *Queer Free*). On balance it seems that social attitudes have shifted in our favor, though perhaps less clearly in the United States than in other parts of the Western world that are less troubled by fears of social disintegration and an evangelical tradition. In America the mood seems to fluctuate between a genuine acceptance of homosexuals as a legitimate minority and a deep and irrational fear that, as Seymour Kleinberg put it: "We will not only destroy the family and seduce the children but also pioneer the corruption of all modesties, all restraints, and most threatening, all privacies. We are speaking of the unspeakable; to do so is already to give it some quarter. To demand that society tolerate the display of sexual variety is to condone it."[2]

One should never underestimate the extent to which social attitudes toward sexuality rest upon irrational fears and fantasies. It is perhaps not surprising that the development of gay consciousness and the expression of homophobia go hand in hand. A few years after Gide published *Corydon* in 1920, the English critic and novelist Edmund Grosse wrote: "No doubt in fifty years this particular subject will cease to surprise anyone, and how many people in the past might wish to have lived in 1974."[3] Grosse was right to forecast large changes, but these changes have been more ambivalent than he expected.

There may be rhetorical value in insisting that homosexuals form a minority like any other, but at the same time we are also seen as a basic threat to some very central assumptions of Western society. To demand acceptance of real diversity in sexuality, in gender roles, and in family structures—all of which are implied in a full acceptance of homosexuality—is to go far beyond the sort of pluralism that American society recognizes. Even within the gay world the demand for acceptance of transvestites, pederasty, sadomasochism, and "public sex" is far from complete, nor is this simply a matter of disputes between gay women and gay men. It was a gay man who wrote, apropos of Mitzel's *The Boston Sex Scandal:* "It seems logical to say that the American people will never accept boy love regardless of how it is presented. The Gay movement has enough problems to cope with already. Acceptance of man-boy affection is many light years away, if ever."[4]

In the early days of the movement, both women and men saw the process of gay liberation as intimately related to the blurring of sexual and gender boundaries, a move toward androgyny, and the triumph of those values traditionally assumed to be feminine (i.e., softness, compassion, cooperation, etc.). Our biggest failure was an inability to foresee the extent to which the opposite would happen and a new gay culture/identity would emerge that would build on existing male/female differences.

That this has happened should not be seen as a purely negative development, though there are certainly aspects to it that are hardly welcome. For part of what has happened has been an exploration of new forms of sexuality and relationships that goes beyond the vague libertarianism of the early seventies. As part of this exploration some of the characteristics of traditional homosexual culture are stressed in a new form. This has been most obvious among certain gay men, who have found many of their sexual practices and institutions under fire from within and without the gay world. But it is also the experience of some lesbians; even some lesbian feminists argue for the importance of traditional butch/fem role playing in developing their primary identity as lovers of other women.[5]

Precisely because the affirmation of being gay is the affirmation of sexual desire, there is something radical about the gay movement that all the attempts of those who would claim respectability for us cannot dispell. Indeed, the very strengthening of the sense of gay identity leads both to claims that we are another minority and to an awareness of the fact that we organize our everyday lives in radical opposition to the sexual norms of this society. This contradiction underlies the complaint of Vito Russo that, "I want what seems like a complete contradiction. I want society to cease viewing gays as defined solely by our sexuality, and at the same time I want the freedom to be as unabashedly sexual as I wish."[6]

One of the ways in which the gay liberation movement of a decade ago differed most from its predecessors was in its insistence that only radical change to society could bring about genuine acceptance of homosexuality. The thrust of the gay movement over the past decade has been away from this perception toward the idea that all that is involved is the granting of civil rights to a new minority. Yet just as the black civil rights movement discovered the limits imposed by the economic structures of America, so the gay movement is discovering the real limits imposed by the sexual order.

Institutionalized racism has its counterpart in institutionalized heterosexism. As Edgar Friedenberg argued some years ago, homophobia is related to the social structure as a whole, and it flourishes in a society "that is dependent on [a] kind of self-mutilation to keep itself going and to keep people self-oppressing in the roles that they need to stay in if the society is to keep going."[7]

The gay movement, using that term in its broadest sense, involves a number of strands that are in a sense contradictory. This is clear in the relationships between gay women and gay men, where the very dynamics of developing an identity based on commitment to one's own sex makes genuine cosexual cooperation difficult to attain. It is clear in the practice of gay politics, where there is often tension between stressing what sets us apart from others as a way of creating gay community, and needing to demonstrate that we are really just like anyone else in order to win support for antidiscrimination ordinances. It is clearest in the apparent contradiction between the creation of a separate gay identity and the liberation of homosexual desire in society as a whole.

There are two discos on the main gay thoroughfare in Sydney, separated by no more than several hundred yards, that sum up this contradiction perfectly. One, which features drag shows and is full of beautiful young men of ambivalent sexuality, has become a favorite of many would-be swinging straights, to the point that many gay men will no longer go there. (Unfortunately gay women often meet with a hostility that is intended for straights.) The other is totally male, and much raunchier, with lots of men in leather. The first of these places represents the breaking down of the rigid dichotomy between gay and straight that is occurring in all Western societies. The second demonstrates the solidification of these distinctions that is equally and simultaneously taking place.

One can find counterparts to these places in most large Western cities, and the same distinctions exist in other parts of the gay world. Ten years ago I would have expected the first, rather than the second, of these discos to be the model for the future. I would also have anticipated that as more of us came out and lived openly as homosexuals, the question of our sexuality would become less rather than more important. That this has not happened is due in part to the depth of hostility toward homosexuality, a hostility only explicable in psychoanalytic terms. It suggests that while the dominant way of dealing with homosexuality in modern America has become the recognition of a homosexual minority, this is not sufficient to deal with the imperatives of homosexual desire. The creation of minority status both contains homosexuality by making it "the other" and simultaneously, by making it visible, poses us as a permanent reminder to nonhomosexuals of the possibility of a less repressed sexuality. This may help explain the preoccupation of the media with elements of gay life, such as leather bars, that can represent both the "otherness" *and* the sexuality of the homosexual (good examples are the films *Windows* and *Cruising*, the former about a predatory lesbian, as well as the CBS documentary "Gay Power, Gay Politics").

Homosexuality is not just the concern of homosexuals, but the emphasis of the past ten years has been to deny this, and almost to reintroduce notions of the third sex, with the assumption that homosexual desire is the exclusive property of self-identified homosexuals. My first book ended with a chapter called "The End of the Homosexual," in which I argued that true sexual liberation would mean the disappearance of the categories heterosexuality and homosexuality. Such claims still surface in gay writing; Lillian Faderman ends her study of female love and friendships with the same sentiment.[8] But in the process of writing this book, and partly due to the arguments of my editor, I have come to suspect that a homosexual identity is likely to persist even if we were able to attain something one might call sexual liberation. (This would not, of course, exclude a recognition that such an identity is a possibility for everyone.) A similar position seems to be adopted by Michel Foucault, who has recently spoken of the myth of polysexual liberation and the development of a gay life style:

Doesn't this introduce a diversification other than that which is due to social class, to job differences, to cultural levels, a diversification which might be also a form of relationship, and a "lifestyle." A lifestyle can be shared between individuals of different ages, positions, social activities. It can lead to intense relationships which don't resemble any that are so far institutionalized and it seems to me that a lifestyle can give birth to a culture and an ethic. To be "gay" is not, I believe, to identify with the psychological traits and visible signs of the homosexual, but rather the search to define and develop a lifestyle.[9]

Increasingly both the gay movement and its moralistic opponents see this as the central issue; the Moral Majority, in newspaper ads in the spring of 1981, proclaimed that "we . . . oppose any attempts by homosexuals to flaunt their perversion as an acceptable lifestyle and/or to attempt to force their lifestyle upon our children."[10]

The development of this new definition of being homosexual creates the possibility for us to be accepted, to be co-opted, or to be scapegoated, and it is in the interplay between these three modes that one can understand the reality of being gay in America today. The contrasts are encapsulated in the story of a San Francisco socialite who called a prominent local gay writer to invite "lots of nice gay men" to a fundraiser for victims of the recent earthquake in Italy. Patron of the fund was the Catholic archbishop of the city, who was at that stage being sued for refusing use of church facilities to the San Francisco Gay Men's Chorus. Ironically, there is in the United States a growing reversal of the position that homosexuality occupies in many so-called primitive societies; whereas, as in much of the Moslem world today, homosexuality is tolerated but homosexuals strongly condemned, now there is a situation in which homosexuals are at least partially accepted while homosexuality itself is feared and hated.

Under existing social conditions, to say someone is homosexual is to describe far more about a person than what he or she does in bed, which, as one wit suggested, may be the one place where homosexuals and heterosexuals do not much differ. An awareness of homosexuality affects us socially, in relationships with family, friends, and coworkers, and indeed on the most intimate levels of everyday life. Until recently there was a tendency to depict homosexuals as just like everyone else, except for the small matter of choice of partner. The burgeoning gay culture is beginning both to delineate—and itself to shape—the ways in which we are *not* just like everyone else.

In the early days of gay liberation, our sense of this difference was expressed in hostility to the family, a hostility that found ideological inspiration in the women's movement but was also shaped by the strong sense of alienation that existed all too often between homosexuals and their families. The sort of ties with one's blood family that are central to the writings of James Baldwin were inconceivable to large numbers of homosexuals, for whom coming out often meant literal rejection by parents and siblings.

Ten years later we are, I think, more aware of the complexities. For one thing, large numbers of homosexuals, women more than men, have turned out to be themselves parents, and it is hardly an accident that the eighties are seeing a proliferation of novels such as Joseph Hansen's *A Smile in His Lifetime* and Gordon Glasco's *Second Nature*, about married and formerly married homosexuals.

But we are becoming aware of the fact that despite the attempts by some of the more conservative and religious gay groups to institute gay marriages, it is precisely in the area of our central emotional relationships that we are most different, and this cannot really change until such time as there is the sort of genuine social acceptance that would allow, for example, the role of First Lady to be played by another man. Since we are still far from the time when even a conventional heterosexual woman can be regarded a serious contender for the presidency, I would not hold my breath waiting for the homosexualization of the White House.

In part because our growing self-assertion has not been accompanied by a corresponding degree of social acceptance, the pressures toward separatism have increased, much as was true for blacks in America in the period following the major push for civil rights in the early sixties. At this level we are experiencing the development of a genuine community, and one that is sometimes able to bridge the very real gaps between gay women and gay men. The very fact that —despite quite different attitudes toward sexuality in the lesbian and gay male worlds—we are both excluded from the social institutions of marriage and the family tends to pull us together. I personally find that even if on some levels my sexuality has more in common with that of straight men than with that of women, I feel more comfortable talking about my sexual and emotional life with lesbians, who are unlikely to believe that our relationships are somehow less real and less important than those sanctified by heterosexual marriage.

As we have become more secure in our identities and less prepared to accept either outright hostility or grudging tolerance, gay women and gay men have tended to spend more time apart from the heterosexual world, not just in search of sex but also for company, for shared humor and perceptions of the world. This has been a feature of homosexual life ever since an awareness of homosexual identity developed, but it has been strongly increased by the growing openness and self-confidence of the last decade. I have noticed in my own life that I willingly spend less time in heterosexual gatherings and depend more on the special intimacy and understanding that comes from being with other gays. In some ways this is an unfortunate development, although it does not prevent individual friendships with nonhomosexuals from persisting. It also seems an inevitable concomitant of the way in which American society is comprised of large numbers of self-conscious groups.

On the surface at least it seems as if the universalism of the early gay liberation movement has given way to a more realistic, and certainly a more American, emphasis on group identity, and the search for social recognition as part of a group. In many ways this has become a model for the rest of the world, as the idea of a discrete homosexual minority has become entrenched in most of the countries of the First World. Anthony Burgess, whose obsession with homosexuality makes him a keen observer of these things, noted in 1979 that "the best homosexuality is in America, like the best everything else, and California, where all national tendencies achieve their most hyperbolic expression, is a living beach of writhing male bodies."[11] (Burgess, apparently, was unaware of or uninterested in female homosexuality.) Whether it is the best or not, America has certainly become a model for many others, a vision of paradise for some, an early warning of perdition for others.

Most of my life since I first became involved in the American gay movement in 1970 and 1971 has been spent outside the United States, largely in Australia, but also in France and for short periods in other European countries and in Canada. Certainly my sense of a gay community extends across national borders; indeed the fact that homosexuals are less often restrained by family ties makes us voracious travelers. There is an important work of homosexual literary criticism waiting to be written around this theme, and the related one of homosexual writers in exile. In a sense the 1970s were a period when the homosexual writer was able to come home.

Most large Western cities today offer at least some of the characteristics of American gay life, and some have areas, like the Rue St. Anne in Paris, that are centers of gay night life. Yet it is also true that there is less social separation elsewhere than is the case in the United States. In Amsterdam, for example, I was told by officers of C.O.C., the principal Dutch gay organization, that they were pushing for housing policies—in most European countries governments are less willing to leave such matters to the benevolence of the market—that would ensure a mixture of gays and straights, singles and families in apartment houses. In Paris and Sydney, despite an extensive gay presence, there are no clearly demarcated gay areas, although homosexuals have played an important part in the restoration of several inner-city neighborhoods. The way in which homosexuals appear to live in a less segregated style in the Netherlands is suggested by the café and pub scenes in the Dutch film *Dear Boys.*

These differences are due in part to different historical and cultural traditions, in part to sheer numbers, and in part to the politics of those homosexuals who have come out (this is particularly important in Italy, in Spain, and in those Latin American countries where there are sufficient civil rights to allow at least some visible gay presence). To a far greater extent than is true in the United States, one finds a rejection of the idea of gay separatism. At its first congress in 1979 the Catalan Gay Liberation Front (F.A.G.C.) adopted "the strategical aim of dissolving the categories 'homosexual/heterosexual' ";[12] the equivalent group in Mexico, F.H.A.R., rejects the idea of "gay cops, or a gay ghetto like San Francisco."[13] The Dutch group, Rooie Flikkers, has argued that "there should no longer be a gay culture, produced by gays and directed at gays in their own safe environment,"[14] and in general openly gay writers in Europe seem less easily dismissed as of interest only to the homosexual minority than is the case in America. This would seem particularly the case in France, where the prestigious Prix Goncourt was awarded in 1980 to Yves Navarre for his openly homosexual novel *Le Jardin d'Acclimatation,* but even here acceptance is sometimes ambivalent: I remember watching a discussion on French television about Christopher Isherwood's *A Single Man* in 1980 that managed to avoid ever mentioning the homosexuality of the central character.

By and large Europeans seem more at ease with the possibility of homosexuality than are Americans, which might seem to reduce the need for homosexual self-assertion of the sort that is common in the United States. Yet there is no doubt that if we can speak of the homosexualization of America, we can also speak of the Americanization of the gay world elsewhere. In 1979, returning to Sydney after a sabbatical of four months, I was tempted to commence my report to the University with the sentence: "In the interests of research I have danced to 'In the Navy' on four continents." In Paris gay bars have adopted American names (the Bronx, the Manhattan, Le Village); across Europe the clone look is proliferating; in Australia lesbians are as familiar with the music of Holly Near and Meg Christian as their American sisters, and a Melbourne collective borrowed the name *Gay Community News* for their publication. It is possible that with time the American model of self-conscious gay separatism will become established elsewhere.

* * * * * * *

It might be argued that the twentieth century has seen homosexuals increasingly defined not just as a minority, but as that minority whose social role is to articulate opposition to repressive sexual norms. While I would be suspicious of so metaphysical a view, which comes close to seeking justification for our existence in some sort of transcendental purpose, it is true that our assertion is a reminder of the constant struggles around sexuality and power that are found in every civilization, and that, *pace* both Freud and sociobiology, explains a great deal about the way in which social life is organized. Over the past decade the very growth of a visible gay minority has helped define the sexual as one of the major current political and cultural battlegrounds.

It is because homosexuality is so central a symbol of the struggle between those who would impose one set of values and morality on all of us, and those who see in diversity a better possibility of creating a more genuinely moral society, that what happens to homosexuals affects all of American society. The murder of gays in the streets of San Francisco and New York has yet to reverberate through America in the same way as did the firebombings and police hoses in Selma, Alabama, in the early sixties, but, as was true of blacks then, we are a reminder to the liberal conscience that freedom and equality are indivisible.

This is not, by the way, a restatement of that rather inane sixties slogan that everyone should be free to do her or his own "thing." For the right to diversity does not give people the right to harm others, nor does it remove the responsibility for making moral choices. Gays can claim equality only if we are ourselves convinced that there is no moral disadvantage to being sexually and emotionally attracted to members of the same sex—that there are *social* disadvantages is the basis for our consciousness of oppression—and that in a good society such preferences would be irrelevant. We can only fight the bigots and their new liberal allies if we do in fact believe that gay is just as good as straight, even when gay behavior does more than mimic heterosexual respectability.

The clash with the New Right often involves a conflict over rights; they argue that parents have the right to oversee their children's reading, that fetuses have the right to be born, that people have the right not to be exposed to pornography or acts of sex. In one sense this is the basic American conflict between individual rights and majority rule, now expressed increasingly around issues of sexual and personal behavior. When the Moral Majority and the Reaganites speak of rights and freedoms they almost always use these words to mean their right to interfere with the lives of others.

The early gay liberation movement defined itself as anticapitalist, arguing that only with the overthrow of capitalism could we find genuine sexual liberation. Certainly homosexuals, especially those who are white and middle class, can find a place within capitalist societies; the advertising columns of *The Advocate* or *Mandate* are testimony to this. But like both feminists and Marxists, I doubt whether liberation means only the right to our own resort areas and leather bars (and even the latter have recently been under real attack from the state). Any liberation movement must confront the way in which its particular oppression is bound up with the general fabric of power and ideology in a given society, and calculate the limits to what can be attained within the confines of the existing system. Only major changes in the social and ideological structures of American society, for example, could achieve a situation where police genuinely protected rather than harassed homosexuals, where openly gay parents were not discriminated against in custody cases, where homosexuality was discussed in a nonprejudicial way in the mass media and schools.

There is no doubt that most American homosexuals remain unconvinced of this position, that many, in fact, are ardent supporters of President Reagan and the unreconstructed conservatism for which he stands. One of the dilemmas for many gay activists is how to reconcile the development of a mass movement with the political conservatism of so many homosexuals. So far those of us who are anarchists or socialists in our politics have been less influential in the way the gay movement is evolving than are the liberals of the N.G.T.F., the gay Democratic clubs, and the various business councils.

It is easy to react to the frequent expressions of conservatism one encounters in the gay world by seeing the whole business of gay politics as very self-indulgent; how can one worry about the closing of bathhouses when people are being slaughtered in El Salvador and dying of hunger in the ghettos (the *real* ghettos). Such a feeling is not uncommon among leftists, and it would be silly to respond purely by branding them as homophobes. If, in fact, it were a matter of simply choosing between whether to save people from napalm or to keep open the bathhouses, such arguments would be convincing, but this is not how politics works; it is the same people by and large who are responsible for both types of oppression. It is a large generalization to say that those people who are committed to a more egalitarian and participatory view of politics are also those least inclined to persecute homosexuals, but since the end of the nineteenth century there has in fact been a fairly consistent link between supporters of homosexual rights and, if not the left (for left authoritarians are as homophobic as their right-wing counterparts), at least those people on the left who believe that socialism means the extension of freedom, not its restriction. In the end I believe homosexuals have reasons of self-interest as well as of ethics to support progressive and egalitarian politics.

The process of liberation implies that our homosexuality becomes both more and less important. More, for the majority of homosexuals are still a long way from accepting themselves as gay, and only the communal sense provided by the gay world can overcome their internalized doubts and hatreds. Less, for were society as a whole also able to accept homosexuality, there would be far less reason to constantly assert our identity. There are times when I am weary of talking about being homosexual, when I resort to small subterfuges with strangers not because I am ashamed, but because I don't want to have to constantly explain myself. (This is undoubtedly one reason why, as more of us become open, we also feel the need to segregate ourselves socially.) Unfortunately, just as blacks cannot escape the constant presence of racism, neither can gays avoid the pressures of a heterosexist society—and what a previous generation felt obliged to ignore we now feel pressured to challenge.

But our attention cannot be concentrated exclusively on the external society. As a growing sense of gay community comes into being, we need develop an internal critique and ethics to deal with the way in which we treat one another. Too often gay radicals have sought to explain away all the features of gay life that we dislike as being the result of either heterosexism or exploitation. These are real factors, and it is certainly true that much of the self-help literature and therapy that has flourished in recent years tends to ignore the way in which social pressures limit our abilities to remake ourselves. It is also true that one of our major tasks, and one at which I suspect gay women have been far more imaginative than gay men, is to construct a value system and a set of institutions that can allow us to live more fulfilling and communal lives.

It is not only homophobes who see the gay world, particularly the gay male world, as cold and unfeeling. The German filmmaker Rosa von Praunheim wrote of the California gay scene:

> It is very difficult to make real contact with people; superficial
> conveyor belt relations are easy enough, but real human relations
> are not what people want here. Men must be hard and cold,
> unfeeling and unsentimental, and you can only stand that for a
> certain length of time. The world in which gays live here is marked
> by a tremendous spiritual impoverishment.[15]

There might be a degree of hyperbole in this observation, but too many people have made it (and not only about California) for me to doubt that there is an element of truth in it. The transition from a commercial gay world to a genuine gay community (which would, of course, include commercial ventures) is by no means an accomplished fact.

Because we are excluded from the conventional means of happiness, because we have no real role models on which to base our lives other than those borrowed from the larger heterosexual world, the need to develop this sense of community and our own morality is all the greater. I am not thinking here of what is usually thrown up against homosexuals, namely our so-called promiscuity and the relatively small number of lifelong relations. The latter is becoming more and more the social norm, and the former is often the mark of a far healthier attitude toward sexuality than is true of society as a whole. What is disturbing is the degree to which much of the gay world rests on a sea of alcohol and drugs, and the inability of so many gays to relate to each other on more than the most superficial level.

That this should be the case is hardly surprising; the self-hatred generated by social oppression is often most clearly reflected in the way people relate to each other. But the process of liberation itself has its casualties, as recent feminist literature has demonstrated. As we come to see traditional moral strictures as repressive and homophobic, we find ourselves in a moral and ethical vacuum. In their very different ways, writers such as Sally Gearhart, John Rechy, Jane Rule, and Doric Wilson are addressing the problems this raises. The development of our own values and ethics, more relevant to our lives than the handed-down shibboleths of conventional morality, is perhaps the chief task of the new gay culture.

This seems to me clearest in regard to two areas: the relationships between women and men, and the quite considerable presence of racism in the gay world. Over the past decade there has been a marked deterioration in the relationships between gay women and gay men, perhaps an inevitable consequence of social separatism, but nonetheless enormously unfortunate in both political and personal terms. Many men who in the early seventies were proud to call themselves feminists now no longer claim that label; many women have wearied of the blindness of gay men to their position and concluded, with Del Martin, that "so long as there's a put-down of lesbians, an indifference to our issues and complete male domination of how things are going to go, then obviously the place for us to be is in the Women's Movement."[16] Sometimes this position is expressed in extraordinarily vituperative terms, as in this claim by an unnamed lesbian-feminist: "Many gay men are not rapists, but murderers . . . by living in a world from which women are excluded, such gay men to all intents and purposes annihilate women."[17]

Yet gay women and gay men need each other, both as political allies and, separatist rhetoric aside, as friends, for a world in which one knows only one sex is that much poorer an environment. With some exceptions, the disinterest of gay men in women's issues and the hostility of gay women to much of the gay male movement are reinforcing this separation, but its roots go far deeper than political differences; undoubtedly for many homosexuals there is something threatening in the idea of intimacy with the other sex (especially, perhaps, for women who have experienced real male aggression). Ironically, it may be easier for gays than for other people to develop a genuinely equal basis for relating between the sexes, for both gay women and gay men are victims of the institutionalized norms of sexuality and sex roles, even if they experience their impact somewhat differently.

Just as there has been a decline in the links between women and men in the gay world over the past decade, so too, I suspect, there has been a decline in relationships between blacks and whites, at least in the male gay world (I am less sure about the female). Perhaps this is only an illusion, and all that has really changed is our awareness of it; only the radical wing of the gay movement shows any concern for the fact that it is disproportionately white. When I attended the Florida Lesbian and Gay Conference in May 1981 there were perhaps three blacks present among several hundred delegates (and as far as I could tell, no Hispanics); what was most striking was that none of the whites seemed concerned or even aware of this. In San Francisco the gay male scene is again very largely white, and both blacks and Asians have organized to protest discrimination from commercial establishments.[18] More insidious is the lack of contact between white and nonwhite homosexuals at a social level; whereas ten years ago I wrote that, even if white homosexuals were as likely to be racist as their heterosexual counterparts, they were also more likely to mix with blacks, I now wonder whether this is really true.

The gay world often seems to exaggerate the characteristics of the broader society, and it would be naive to expect it to be free of class division, racism, sexism, exploitation, and drug dependence. It is not, however, naive to argue that the creation of a real gay community means struggling with these issues, nor to question a celebration of our life style that ignores such inconvenient questions as discrimination and alcoholism. If there is to be a politics and a culture based on the "gay minority," it must go beyond the image of young, affluent, white males that is the dominant picture presented by the commercial gay media.

When the idea of coming out was first postulated ten years ago as the basic meaning of gay liberation, we tended to think of it as a one-off, dramatic action that would transform our individual lives and collectively revolutionize the society. Over the past decade it has become clear that coming out is a long and complex process, one that involves not merely the assertion of a gay identity but the creation of new standards of behavior that will allow us to live in ways we are only beginning to imagine. Most minorities are held together by a desire to preserve their past against the encroachments of centralization and "modernization." The gay minority may be the only one that is held together by the attempt to create a *new* identity and a *new* sense of community. We are a product of both social pressures and our own responses to these pressures; as hostility to our self-assertion increases, it has the effect of strengthening the sense of identity it wishes to deny.

* * * * * * *

It may seem odd to assert that America is being homosexualized while pointing to the growth of gay separatism. It is true, however, that the recognition of group identity allows minorities to influence the broader culture; in this sense one can see that gays are following in the tradition of those ethnic groups, such as Jews and blacks, whose self-assertion dramatically increased their social and cultural impact. The gay impact is immediately obvious if one looks at a book like Fran Lebowitz's *Metropolitan Life* or the cartoons in *Christopher Street* magazine: in one cartoon collection from the latter I found references to gay themes in gentrification, fashion, disco, high culture, and the cult of Bette Midler.[19] Urban life in the eighties bears the very considerable mark of gay influence.

But by homosexualization I have meant something broader and probably more significant. The conditions of consumer capitalism have provided the opportunities for an unprecedented variety of life styles, in which gay women and gay men are often the most adventurous pioneers. Of course the traditional canons of sexual and familial morality have always been more honored in rhetoric than in reality. Nevertheless it is only over the past fifteen years or so that one could really speak of their collapse, both in terms of behavior

and as a legitimizing and unifying value system. It is precisely because there is no longer one dominant set of standards for social and
emotional life that homosexuals can successfully challenge the view
of us as deviants, and that the Moral Majority is mounting so
hysterical a counterattack. America—and other Western societies—
is becoming homosexualized in the sense that more people are
behaving in the way traditionally ascribed to homosexuals, and that
lesbians and gay men are exploring models for living everyday life
that are relevant to everyone.

Prophecy is a dangerous venture. Ten years ago I would have
expected a greater integration of homosexuality and homosexuals
into the mainstream than has in fact occurred; who is to say that the
present trend, which by and large is in the opposite direction, might
not be reversed? Such reservations aside, I suspect at least three of
the present trends will continue for the foreseeable future, both in
the United States and, with some modifications, in those countries
where there is sufficient space, both social and political, to allow
homosexuals to exist. Gay women and gay men will continue to
assert an identity and a culture, and through this assertion we will
ensure that our minority status is strengthened. The gay minority
and culture that is developing will impinge more obviously on the
larger society, in particular because unlike other minorities we are
not restricted by barriers of class or geography. And sexuality will
remain a battleground for much of our politics, a battleground in
which homosexuals will inevitably remain in the front lines.

If the idea of the homosexual is a product of the nineteenth
century, then the idea of seeing her/him in sociological rather than
psychological terms, as a member of a minority rather than as an
aberrant individual, is largely a product of the 1970s. It is the gradual
working through of this new perception, which simultaneously creates and delimits us, that Jean-Paul Aron had in mind when he spoke
of homosexuals being "acclaimed, proclaimed and at the same time
straight-jacketed."[20] In the short run the changes are positive, for
they have greatly expanded our possibilities and created a new sense
of identity and self-worth for millions of people who previously were
badly scarred by internalized oppression. It may be, as Jean-Paul
Sartre said shortly before his death, that: "Homosexuals should reject this society, but the only thing that they can hope for at present
in certain countries is a kind of free space, where they can come
together among themselves, as in the United States."[21] In the long
run it would be nice to hope that we can escape the limitations on
individual potential and diversity that all categories impose.

NOTES

1 Rosemary Pringle, "Sexuality and Social Change," *Island* magazine (Hobart, Tasmania), No. 7, June 1981, p. 35.

2 Seymour Kleinberg, *Alienated Affections* (New York: St. Martin's Press, 1980), p. 179.

3 Quoted in Ted Morgan, *Somerset Maugham* (New York: Simon and Schuster, 1980), p. 81.

4 Frank Howell, "Boy/Man Love Goes Public," *Bay Area Reporter*, June 18, 1981.

5 See, for example, Joan Nestle, "Butch-Fem Relationships," *Heresies* (New York), No. 12, 1981.

6 Vito Russo, "Glad to Be a Clone," *Gay News* (London), No. 197, August 21, 1980.

7 Edgar Friedenberg, "Homophobic Society," in *The Universities and the Gay Experience*, Proceedings of the Gay Academic Union, November 1973, p. 42.

8 Lillian Faderman, *Surpassing the Love of Men* (New York: William Morrow, 1981), p. 415.

9 Interview with Michel Foucault, "De l'Amitié comme mode de vie," *Le Gai Pied*, No. 25, April 1981, p. 39.

10 Quoted by Scott Tucker, "Gays to Canada: No More Shit!" *New York Native*, No. 11, May 4, 1981.

11 Anthony Burgess, "Notes from the Blue Coast," *Saturday Review*, April 28, 1979, p. 10.

12 F.A.G.C. International Monthly Newsletter, No. 3, September 1979.

13 Quoted by Scott Tucker, "Gays and Lesbians and Latin America," *Gay Community News*, May 16, 1981, p. 9.

14 Quoted by Terry Helbing, "Gay Plays, Gay Theatre, Gay Performance," *The Drama Review*, No. 89, March 1981, p. 42.

15 Rosa von Praunheim, *Army of Lovers* (London: Gay Men's Press, 1980), p. 21.

16 Interview with Del Martin, "Twenty-four Years of Activism," *Gay Community News*, May 5, 1979, p. 10.

17 Quoted by Johanna H. Stuckey, "The Politics of Powerlessness," *Body Politic*, No. 63, May 1980, p. 29.

18 See Scott Anderson, "Discrimination," *The Advocate*, February 19, 1981.

19 See Fran Lebowitz, *Metropolitan Life* (New York: E. P. Dutton, 1978), and Charles Ortleb and Richard Fiala, *Le Gay Ghetto* (New York: St. Martin's Press, 1980).

20 Jean-Paul Aron and Roger Kempf, "Triumphs and Tribulations of the

Homosexual Discourse," George Stambolian and Elaine Marks, eds., *Homosexualities and French Literature* (Ithaca N.Y.: Cornell University Press, 1979), p. 156.

21 Jean-Paul Sartre, "The Final Interview," *Christopher Street*, July–August 1980, p. 37 (originally published in *Le Gai Pied*, April 1980).

Bibliography

Note: This bibliography lists those works that I have found most useful in working on this book. For the sake of brevity I have omitted almost all articles, though a complete bibliography would rely heavily on such publications as *Body Politic, The Furies,* and *Christopher Street* magazine. In most cases I have also omitted those works that are already listed in the bibliography to my earlier book, *Homosexual: Oppression and Liberation.*

Adam, Barry. *The Survival of Domination.* New York: Elsevier, 1978.

Altman, Dennis. *Coming Out in the Seventies.* Sydney: Wild and Woolley, 1979; also shortened version, Boston: Alyson Publications, 1981.

————. *Homosexual: Oppression and Liberation.* New York: Avon Books, 1973.

Andrews, Terry. *The Story of Harold.* New York: Avon Books, 1975.

Austen, Roger. *Playing the Game: The Homosexual Novel in America.* Indianapolis: Bobbs Merrill, 1977.

Baldwin, James. *Giovanni's Room.* New York: The Dial Press, 1956.

————. *Just Above My Head.* New York: The Dial Press, 1979.

Barbadette, Gilles, and Carassou, Michel. *Paris Gay 1925.* Paris: Presses de la Renaissance, 1981.

Barnett, R. *Sexual Freedom and the Constitution.* Albuquerque: University of New Mexico Press, 1973.

Bayer, Ronald. *Homosexuality and American Psychiatry.* New York: Basic Books, 1981.

Becker, Howard. *Outsiders: Studies in the Sociology of Deviance.* New York: The Free Press, 1964.

Bell, Alan, and Weinberg, Martin. *Homosexualities.* New York: Simon and Schuster, 1978.

Bell, Alan, Weinberg, Martin, and Hammersmith, Sue Kiefer. *Sexual Preference: Its Development in Men and Women.* Bloomington: Indiana University Press, 1981.

Bell, Arthur. *Kings Don't Mean a Thing.* New York: William Morrow, 1978.

Bengis, Ingrid. *Combat in the Erogenous Zone.* New York: Alfred A. Knopf, 1972.

Benson, E. F. *Make Way for Lucia.* New York: Thomas Y. Crowell, 1977.

Birdstone, Alabama. *Queer Free.* New York: Calamus, 1981.

Birkby, Phyllis et al. *Amazon Expedition.* New York: Times Change, 1973.

Blais, Marie-Claire. *Le Loup.* Montreal: Editions du Jour, 1972.

———. *Nights in the Underground.* Don Mills, Ontario: Musson, 1979.

Bocock, Robert. *Freud and Modern Society.* London: Nelson, 1978.

Bory, Jean-Louis, and Hocquenghem, Guy. *Comment Nous Appelez Vous Déjà?.* Paris: Calmann-Levy, 1977.

Boswell, John. *Christianity, Social Tolerance, and Homosexuality.* Chicago: University of Chicago Press, 1980.

Bradley, Marion Zimmer. *The Catch Trap.* New York: Ballantine Books, 1979.

———. *The Ruins of Isis.* New York: Pocket Books, 1979.

Brown, Rita Mae. *A Plain Brown Rapper.* Oakland, Ca.: Diana Press, 1976.

———. *Rubyfruit Jungle.* Plainfield, Vt.: Daughters, Inc., 1973.

Burgess, Anthony. *Earthly Powers.* London: Hutchinson, 1980.

Burroughs, William. *Cities of the Red Night.* New York: Holt, Rinehart & Winston, 1981.

Califia, Pat. *Sapphistry: The Book of Lesbian Sexuality.* Tallahassee, Fla.: Naiad Press, 1980.

Callenbach, Ernest. *Ecotopia.* Berkeley, Ca.: Banyan Tree Books, 1975.

Chodorow, Nancy. *The Reproduction of Mothering.* Berkeley, Ca.: University of California Press, 1978.

Crawford, Alan. *Thunder on the Right.* New York: Pantheon Books, 1980.

Crew, Louie. *The Gay Academic.* Palm Springs: Etc. Publications, 1976.

Crisp, Quentin. *The Naked Civil Servant.* New York: New American Library, 1978.

Crowley, Mart. *The Boys in the Band.* New York: Farrar Straus & Giroux, 1968.

Daly, Mary. *Gyn/Ecology: The Metaethics of Radical Feminism.* Boston: Beacon Press, 1978.

Dannecker, Martin. *Theories of Homosexuality.* London: Gay Men's Press, 1981.

Delaney, Samuel. *Dahlgren.* New York: Bantam Books, 1979.

———. *Tales of Nevèrÿon.* New York: Bantam Books, 1979.

DeLynn, Jane. *Some Do.* New York: Macmillan, 1978.

Denneny, Michael. *Lovers: The Story of Two Men.* New York: Avon Books, 1979.

Dick, Philip. *The Man in the High Castle.* New York: Berkley, 1974.

Dreuilhe, A. E. *La Société Invertie.* Montreal: Flammarion, 1979.

Duvert, Tony. *Le Bon Sexe Illustré.* Paris: Editions de Minuit, 1974.

———. *L'Ile Atlantique.* Paris: Editions de Minuit, 1979.

Dyer, Richard, ed. *Gays and Film.* London: British Film Institute, 1977.

Evans, Arthur. *Witchcraft and the Gay Counterculture.* Boston: Fag Rag Books, 1978.

Faderman, Lillian. *Surpassing the Love of Men.* New York: William Morrow, 1981.

Faust, Beatrice. *Women, Sex and Pornography.* New York: Macmillan, 1981.

Fernandez, Dominique. *L'Etoile Rose.* Paris: Grasset, 1978.

———. *Une Fleur de Jasmin à l'Oreille.* Paris: Grasset, 1980.

Fernbach, David. *The Spiral Path*. Boston: Alyson Publications, 1981.

Fierstein, Harvey. *The Torchsong Trilogy*. New York: Gay Presses of New York, 1981.

Fisher, Pete, and Rubin, Marc. *Special Teacher/Special Boys*. New York: St. Martin's Press, 1979.

Forster, E. M. *The Life to Come and Other Stories*. New York: W. W. Norton, 1973.

————. *Maurice*. New York: New American Library, 1975.

Foucault, Michel. *The History of Sexuality, Vol. I*. New York: Vintage Books, 1980.

————. *The Order of Things: An Archaeology of the Human Sciences*. New York: Pantheon Books, 1970.

Freud, Sigmund. *The Standard Edition of the Complete Psychological Works*. Edited by James Strachey. 24 vols. London: Hogarth Press, 1953–1973.

Fricke, Aaron. *Reflections of a Rock Lobster*. Boston: Alyson Publications, 1981.

Gagnon, J. H., and Simon, William. *Sexual Conduct*. Chicago: Aldine, 1973.

Gay Left Collective. *Homosexuality: Power and Politics*. London: Allison & Busby, 1980.

Gearhart, Sally. *The Wanderground*. Watertown, Mass.: Persephone, 1979.

Genet, Jean. *Funeral Rites*. New York: Grove Press, 1969.

Gibson, E. Lawrence. *Get Off My Ship: Ensign Berg vs. the U.S. Navy*. New York: Avon Books, 1978.

Glasco, Gordon. *Second Nature*. New York: St. Martin's Press, 1981.

Goffman, Erving. *Stigma: Notes on the Management of Spoiled Identity*. Englewood Cliffs, N. J.: Prentice-Hall, 1963.

Grahn, Judy. *The Work of a Common Woman*. New York: St. Martin's Press, 1978.

Grumbach, Doris. *Chamber Music*. New York: E. P. Dutton, 1977.

Hall, Radclyffe. *The Well of Loneliness*. New York: Pocket Books, 1975.

Hall, Richard. *The Butterscotch Prince.* New York: Pyramid Books, 1975.

Hamilton, Wallace. *Kevin.* New York: St. Martin's Press, 1980.

Hansen, Joseph. *A Smile in His Lifetime.* New York: Holt, Rinehart & Winston, 1981.

Harris, Bertha. *Lover.* Houston: Daughters, 1976.

Harris, Bertha, and Sisley, Emily. *The Joy of Lesbian Sex.* New York: Crown, 1977.

Hebdige, Dick. *Subculture: The Meaning of Style.* London: Methuen, 1979.

Heger, Heinz. *The Men with the Pink Triangle.* Boston: Alyson Publications, 1980.

Heresies. No. 12 ("sex issue"). New York, 1981.

Highsmith, Patricia. *Strangers on a Train.* Baltimore: Penguin Books, 1979.

Hoch, Paul. *White Hero, Black Beast.* London: Pluto Press, 1979.

Hocquenghem, Guy. *Homosexual Desire.* London: Allison & Busby, 1978.

Hoffman, Martin. *The Gay World.* New York: Basic Books, 1968.

Hoffman, William, ed. *Gay Plays.* New York: Avon Books, 1979.

Holleran, Andrew. *Dancer from the Dance.* New York: William Morrow, 1978.

Horowitz, Gad. *Repression.* Toronto: University of Toronto Press, 1977.

Humphreys, Laud. *Tearoom Trade: Impersonal Sex in Public Places,* new ed. Hawthorn, N. Y.: Aldine Publishing Co., 1975.

Hunt, Morton. *Sexual Behavior in the 1970s.* Chicago: Playboy Press, 1974.

Isherwood, Christopher: *Christopher and His Kind.* London: Methuen, 1977.

———. *A Single Man.* London: Methuen, 1964.

Jay, Karla, and Young, Allen. *After You're Out.* New York: Pyramid Books, 1975.

———. *The Gay Report.* New York: Summit Books, 1979.

———. *Lavender Culture.* New York: Jove/HBJ, 1979.

Katz, Jonathan. *Gay American History.* New York: Thomas Y. Crowell, 1976.

Kinsey, A. C., Pomeroy W., and Martin, C. E. *Sexual Behavior in the Human Male.* Philadelphia: W. B. Saunders, 1948.

Kinsey, A. C. et al. *Sexual Behavior in the Human Female.* Philadelphia: W. B. Saunders, 1953.

Klaich, Doris. *Woman Plus Woman: Attitudes towards Lesbianism.* New York: William Morrow, 1978.

Kleinberg, Seymour. *Alienated Affections.* New York: St. Martin's Press, 1980.

Kramer, Larry. *Faggots.* New York: Random House, 1978.

Lahr, John. *Prick Up Your Ears: The Biography of Joe Orton.* New York: Alfred A. Knopf, 1978.

Lasch, Christopher. *The Culture of Narcissism.* New York: W. W. Norton, 1978.

Le Guin, Ursula K. *The Dispossessed.* New York: Harper & Row, 1974.

Levine, Martin, ed. *Gay Men.* New York, Harper & Row, 1979.

Leyland, Winston, ed. *Gay Sunshine Interviews.* San Francisco: Gay Sunshine Press, 1978.

————, ed. *Now the Volcano.* San Francisco: Gay Sunshine Press, 1979.

Mackenzie, Compton. *Extraordinary Women.* London: Martin Secker, 1928.

Marcuse, Herbert. *Eros and Civilization.* Boston: Beacon Press, 1955.

Marmor, Judd, ed. *Homosexual Behavior.* New York: Basic Books, 1980.

Martin, Del, and Lyons, Phyllis. *Lesbian/Woman.* New York: Bantam Books, 1972.

Martin, Robert. *The Homosexual Tradition in American Poetry.* Austin: University of Texas Press, 1979.

Masters, William, and Johnson, Virginia. *Homosexuality in Perspective.* Boston: Little, Brown, 1979.

Maupin, Armistead. *Tales of the City.* New York: Harper & Row, 1978.

Mieli, Mario. *Homosexuality and Liberation.* London: Gay Men's Press, 1980.

Millett, Kate. *Sexual Politics.* New York: Doubleday, 1970.

———. *Sita.* New York: Farrar Straus & Giroux, 1977.

Mitchell, Juliet. *Psychoanalysis and Feminism.* London: Allen Lane, 1974.

Mitzel, John. *The Boston Sex Scandal.* Boston: Glad Day Books, 1980.

———, ed. *Myra and Gore.* Dorchester, Mass.: Manifest Destiny, 1974.

Morgan, Robin. *Monster.* New York: Vintage Books, 1972.

Morgan, Ted. *Somerset Maugham.* New York: Simon and Schuster, 1980.

Morris, Meaghan, and Patton, Paul. *Michel Foucault: Power, Truth, Strategy.* Sydney: Feral Publications, 1979.

Padgug, Robert, ed. *Radical History Review* (sexuality issue). Spring/Summer 1979.

Pasolini, Pier Paolo. *A Violent Life.* London: Jonathan Cape, 1968.

Patrick, Robert. *Mercy Drop and Other Plays.* New York: Calamus, 1981.

Peyrefitte, Roger. *The Exile of Capri.* London: Secker & Warburg, 1961.

Picano, Felice. *The Lure.* New York: Delacorte Press, 1979.

———, ed. *A True Likeness.* New York: Sea Horse Press, 1981.

Plummer, Ken, ed. *The Making of the Modern Homosexual.* London: Hutchinson, 1981.

von Praunheim, Rosa. *Army of Lovers.* London: Gay Men's Press, 1980.

Price, Richard. *Ladies' Man.* New York: Houghton Mifflin, 1978.

Puig, Manuel. *Kiss of the Spider Woman.* New York: Alfred A. Knopf, 1979.

Ramsey, Lynn. *Gigolos.* Englewood Cliffs, N.J.: Prentice-Hall, 1978.

Raymond, Janice. *The Transsexual Empire.* Boston: Beacon Press, 1979.

Rechy, John. *City of Night.* New York: Grove Press, 1963.

———. *Rushes.* New York: Grove Press, 1979.

———. *The Sexual Outlaw.* New York: Grove Press, 1977.

Renault, Mary. *The Charioteer.* London: Longmans, 1953.

———. *The Persian Boy.* New York: Pantheon Books, 1972.

Rich, Adrienne. *On Lies, Secrets and Silence.* New York: W. W. Norton, 1979.

Richmond, Len, and Noguera, Gary. *The New Gay Liberation Book.* Palo Alto: Ramparts Press, 1979.

Roazen, Paul. *Freud and His Followers.* New York: Alfred A. Knopf, 1975.

Robinson, Paul. *The Freudian Left.* New York: Harper & Row, 1969.

————. *The Modernization of Sex.* New York: Harper & Row, 1977.

Rodgers, Bruce. *The Queen's Vernacular: A Gay Lexicon.* San Francisco: Straight Arrow, 1972.

Rossner, Judith. *Looking for Mr. Goodbar.* New York: Simon and Schuster, 1975.

Roth, Philip. *Our Gang.* New York: Random House, 1971.

Rowbotham, Sheila, and Weeks, Jeffrey. *Socialism and the New Life.* London: Pluto, 1977.

Rule, Jane. *Desert of the Heart.* New York: W. W. Norton, 1976.

————. *Lesbian Images.* New York: Doubleday, 1975.

Russ, Joanna. *The Female Man.* Boston: Gregg Press, 1977.

Russo, Vito. *The Celluloid Closet.* New York: Harper & Row, 1981.

Sarton, May. *A Reckoning.* New York: W. W. Norton, 1978.

————. *Mrs. Stevens Hears the Mermaids Singing.* New York: W. W. Norton, 1975.

Sartre, Jean-Paul. *Intimacy.* New York: New Directions, 1948.

Seabrook, Jeremy. *A Lasting Relationship.* London: Allen Lane, 1976.

Semiotext(e). Loving Boys (special issue). New York, June 1980.

Sennett, Richard. *The Fall of Public Man.* New York: Alfred A. Knopf, 1977.

Sherman, Martin. *Bent.* New York: Avon Books, 1980.

Shilts, Randy. *The Mayor of Castro Street.* New York: St. Martin's Press, 1982.

Shorter, Edward. *The Making of the Modern Family.* New York: Basic Books, 1975.

Silverstein, Charles. *Man to Man: Gay Couples in America.* New York: William Morrow, 1981.

Silverstein, Charles, and White, Edmund. *The Joy of Gay Sex.* New York: Crown, 1977.

Simpson, Ruth. *From the Closets to the Courts.* New York: The Viking Press, 1976.

Singer, Rochelle. *The Demeter Flower.* New York: St. Martin's Press, 1980.

Sisley, Emily. *The Novel Writers.* New York: Mosaic Press, 1980.

Slater, Philip. *Footholds: Understanding the Shifting Sexual and Family Tensions in Our Culture.* New York: E. P. Dutton, 1977.

Snyder, William. *Tory's.* New York: Avon Books, 1981.

Soble, Alan, ed. *Philosophy of Sex.* Totowa, N.J.: Littlefield, Adams, 1980.

Sontag, Susan. *Against Interpretation.* New York: Farrar Straus & Giroux, 1966.

―――. *Under the Sign of Saturn.* New York: Farrar Straus & Giroux, 1980.

Stambolian, George, and Marks, Elaine, eds. *Homosexualities and French Literature.* Ithaca, N.Y.: Cornell University Press, 1979.

Stevenson, Richard. *Death Trick.* New York: St. Martin's Press, 1981.

Steward, Samuel. *Chapters from an Autobiography.* San Francisco: Grey Fox, 1981.

Stoller, Richard. *Perversion: The Erotic Form of Hatred.* New York: Basic Books, 1975.

Szasz, Thomas. *The Manufacture of Madness.* New York: Harper & Row, 1970.

Symons, Donald. *The Evolution of Human Sexuality.* New York: Oxford University Press, 1979.

Talese, Gay. *Thy Neighbor's Wife.* New York: Doubleday, 1980.

Taylor, G. Rattray. *Sex in History.* New York: Ballantine Books, 1954.

Tripp, C. A. *The Homosexual Matrix.* New York: McGraw-Hill Book Co., 1975.

Vidal, Gore. *Homage to Daniel Shays.* New York: Random House, 1972.

————. *Myra Breckinridge.* Boston: Little, Brown, 1968.

————. *Sex is Politics: An Essay.* Los Angeles: Sylvester & Orphanus, 1979.

Walker, Gerald. *Cruising.* New York: Stein and Day, 1970.

Walters, Margaret. *The Nude Male.* New York: Paddington Press, 1978.

Warren, Patricia Nell. *The Beauty Queen.* New York: William Morrow, 1978.

————. *The Fancy Dancer.* New York: William Morrow, 1976.

————. *The Front Runner.* New York: William Morrow, 1974.

Weeks, Jeffrey. *Coming Out.* London: Quartet, 1977.

Weinberg, George. *Society and the Healthy Homosexual.* New York: St. Martin's Press, 1972.

Welles, Paul. *Project Lambda.* Port Washington, N. Y.: Ashley Books, 1979.

White, Edmund. *Nocturnes for the King of Naples.* New York: St. Martin's Press, 1978.

————. *States of Desire.* New York: E. P. Dutton, 1980.

Whitmore, George. *The Confessions of Danny Slocum.* New York: St. Martin's Press, 1980.

Williams, Tennessee. *Hard Candy.* New York: New Directions, 1959.

————. *Memoirs.* New York: Doubleday, 1975.

Willis, Ellen. *Beginning to See the Light.* New York: Alfred A. Knopf, 1981.

Wilson, Doric. *Two Plays.* New York: Sea Horse Press, 1979.

Wilson, Edward. *On Human Nature.* Cambridge, Mass.: Harvard University Press, 1978.

Wittig, Monique. *The Guérillères.* London: Peter Owen, 1971.

Wittig, Monique, and Zeig, Sande. *Lesbian Peoples: Materials for a Dictionary.* New York: Avon Books, 1979.

Wolf, Deborah. *The Lesbian Community.* Berkeley, Ca.: University of California Press, 1979.

Index

Abzug, Bella, 116
Adam, Barry, 89
Advertising, 95, 199
Advocate, The,
  (newspaper), 164, 165
After Dark (magazine), 17
Albee, Edward, 160
Allen, Woody, 87
Alternative life style,
  homosexuality as an, 6.
  See also Life style
American Psychiatric
  Association, 5, 26
Amory, Richard, 152
Anal intercourse, 177,
  178
Anderson, Robert, 57
Anderson, Scott, 20
Andrews, Terry, 193
Antidiscrimination
  ordinances, 3, 24, 25,
  110, 124, 131
Antisodomy statutes, (laws
  prohibiting homosexual
  behavior), 24, 25, 109,
  110, 124, 131
Apuzzo, Virginia, 128
Argentina, 50, 109
Aron, Jean-Paul, 224
Artists, 147
Askew, Reuben, 26
Auden, W. H., 148
Australia, 24, 25, 90, 101,
  154
Austria, 24
Authoritarian societies
  (totalitarian states), 51,
  62, 90, 109

Bachelors for Wallace,
  112–13

Backlash against gays in
  the 1980s, 128–31, 140
Bahlmann, Lynn, 15
Baldwin, James, 64, 135
Ballet, 154
Barnes, Djuana, 150
Bars, 21
Baths, 17, 79–83
Bayer, Ronald, 26
Bayh, Birch, 128
Beach, Frank, 48
Bearchell, Chris, 163
Bell, Alan, 52, 57, 62,
  178, 189
Bell, Arthur, 30
Ben, Lisa, 164
Benkert, Karoly, 4, 111
Bentley, Eric, 150
Bieber, Irving, 40
Biological basis for
  homosexuality, 44
Bisexuality, 15–16, 41–43,
  45–47, 55, 71
Biskind, Peter, 89
Black and White Men
  Together (B.W.M.T.),
  134
Black movement, 121–23
Blaker, Roger, 9–10
Body building, 13, 14
Body Politic (newspaper),
  138, 164, 199
Bonding, male, 61, 62
Bookstores, 165–66
Boozer, Mel, 117
Boswell, John, 4, 48–49,
  66, 71, 109
Boyers, Robert, 80, 81
Boy/man sex. *See*
  Child/adult sex
Bradley, Tom, 20

Brazil, 50, 58, 139
Briggs Initiative, 126–28
Britt, Harry, 32, 127, 131
Bronski, Michael, 154
Brooks, Romaine, 158
Brown, Howard, 26
Brown, Jerry, 25, 124
Brown, Rita Mae, 184–85
Bryant, Anita, 120–21, 128
Burgess, Anthony, 151–52,
  168, 216
Burke, Tom, 2
Businesses, 17–21

Cage aux Folles, La, 3,
  153
Califia, Pat, 54, 121, 179,
  182, 193, 195, 197
Callas, Maria, 154
Callenbach, Ernest, 196
Camp, 152–55
Canada, 24, 25, 139, 164
Capitalism. *See* Consumer
  capitalism
Carpenter, Edward, 112,
  149
Carter, Jimmy, 117
Catalan Gay Liberation
  Front (F. A. G. C.), 217
Catholic Church, 4, 27,
  62, 66
Chambers, Jane, 12
Child/adult sex, 199–202,
  210–11
Child molestation, 173
Children, 69
  sexuality of, 198–200
Chile, 109
China, 109
Chodorow, Nancy, 46–47,
  61

Christian Voice, 129
Christopher Street
(magazine), 130, 165, 223
Churches, 4, 26–27,
62–63, 66–67
Churchill, Wainwright, 66
Civil rights, 121, 134–35
Cixous, Hélène, 163
Clift, Montgomery, 65
Coburn, Judith, 201–2
Colquhoun, Maureen, 30
Coming out, 22–23
Commercialization of sex,
80–85. *See also*
Consumer capitalism
Commercial world, 17–21
Community, sense of, 7–9,
18, 125, 215, 216,
220–23
Compton-Burnett, Ivy,
151
Concealment, experience
of, 150–52
Concerned Republicans
for Individual Rights,
126, 127
Conservatism, 219–20
Consumer capitalism,
82–85, 88–97, 109–10,
199
emergence of a
homosexual identity
and, 93–95
narcissism and, 92, 95
Cowan, Paul, 97–98
Crisp, Quentin, 3
Cruising, 174–75
Culture, gay. *See* Gay
culture; Subculture,
homosexual

Daughters of Bilitis, 113
Davidson, Michael, 3
da Vinci, Leonardo, 149
Dayton, Ohio, 30
Decter, Midge, 130
Delaney, Samuel, 196
DeLynn, Jane, 12
Democratic National
Convention (1980),
115–18

De Mott, Benjamin, 150
Denneny, Michael, 73
Deviance or perversion,
homosexuality as, 2, 4–6
Di Sabato, Joe, 126
Discos, 18–19, 21
Discrimination, 110. *See
also* Antidiscrimination
laws; Employment
discrimination
Drag queens (drag
culture), 58, 153–55
Drugs, 18–19
Duberman, Martin, 177
Dyer, Richard, 152, 153,
157

East Germany, 24
Eglinton, J. Z., 202
Ehrenreich, Barbara, 89
Ellis, Havelock, 40, 112
Employment
discrimination, 25–26
England. *See* Great
Britain
Evans, Arthur, 125, 161
Experts, 5, 52–54
Eysenck, H. J., 100

Faderman, Lillian, 48, 69,
213
Fairlie, Henry, 82
Fairy movement, 133, 161
Falwell, Rev. Jerry, 99
Fameny, Frank, 113
Family, the, 86, 89–90
homophobia and, 64, 69
Family Protection Act,
129
Fashion, 33–34, 166–67
Fassbinder, Rainer, 158,
160
Faust, Beatrice, 163, 183
Feingold, Michael, 151
Femininity, 55–59
Feminism (feminist
movement), 1, 11–12, 14,
15, 22, 94, 96, 221–22
civil rights and, 135
gay political movement
and, 113, 131, 132

homophobia and,
68–69, 92
pornography and, 183
Fernandez, Dominique,
156
Fernbach, Davoid, 56–57,
70
F. H. A. R., 217
Fiedler, Leslie, 69–70
Films, 29, 87, 159–61,
167–68, 199
FitzGerald, Frances, 98
Fliess, Wilhelm, 41
Flikkers, Rooie, 217
Florida Task Force, 125
Fone, Bryne, 155
Ford, Clellan, 48
Forster, E. M., 22, 149,
159–60, 186
Foucault, Michel, 5,
48–50, 52, 81, 213
France, 24, 90, 112, 139,
140, 202
Franklin, Patrick, 65
Freedman, Mark, 63
Freud, Sigmund, x, xi, xiii,
39–41, 54, 55, 58, 71,
84, 193
repression thesis of,
60–63
on sadomasochism, 191
Fricke, Aaron, 124
Friedenberg, Edgar, 212
Friendships, 189–90
Fromm, Erich, 197–98
Fuller, Buckminster, 71
Fuori (newspaper), 164
Fundamentalists, 128–29
Furies, The (magazine),
165

Gagnon, J. H., 41, 48
Gai Pied, Le, 73, 165
Gallagher, Nora, 130
Gardner, Kay, 162
Garfinkle, Ellen, 68
Gay, use of the word, 6
Gay Academic Union, 160
Gay and Lesbian Lifestyles
Expo (1980), 20, 120
Gay chic, 19

Gay Community News,
73, 164, 165
Gay culture, 18, 146–68,
214, 222
    camp, 152–55
    definition of, 146–49
    drag, 152–55
    experience of
        concealment and,
        150–52
    gay sensibility and, 146,
        148–51
    idolization of women
        singers and actors, 154
    language, 151–52
    lesbians and, 153, 154,
        156–58, 161–63, 165
    as middle-class, 157–58
    new, 155–63
    opera and ballet, 154
    publications, 164
Gay Left, 1
Gay Liberation Front, 6,
164
Gayness, homosexuality
    distinguished from,
    56–57, 70–71
Gay political movement,
110–42, 209, 211–14,
218–19. *See also specific
organizations*
    alliances and, 137
    antigay backlash of the
        1980s and, 128–31
    black movement
        compared to, 121–23
    civil rights strategy and,
        121, 134–35
    elite/mass-politics
        division within,
        124–25
    in Europe, 111–13,
        139–41
    fairy movement, 133,
        161
    feminism and, 113
    functions of, 118
    lesbian feminist
        criticism of, 131–32
    lesbian separatism and,
        132

links between gay
    women and men,
    135–36
Marxist view of, 132–33
the media and, 136–37
national organization,
    absence of, 123–24
in other countries,
    111–13, 139–41
publications, 164
radical, 1–2, 113–14,
    121–22, 127, 137
Gay Press Convention,
126
Gay Pride Day, 113, 114
Gay Rights National
    Lobby (G.R.N.L.), 124
Gay Sunshine (magazine),
165
Gearhart, Sally, 131–32,
161, 179, 180
Gender, confusion
    between sexuality and,
    54–60
Gender roles. *See* Sex
    roles
Genet, Jean, 65, 158
Gentrification, 32–33
Germany, 24, 109,
    111–12, 139–40, 194
Ghettos. *See*
    Neighborhoods, gay
Gide, 210
Goldman, Emma, 112
Goodman, Paul, 167
Goodstein, David, 125–26
Gordon, Linda, 135
Great Britain, 24, 30, 95,
    111, 112, 134, 140
Grosse, Edmund, 210

Hall, Richard, 72–73, 138
Hammersmith, Sue Kiefer,
57
*Hammond World
    Almanac*, 167
Harrington, Michael, 130
Harris, Bertha, 158
Haskell, Molly, 88
Hay, Harry, 112–13, 119,
133

Hefner, Hugh, 91
Heller, Joseph, 100
Hemingway, Ernest, 148
Hiller, Kurt, 138
Hirschfeld, Magnus, 111,
112
Hite, Shere, 46, 177
Hoch, Paul, 14, 62
Hocquenghem, Guy, 15,
63, 65, 173, 175
Hoffman, Martin, 8, 63,
183
Holland, 24, 25, 139, 140,
216
Homophobia, 63–70, 210.
See also Religious
    condemnation of
    homosexuality; Violence,
    antihomosexual
    definition of, 63
    the family and, 64, 69
    feminism and, 68–69, 92
    language of, 64
    political aspects of,
        98–102, 109
    repression of
        homosexuality and,
        63–65
Homosexualization of
    American society, 33, 35,
    204, 223–24
Homosexual rights
    movement. *See* Gay
    political movement
Hostility to homosexuality.
    See Homophobia
Hotchner, Beverley, 90
Hunt, Morton, 87–88

Identity, homosexual, 5, 9,
    10, 12, 13, 16, 43–45,
    47, 72–73, 212, 213
    consumer capitalism and
        emergence of, 93–95
    emergence of
        homosexuals as a social
        category and, 48–51
    experts' views and,
        52–54
    gay political movement
        and, 118–20

restrictions on freedom
and, 103–4
sex roles and, 55–56
Illness, homosexuality as
an, 4–5
Imperialism, 51–52
International Committee
for Sex Equality, 166
International Gay
Association (I.G.A.),
140–41
Iran, 51, 66, 109
Ireland, Doug, 130
Isherwood, Christopher,
74, 136, 148
Islamic societies, 47, 48
Israel, 66
Italy, 30, 140, 154

Jay, Karla, 11, 17, 46,
59–60, 155, 161–63, 174,
177, 178, 186
Jefferson, Thomas, 64
Jews, 69, 146
Johnson, Haynes, 82
Johnson, Virginia, 42, 44,
45, 177–78
Johnson, Rev. William, 27
Jong, Erica, 81, 83
Judaeo-Christian tradition,
4, 66–67

Kennedy, Ted, 116
Kepner, Jim, 119
King, Billy Jean, 23
Kinsey, Alfred, 42, 54
Kinsey's studies, 42–44,
52, 87
Kleinberg, Seymour, 157,
210
Knight, John, 65
Kopkind, Andrew, 62
Kotulak, Ronald, 86
Kramer, Larry, 180, 188

Lachs, Stephen, 124
Language
gay, 151–52
of homophobia, 64
Lasch, Christopher, 92–93,
95

Latin America, 24, 30, 50
Lavender Left, 133
Law reform, 24–25, 131,
134. See also
Antidiscrimination
ordinances; Civil rights
Laws prohibiting
homosexual behavior
(antisodomy statutes), 24,
25, 109, 110, 124,
131
Leadership Conference on
Civil Rights, 130
Legal protection of
homosexuals, 24–25. See
also Antidiscrimination
ordinances
Lem, Stanislaw, 91–92
Leo, John, 11
Levine, Martin, 59
Liberals, attacks on
homosexuals by, 129–30
Life style, 6, 146, 147,
160, 213
Living arrangements, 166
Los Angeles Gay and
Lesbian Community
Services Center, 163–64
Los Angeles Times, 87
Lotringer, Sylvère, 200–1
Love, 186, 189
Lucie-Smith, Edward, 167

McCullers, Carson, 150
McDonald, Larry, 129
Macho cult (macho style),
13–15, 34
MacKenzie, Compton, 8
McWhirter, David, 188
Magazines, gay, 164
Mailer, Norman, 14, 42
Marcuse, Herbert, 72, 84,
94
Marmor, Judd, 53
Marriage, 83, 86–88, 172,
175, 185–87
Martin, Del, 221
Marx, Karl, xiii
Marxism, gay political
movement and, 132–33
Masculinity, 55–59

Masochism. See
Sadomasochism
Masters, R. E. L., 118,
166
Masters, William, 42, 44,
45, 177–78
Matlovich, Sergeant, 26
Mattachine Society, 113,
119
Mattison, Andrew, 188
Maugham, Somerset, 3
Maupin, Armistead, 32
Media, the, 27–29, 213.
See also Films; Press, the
gay political movement
and, 136–37
Mendola, Mary, 185
Metropolitan Community
Church (M.C.C.), 7, 27,
123
Michelangelo, 149
Midler, Bette, 154
Mieli, Mario, 71–72
Military, the, 62, 70
Milk, Harvey, 29–30, 126,
127
Millett, Kate, 16, 46,
110–11
Minority, homosexuals as
a, 6, 9, 18, 72, 211–13,
217–18, 223, 224
legal aspects of, 24, 25
Mitterrand, François, 140
Mitzel, John, 62, 102,
122, 210
Monaco, James, 159
Monette, Paul, 64–65,
178
Money, John, 65
Monogamy, 175, 176
Moral Majority, 128–29,
213–14, 218
Morin, Stephen, 68
Morris, Jan, 58, 69
Mort, Frank, 108–11
Moscone, George, 29, 127
Movement, the. See Gay
political movement
Municipal Elections
Committee of Los
Angeles (MECLA), 124

Narcissism, 92–93, 95, 150

National Association of Business Councils (NABC), 20

National Gay Task Force (NGTF), 123, 124, 126, 135

National Organization of Lesbians and Gays (NOLAG), 123, 138, 179

National Organization of Women, 113, 136, 179

Navarre, Yves, 217

Near, Holly, x

Neighborhoods, gay (ghettos), 30–33

Nestle, Joan, 12

Netherlands, the, 24, 25, 139, 140, 216

Newspapers. See Press, the

New Yorker, The, 130

New York Native (magazine), 165

New York Times, The, 6, 28, 137

New Zealand, 25, 154

Norway, 24, 25

One, Incorporated, 113

Opera, 154

Oraison, Marc, 47

Paedophile Information Exchange, 199

Pasolini, Pier Paolo, 65

Pedophilia. See Child/adult sex

Perreault, John, 147

Perry, Rev. Troy, 27, 123

Personal relationships. See Relationships

Petit, Roland, 148

Phoenix, Arizona, 7

Picano, Felice, xiii, 34

Plummer, Ken, 43

Podhoretz, Norman, 129–30

Police, 24

Politics, 29–30. See also Gay political movement

homophobia and, 98–102, 109

sexuality and, 108–11

Ponse, Barbara, 53

Popert, Ken, 173–74

Pornography, 88, 183

Press, the, 28–29

gay, 164–65

Price, Richard, 87

Pringle, Rosemary, 208

Promiscuity, 16–17, 59, 79–80, 173–76, 180, 183–85

Prostitution, 81, 83

Protestantism, 66, 69

Proust, Marcel, 148

Psychiatrists and psychologists, 5, 26. See also Experts

Psychoanalysis, 40, 44, 155. See also Freud, Sigmund

Publishing houses, 165

Puig, Manuel, 50, 54–55

Queens. See Drag queens

Racism, 134, 221, 222

Radical gay movement, 1–2, 113–14, 121–22, 127, 137

Reagan, Ronald, 9, 91, 101

Rechy, John, 56, 58, 68, 84, 148–50, 158, 173, 175, 190, 193

Reich, Wilhelm, 52

Relationships, 172, 185–90. See also Marriage

friendships, 189–90

in gay literature, 187–88

love and, 186, 189

promiscuity and, 175–76

sex and, 179, 180, 183–85, 188

Religious condemnation of homosexuality, 4, 27

Renault, Mary, 6–7, 44, 51, 159

Repression of

heterosexuality among homosexuals, 71–72, 154

Repression of homosexuality (repression theory of homosexuality), x, xi, 22, 41–42, 60–65, 71. See also Sublimation of homosexuality

homophobia and, 63–65, 68

male bonding and, 61, 62

team sports and, 61–62

Rich, Adrienne, 168

Ritter, Rev. Bruce, 88

Robinson, Paul, 3, 43, 44

Rosenberg, Samuel, 41

Roth, Philip, 61

Rothenberg, David, 28

Ruitenbeek, Hendrik, 45

Rule, Jane, 175–76

Russo, Vito, 55, 118, 167–68, 211

Sabol, Blair, 97

Sadomasochism, 13, 34, 59, 180, 182, 190–98, 203

Freud on, 191

among heterosexuals, 197

male-female differences, 197

self-hatred and, 193, 196

therapeutic social role of, 195–96

Sagarin, Edward, 103

San Francisco, 29, 31, 32

Sanzio, Alain, 32

Sarria, Jose, 113

Sartre, Jean-Paul, 195, 224

Scientific Humanitarian Committee (Germany), 111–12

Seabrook, Jeremy, 94–95

Self-assertion, 12, 14, 17

Self-hatred of homosexuals, 3, 7, 221

sadomasochism and, 193–96

Sennett, Richard, 93, 95
Sensibility, gay, 146, 148–51
Separatism, 215, 217, 223
Sex roles, 54–57, 68, 95, 153
Sexual freedom (sexual liberation; "sexual revolution"), 81–85, 89, 91–94, 98–100
Sexuality (sexual behavior), 172–85, 224
  child/adult sex, 199–202, 210–11
  of children, 198–200
  cruising, 174–75
  male-female differences in, 174, 178–79, 182–83
  pornography and, 183
  promiscuity, 16–17, 59, 79–80, 173–76, 180, 183–85
  in public areas, 180–82
  relationships and, 170, 180, 183–85, 188
  sadomasochism, see Sadomasochism
  socialization and, 182–83
Sexual mores and values, changes in, 85–96
Shakespeare, William, 147–48
Sherman, Martin, 112
Sherrill, Kenneth, 67–68
Shewey, Don, 59
Shields, Brooke, 199
Shively, Charles, 185
Silverstein, Charles, 62
Simon, William, 41, 48
Singles (singles scene), 87, 89
Sisely, Emily, 190
Slater, Philip, 93, 100
Snyder, William, 83
Social category, emergence of homosexuals as a, 48–51

Social mobility, 157
Society for Human Rights, 112
Sontag, Susan, 146, 148, 150–52, 192, 194
South America, 154
Soviet Union, 53, 109
Spain, 30, 90, 139, 140
Spiritual Conference for Radical Fairies, 133
Spiritualism, 161
Sports, 20, 61–62
State, the, sexuality and, 108–11
Stein, Gertrude, 152
Steiner, George, xiii, 146, 150
Stevenson, Richard, 8
Stoller, Robert, 149
Subculture, homosexual, 48–51, 96
Sublimation of homosexuality, 61–63, 71
Sweden, 25

Talese, Gay, 81, 84, 87–88, 91
Tanner, Donna, 189
Tavernier, Bernard, 90
Taylor, Gordon Rattray, 90
Television, 27–28
Third World countries, 51, 90
Thomas, D. M., 155
Time magazine, 28
Tocqueville, Alexis de, 85–86
Toffler, 186
Transsexualism, 57–58
Transvestism, 57–58
Tripp, C. A., 46, 59

Ulrichs, Karl, 5, 39–40, 50

Vidal, Gore, 42–43, 102, 147, 167
Village People, 1, 2, 13
Village Voice, 6

Violence, antihomosexual, 65, 100–1, 130
Visconti, Luchino, 150
Visibility of homosexuals, 1, 3, 7, 130, 172. See also Coming out
Voeller, Bruce, 176
Von Praunheim, Rosa, 167–68, 220

Walker, Gerald, 175
Warren, Patricia Nell, 17–18, 197
Washington Post, 30
Waters, Charlotte, 187
Wechsler, Anne, 117–18
Weeks, Jeffrey, 203
Weinberg, George, 63, 65–67, 69
Weinberg, Martin, 52, 57, 62, 178, 189
West Germany, 24, 139–41, 157
White, Dan, 29, 127
White, Edmund, 67, 83, 97, 122, 150, 152, 154–56, 166, 181–82, 192, 194
White, Patrick, 56
Whitman, Walt, 70
Whitmire, Kathryn, 138
Whitmore, George, 203
Wilde, Oscar, 156
Williams, Tennessee, 65
Willis, Ellen, 182–83
Wilson, Edward O., 41–42
Wilson, G., 100
Wolf, Deborah, 15
Wolfe, Tom, 82, 84
Wolff, Charlotte, 46
Women's movement. See Feminism
Wrangler, Jack, 13
Wright, Stephen, 147

Young, Allen, 17, 46, 59–60, 174, 177, 178, 186
Young, Andrew, 138
Young, Ian, 196, 198–99